In *Runners of the Nish,* Alex Cyr leads us viscerally into the grueling sport of cross-country running. It's a true 'view from the inside' as the St. F.X. men's team trains for the next race, running their tried and true courses and their harrowing hills, always striving towards a personal best and a victory at the national championships.

Cyr describes his teammates with such compassion and wit that we intimately get to know them as the high-achieving individuals they are. In a story chockfull of drama, we experience them in the thrill of victory and the pain of season-threatening injuries. We also see candidly into their daily routines and the personal and team obsessions that keep them on track to achieve ever better performances. As only an insider can do, Cyr has written a classic sports book and a personal homage to a team and a beloved coach, the uniquely dedicated and highly respected Bernie Chisholm. It is well worth the run and the read!

Danny Gillis
author of *Where the Rivers Meet*

RUNNERS OF THE NISH

A Season in the Sun, Rain, Hail, and Hell

BY
ALEX CYR

[signature]

FOREWORD BY
3-TIME OLYMPIAN ERIC GILLIS

 FriesenPress

Suite 300 - 990 Fort St
Victoria, BC, V8V 3K2
Canada

www.friesenpress.com

ISBN
978-1-5255-2958-0 (Hardcover)
978-1-5255-2957-3 (Paperback)
978-1-5255-2959-7 (eBook)

1. BIOGRAPHY & AUTOBIOGRAPHY, SPORTS

Distributed to the trade by The Ingram Book Company

Table of Contents

Acknowledgements

I first want to thank my head coach Bernie Chisholm for planting in my mind the idea of writing a chronicle of our last season together. When the going got tough, and I wanted to lay the pen down, I swear I could hear his voice creeping out of my subconscious, saying: "Cyr, do you want to write, or do you want to make excuses?"

Thank you to Kevin Grant, our assistant coach, for offering his support throughout the process and helping me make valuable connections that has helped me move forward in this endeavour.

Thank you to Danny Gillis, author of *Where the Rivers Meet and A Treasure for the Taking*. Your guidance, pointers and editing propelled this project to new heights, and I am extremely grateful for your mentorship.

Thank you to Eric Gillis. Between endless miles, dad chores and coaching hours, you found the time to contribute to this project and offer your insightful words.

Thank you to my main sponsors, supporters and first readers: my parents Paul and Odette. While Mom agreed to use her eye for language to offer a round of editing, Dad asked to be my first official reader, as long as I bring him only the final, polished product. He proceeded to exhale through his nose and lean back in his living room chair while diving into some James Patterson novel.

Thank you to two of my expert editors, Riley Johnston and Scott Donald. Riley's knowledge of running literature and capacity for storytelling, along with Scott's critical eye and precise recall helped complete this story from two, distinct angles.

Thank you to Warren Ferguson, Scott Donald, Patrick Marlow, Hana Marmura and Catherine Thompson for providing me with photo evidence of the happenings of this story. I wish to send a special Thank You to Hana and Catherine for locating a precious photo of "The Snowman" for me.

Thank you to my publicist, Friesen Press. Your excellence in publishing, fast turnover and care for this work was very much appreciated, cherished and crucial to our success. Specifically, to Christoph, Sammy, Joshua and Ellie – thank you for leading me through the creation of my first book.

Lastly, I want to thank every member of the 2016 X-Men for kind of agreeing (alluding to you, Favero) to become subjects of this story without really knowing where I was going with this project. I hope this work helps in preserving precious memories, and prevents us from slowly stretching the truth about them as time goes by. Thanks for allowing me to publicize a snapshot of our time together.

Foreword

By: 3-time Olympian in the 10 000m and marathon,
and current St. FX cross-country and track and field head coach Eric Gillis

If there's anyone who should have been following the success of the St. FX cross-country team after graduating, that person probably should have been me. Having spent a lengthy seven years as an X-Man and having continued on in the sport, I am surprised at myself for not immediately keeping up with the team's results. Anybody who has run at St. FX - or anywhere at the varsity level – knows how the day-to-day running triumphs and challenges happen in a world that feels so large when we live in it, but that in reality is small. For that reason, anybody who moves away from this environment will, unfortunately, quickly lose touch with it.

It was only one short year removed from my own varsity career when the world of CIS (then CIAU, now U Sports) cross-country all of a sudden felt very much behind me. All my years at St. FX seemed to have blended into one, and while a few of my best race results stood out, memories and storylines from when I was an athlete were getting harder to remember. That is until a young Mr. Alex Cyr joined the St. FX X-Men cross-country team and started blogging about life on the run in his new home of Antigonish. His style I liked, the content I ate up, and once again my passion for the Blue and White and the Canadian university running scene was shining through. That is what this book did for me, and I hope it has the same effect on you.

Like Alex mentions, he began this project with the goal of gifting the final product to his coach at St. FX, Bernie Chisholm, who has recently retired after thirty-one years of coaching. Such a gift is well deserved; thirty-one years is a long time to do anything. To coach university-level athletes for such a stretch of time is something else. For that, I take my hat off to Bernie. In the fall of 2017, I began my time as a coach with the X-Men in the twilight of his illustrious career. Luckily, I was able to spend that year shadowing Bernie before becoming the head coach and leader of the school's running programs.

My learning began right away. Sitting on the Oland Centre bleachers in early September listening to Bernie welcoming the newest crop of athletes with enthusiasm set the tone for the season, and reminded me of what I had been missing for the past 11 years. As I sat in front of him with my seven-year-old daughter, surrounded by a couple dozen runners, I was immediately reminded of just how much he enjoys coaching. Coach Bernie was in his element – his message was equally enthusiastic as it had been 18 years prior when I first heard it as a rookie. Right at that moment, I wondered what the secret was to coaching with passion for such a length of time, and hoped to learn from this great man so that I, too, can enjoy these moments as much as he does one year from now, and thirty-one years from now!

Congratulations, Bernie, on such a great career! I am honoured to stand on the shoulders of a running giant and am thrilled about the opportunity to keep building on what you have created here at St. FX.

Prologue (and Dedication)

Once a Runner; Running with the Buffaloes; The Animal Keepers

Consuming these three cult classics of cross-country running literature was all the (albeit unconventional) preparation I had leading into the writing of this book. My lack of formal writing experience at first made me feel hesitant to undertake the project. I worried that documenting my team's cross-country season would simply come across as a feeble attempt to replicate the more refined work of others. My challenges were: How do I make readers understand the beauty and unity of a cross-country team, as Chris Lear did in *Running with the Buffaloes*? How can I instill personality into my characters, as John L. Parker did for his character, Quenton Cassidy? Cumulatively, the question became: How can I make this work my own?

Then it dawned on me. These three colorful narratives, fictitious or factual, share one trait. They are all told through the eyes of an outsider. Parker's story, although inspiring, is fictitious, Donn Behnke narrates *The Animal Keepers* from the viewpoint of a coach, and Chris Lear tells the story of the Colorado Buffaloes by chronicling the team's day-to-day trials from the standpoint of an observer. While the narrators of these great works tend to be removed from the action, my interpretation will be that of a protagonist. Because I am not a coach, an observer, or the creator of my story, the narration comes from a more personal place. The anecdotes I provide about the St. Francis Xavier University cross-country team will be as honest and forthright as I can make them. After all, I was a member of this team. The characters I describe are my rivals, my best friends, my students, and my mentors all at once. Despite taking the liberty of placing my own perspective twist on one season's events, my intent was always to speak on behalf of our group of sixteen guys.

The idea to undertake this project came out of a discussion with my coach, Bernie Chisholm, in August of 2016. He thought it would be a good idea to chronicle the happenings of the upcoming cross-country season. Bernie had been coaching since 1986. When I asked him why 2016 should be the year he suggested this project to one of his athletes, he claimed that our group was special, and that it was an era he never wished to forget.

Bernie wasn't lying to me – he was just hiding an important part of the truth. He was soon retiring from coaching. I suspected it, and along with the fond feelings I had for this team and school, this suspicion pushed me to duly apply myself to this project. Besides, I had always wanted to try my hand at writing. The timing was right, and the idea appealed to me: What could be more appropriate for my inaugural work than a chronicle of my everyday climate? It was a climate in which I had become so comfortable, a climate in which I had met a mercurial, yet synergistic group of guys and girls, who had become my best friends. It was a climate I cherished.

I like to think our cross-country group was special in a few ways. We were comprised of an unusual concoction of overachievers (though perhaps not so unusual within endurance sports). We were an inter-competitive bunch, but also shared a mutual admiration for one another. This admiration stemmed from our understanding that the desire for success, in whichever aspect of life, was shared in our roots. To most of us, running was a vehicle we used to concretize this desire for success – some of us might even have called upon running as our artistic expression. But, despite the time and effort we put into our craft, no matter how fierce the competition between teammates could become, respect for one another overtook any feeling of jealousy, bitterness, or resentment. Simply put, this shared drive, inside or outside of running, had unified our team.

Although I am hopeful that this work provides you with a source of entertainment – given the subjects of this narrative – no outline was followed in its development. I began writing with our season still a white canvas, unable to guarantee a fairy tale ending for the team, for myself, or for any other particular teammate. All I could promise was a genuine and real investigation of the ebbs, flows, highs, and lows of a CIS[1] cross-country campaign, by

---

[1]   CIS – Canadian Interuniversity Sport – now known as U-Sports

giving an honest rendition of the season that I regretfully call my last here at St. Francis Xavier University.

I would like to dedicate this work to my teammates from years one through four: Stephen Deering, William Forsey, Gabe Quenneville (even though I doubt he'll read it), Bryden Tate, Ryan Hatchard, Riley Johnston, Scott Donald, Lee Wesselius, Stuart MacPherson, Patrick Marlow, Brandon MacDonald, Cal DeWolfe, Alex Neuffer, Nic Favero, Ryan O'Regan, Warren Ferguson, Nathan Jeffs, Matt Eliot, Ryan Fuller, Edward MacDonald, Corey McNamara, Vaughn Saunders, Paul MacLellan, Angus Rawling, Cullen MacInnis, Addison Derhak, David MacDonald, and Leo Jusiak.

Also, to my female teammates who have been almost equally present in our everyday activities. Thanks to our meal hall chats, cheering sessions up South River Hill, and lengthy bus rides, our two teams truly feel like only one. This work primarily focuses on the boys' team for simplicity's sake. But I hear that Kendra MacNeil is working on a girls' version, so hang tight.

Finally, I dedicate this story to my coaches, Bernie Chisholm and Kevin Grant. Your guidance in matters of running and beyond is something I hold close and value highly.

To all of you (even Bryden), thank you for making my years at St. FX a time I will cherish for a lifetime. I hope you all enjoy.

2016-2017 St. FX XC team

Athletes

Alex Cyr (me) – Fourth year student, third year eligibility. AUS[2] silver medalist in the 3000 metres and bronze medalist in the 1500 metres in 2016. Looking to translate track times into a high finish at the CIS cross-country championship. Fourth at AUS conference cross-country championship last year and aiming for a podium finish in 2016. Residence: 18 Greening Drive.

Addison Derhak – First year student, first year eligibility. On paper, he is the top recruit coming into the program. The business student from Waterloo, Ontario gained most of his running experience on the track, and still lacks the grit and toughness only obtained with real life cross-country experience. His youth and natural talent suggest that he has a bright future in the sport. He boasts a personal best 5k of 15:55 out of high school. Residence: Lane Hall.

Cal DeWolfe – Fourth year student, fourth year eligibility. After a breakthrough 2015 season, which saw him earn a bronze medal at the AUS championship and rewrite his personal bests in track and field, 2016 did not start as planned. A bout with staleness and burnout slowed him down in the winter, and he struggled to find his step in the spring. Now over the hump, Cal has been running high mileage over the summer, in the hopes of regaining his spot on the podium. A bright philosophy student aspiring to become a lawyer, Cal is a vocal presence on the team, willing to playfully argue about anything and everything with teammates. Meticulous in his training methods, Cal is taking his final year as an X-Man very seriously. Residence: 18 Greening Drive.

---

2   AUS – Atlantic University Sport – the conference in which St. FX competes within the CIS

Scott Donald – Fifth year student, fifth year eligibility. Team captain and team senior, Scott was an unexpected addition to this year's group. A last-minute decision to return to St. FX and work on an honours thesis brought him back, and the team could not have had a better fate. The sixteenth place finisher at the 2015 CIS championship missed the 2016 indoor track season due to illiotibial band syndrome but is poised to make a comeback. He will be chasing his second career individual AUS cross-country championship, having taken home the gold medal in 2014. Charismatic and easy-going, Scott is a popular and respected presence among his peers. Residence: 18 Greening Drive.

Matt Eliot – Fourth year student, third year eligibility. Having spent the first half of the calendar year in Norway, Matt has some catching up to do in terms of training. Looking to earn his spot on the travel team for the first time, he has been running high-mileage weeks since his return from Scandinavia. Owner of fast high school personal bests, he has yet to rekindle the magic at St. FX, and hopes to find what works for him. Also a frequent participant in team debates, Matt has a brain for statistics and spews facts like no other. Now a senior, he wants to leave with a bang. Residence: 25 Acadia Street.

Nic Favero – Fourth year student, fourth year eligibility. Known to become totally immersed in the lifestyle of a cross-country athlete come September, Favero is a lover of the sport. His approach to the fall running season is a thing of beauty. Predominantly aerobically responsive, he runs many miles. This tendency makes him flirt with the fine line between optimal performance and harrowing burnout. A fervent reader of the campus library's sociological volumes, who is often aloof from the latest inter-team gossip; he was once described as a crossover between an academic and a hippie. An expected member of the top seven, he will have a few young runners on the cusp of a breakthrough challenging him for a scoring spot. His penchant for forming interesting opinions on hot topics makes him a popular and fun presence at team gatherings. Residence: 25 Acadia Street.

Warren Ferguson (Ferg) – Fourth year student, third year eligibility. A physics major and medical school hopeful, Warren likes a challenge. We suspect this is why he got into running in the first place. What he lacks in natural talent, he makes up for in plain hard labour. He has yet to make the travel team, but a productive summer of training without an injury could propel him to new heights. A model student with an impressive academic pedigree, his preference for doing things right guilts his teammates into not cutting corners in his presence. His traditional political views, along with his ability to carry out a debate for hours, usually put him in the heart of post-practice conversations. Though not a front-runner, he is expected to assume a leadership role this year. Residence: Governor's Hall.

Ryan Fuller – Third year student, second year eligibility. Perhaps the team member most consumed by the world of cross-country and track and field, he is an encyclopaedia of running facts. Unfortunately, his zest and love for the sport has not yet translated into fast racing times. After earning his spot on the top twelve in his first year, injuries (and university cafeteria desserts) struck hard. Finally feeling healthy, he hopes to regain form to give teammates a run for their money for one of the last travel team spots. At 6'5'' and 215 lbs., the only thing more imposing than Ryan Fuller himself may be his desire to one day run fast. Residence: 84 Church Street, Apt. 3

Nathan Jeffs – Fourth year student, first year eligibility. After a brief stint with the team in his first year, Nathan took some time off from running and focused on cycling and triathlon events. Following a summer of solid training where he tested the waters, he feels ready to make his mark on the running circuit. Already a part of the team's social nucleus – partly due to his sense of humour, partly due to the popularity of his haircutting business – his presence at both practice and team gatherings will be welcome. Residence: 25 Acadia Street.

Leo Jusiak – First year student, first year eligibility. An international student from France who had no intention of running during his year abroad, Leo decided to give running another shot after learning that St. FX had a strong cross-country program. He was a French national team member in mountain running and boasts a 3:56 1500m personal best. He has not run in the summer, however, and he finds himself out of shape. Talented and experienced in the sport, Leo is still expected to place some pressure on the scorers. Residence: 77 Hawthorne Street.

David MacDonald – First year student, first year eligibility. A local engineering student from Antigonish, David kick-started his running career with the Antigonish Track Club and got to tag along at team practices over the course of the last few years. Now a freshman, David will be expected to make a more consistent commitment to the team. Quirky and intelligent, he remains an enigma to most seniors. Residence: Plessis House.

Edward MacDonald – Third year student, third year eligibility. A local runner from Antigonish with a diminutive frame, Edward has been a member of the travel team for both his years at St. FX. A hard-working lobster fisherman in the summers, he thankfully compensates for his lack of training during his months on the boat with natural ability. If consistent, he will challenge for an alternate spot, and may even close in on the top seven. Bernie is looking for him to increase his mileage, so that he can become an immediate threat to usurp our current scorers. Charitable and humble, Edward is well liked by his peers. Residence: 84 Church Street, Apt. 3

Cullen MacInnis – First year student, first year eligibility. A natural athlete from Cape Breton who displays an impressive level of focus, Cullen looks to make big jumps over the next few years. His running career is still in its infancy, but he is a hard worker and student of the sport. A nursing student with God-given dance moves, Cullen is eager to tackle the high-mileage lifestyle that comes with cross-country season. This year will likely be one of adjustment and education for him. Residence: Mount Saint Bernard.

Paul MacLellan – Second year student, second year eligibility. Paul is a local student-athlete who had his sight set on St. FX from a young age. A successful rookie year saw Paul toe the line at the AUS championship as the team's seventh runner. Still learning about the ups and downs of a year-long training regime, Paul hopes to keep improving. He has demonstrated considerable talent by breaking nine minutes for 3000 metres as a freshman. An amusing presence for his bashfulness and his youth, Paul still very well plays the role of rookie. Residence: Plessis House.

Alex Neuffer – Fourth year student, third year eligibility. He has struggled with injuries but remains one of the top runners on the team. If healthy, he will be considered amongst the favourites to win the AUS championship.

Through his inability to handle high mileage, Neuffer learned to thrive on cross training, performing part of his aerobic work on the bicycle and in the pool. Cool, calm, and collected, he oozes confidence in his athletic ability. Known for his capacity to handle pain while racing and working out, he is expected to keep the pace honest and the intensity high from one practice to the next. Residence: 18 Greening Drive.

Ryan O'Regan (DJ) – Fourth year student, third year eligibility. Having found more success on the track than on the cross-country trails, the one we affectionately call DJ hopes that his summer in Antigonish will have ignited some aerobic gains. Athletically built and most suited for shorter, faster distances, O'Regan hopes to become a member of the travel team for the first time. Good-hearted and carefree, his extreme Type-B personality makes him nothing short of a case study for the more high-strung individuals often puzzled by his dysfunctional living habits. Residence: 18 Greening Drive.

Angus Rawling (Beef) – Second year student, second year eligibility. Last year's AUS rookie of the year is coming off a podium finish at the Canadian Junior Track and Field Nationals 5000m, nabbing bronze. A big part of the future of the St. FX cross-country program, the one we call Beef was taken under the wing of several upperclassmen. No longer a rookie, he is expected to use his fearless racing style to keep the seniors on their toes and challenge team hierarchy. Passionate for the sport, and fairly opinionated, he has not required much time to become a member of the team's social nucleus. His motto: Just bury yourself. Residence: 18 Greening Drive.

Coaches:

Bernie Chisholm: Head coach – Bernie is entering his thirty-first year as X-Men and X-Women's cross-country coach. He is the winningest coach in the AUS conference, with seventeen AUS titles under his belt. Known for his recruiting ability, Bernie has recently assembled a dynasty on the men's side – his X-Men are five-time defending AUS champions. His consistent prescription of tempo runs, long hills and hard three to five minute intervals has done wonders to grow a successful program. With a background in education, – he taught high-school English – his tough, but fair coaching style instills discipline and tenacity in his athletes. Reserved but quick-witted, Bernie is well-respected among the team, and widely known and liked in the Antigonish community. As a coach, he is a member of the St. FX Hall of Fame.

Kevin Grant: Assistant coach – Kevin is in his eighth year with the X-Men and X-Women, and assists in coaching, managing, and carrying out every-day tasks for the team. A retired teacher still very active in the Antigonish running community, his passion for the sport is evident. He has coached the local middle school team for years, and many of his athletes have eventually developed into fine varsity runners. A friendly presence at practices and races, Kevin always has a word of advice or a listening ear to offer.

Plains of Abraham, Quebec City

November 12th, 2016

I'm quivering. From the cold, I think. I don't know. Maybe it's just my rapid breathing that is making my chest twitch almost rhythmically. Either way, I'm beat, mangled. I can open my eyes, but not for long. Long enough to feel the wind on my eyeballs – a continuously present wind – that my somatosensory receptors have selectively ignored for over half an hour now. I cover my eyes to shield them. My hands are pulsing, but so is my forehead. They synchronize and throb together as I roll over to my backside, face still twisted in complete agony.

The Plains of Abraham have not seen such a spectacle for 258 years, but history has a weird way of repeating itself. The battle for land, between the French and the English, turned soldiers against each other. Multiple clans, fighting for the same purpose – to extinguish the opponent – depleted their resources, so much so that it was difficult to distinguish the winners from the losers. The line was blurred. Everyone looked the same. Teams were broken down to their purest forms – handfuls of individuals – sprawled out on the battlefield, waiting to learn if their self-sacrifice was worthwhile. Waiting to know if their self-sacrifice was honest enough. Today is not much different.

Here I am, a French-Canadian lying lifelessly, soon listlessly. I'm Montcalm reincarnate. Defeated on the Plains, a heaping pile of war residue. Next to me lies Wolfe, – no, Dewolfe – equally as trashed. We're unsure of who crossed the finish line before us. We have no idea what's happened behind. I think

Bernie is close by, and the look on his face would be telltale. Too bad I can't get up. Too bad I can't see.

I need something – food, maybe. Water…something to make my stomach stop turning. My homeostatic levels are severely threatened from all angles. I feel empty in more ways than one. But there will be a banquet – there will be drinks. We will soon feel alive again. Sustenance is not an issue. I need reassurance. I need comfort so direly that I pick my arms up from the ground and use them as support to push my body up into a sad Vinyasa pose. I open my eyes, and look at Cal Dewolfe, sitting with his head between his knees – beat, distraught, confused. Thank God he is close. I would surely collapse under the weight of my chest and blood-filled head in seconds. I open my dry mouth, knowing that the moment will unveil the value – the significance – of these last months, of these last years. This moment of clarity and truth will be the one I remember. I sacrificed countless hours for this mid-November moment to be a good one. Hoping that he knows better, I turn towards my lanky training partner, roommate, friend, and rival and hope – wish – for some good news.

"How'd we do?"

18 Greening Drive, Antigonish, Nova Scotia

August 31st, 2016

"Heyyy! Anyone in here?? Oh my gosh, it doesn't smell like dirty shoes in here anymore!" The sound of three animated girls walking into my house was alarming enough for me to run up the stairs to anxiously greet them. My five other roommates raced me from their respective rooms. Nothing rounded up a group of college guys quite like a group of college girls. Cal Dewolfe, Angus Rawling, and Ryan O'Regan soon sat on our big green couch. Scott Donald and I shared a two-person red sofa, and Alex Neuffer sat on a little, homely-looking wooden chair as we greeted three of our female teammates. Ellen Burnett, Heidi MacDonald, and Leah Gouthro were overjoyed by the fact that Neuffer had hired a cleaning lady to take her mop to the floors of 18 Greening Drive. The five-person house was currently occupying six runners, and it showed. What I playfully called the "scent of champions and hard work" regularly attracted a legion of fruit flies.

"Yeah, we cleaned this all ourselves," said O'Regan, king of the white lies. Somehow, the girls didn't believe us. They were, however, used to the inherent stench of our running home by now. For the third year in a row, the house on top of the hill overlooking a rundown trailer park was housing an important portion of the St. FX X-Men cross-country team. We had hosted team gatherings, pre-race meals, and X-Box tournaments between these walls, and mementos from races and parties past were slowly accumulating in the form of bottles, medals, and bloodied track spikes. The abode had been the home of three football players when Stuart MacPherson, a past teammate, had come across its advertisement when searching for a home for the 2014-2015 academic year. Along with Cal, Neuffer, Lee, and me, he moved in. Since then, the house had gained hardwood flooring and lots of character. Its off-white walls were covered with rag-tag posters collected at the yearly campus poster fair. Kim Kardashian overlooked the television, which had its wires tangled in those of the X-Box One. Couches surrounded the T.V. and worked well to hide the occasionally dirty floors. Directly above the biggest couch, a red-three seater, which was currently unoccupied – likely due to the brownish stain gracing its middle cushion – were two identical black and white posters of Model A Cadillacs. I did not know where either of them came from. Interspersed between the couches were foam rollers, therapy bands, and the odd running shoe that had found its way out of the veranda. Our three guests took their shoes off and made their way to the maze of couches. Ellen and Leah sat at the right of the stain, Heidi on its left.

Leah rolled her eyes at our shabby abode. "Wow, I really missed this house. Now there are six of you crammed in this living room. Angus, why did you decide to throw yourself in this mess?"

"Come on Leah, you know how it is. Anything to run fast," said the sophomore runner. "No way I was living with a bunch of frosh in Plessis Hall again. I don't know how Paul is going to do it, honestly."

"He's in Plessis again?" asked Heidi. "Wow, that kid has patience. I never could have stayed in residence for two years. No way he can keep up with those residence people who drink all the time."

"I don't know, but Paul loves it." Angus giggled. "He says he's a 'Plessis Panther at heart.'"

"Oh, Plessis Hall," said Heidi. "So happy I'm out of there."

"Hey, living in residence was not that bad," I answered.

"Yeah, for you. You were not surrounded with friends who wanted to drink all the time."

"Hey, look at it this way." I turned to Heidi. "Now, you and Angus have learned how to get through a cross-country season with barely any sleep. Now, you're hardened and will run way faster this year." With that comment, I had opened up the floodgates. The topic of discussion quickly shifted towards the inevitable—how fit is everyone right now? The question that was all but taboo between team members during the summer months was now addressed, knowing that the answers would be empirically revealed soon enough.

"I'm slow now," said Heidi. "I've been in the pool with you almost every day of August." She had recently been plagued with injury.

"And how's the foot?" asked Scott.

"Still not great. I'm just going to run through it at this point. I'll have to if I want to make top seven. Heard some new girl is coming in fit." Even though the girls tended not to speak of our sport as frequently as did we, something about being apart for an extended period of time did something to spike their interest in the topic. Summer racing times were shared, seasonal goals were revealed, and of course, gossip and hearsay were perpetual in conversation. It was a typical first gathering.

"Yeah," said Ellen. "Apparently this girl joining us from the soccer team is supposed to be really fast."

That was enough to send Scott on a lengthy Internet hunt to try and find the best times recorded by Mary MacDonald, a former captain of the varsity soccer team. On the boys and girls teams alike, the thought of gaining a strong athlete was bittersweet. A possible low stick came at a price for middle of the pack runners; the possibility of falling one spot down the depth chart. I had known all about this in the past years, but it was no longer a cause for concern for most of the 18 Greening boys. Naturally, those of us who attributed great importance to our running had migrated to the same house. Unless Nic Favero was to stir the pot and usurp Angus as the fifth runner, which would be possible, our residence would likely be hosting the top five male runners on the team. The playful ponderings between roommates were no longer about who would make the team, as they had been back in 2015, but rather about who would emerge on top of it.

Leah Gouthro was uncharacteristically quiet. The AUS rookie of the year of 2014 had recently been slowed down by a bout with iron deficiency anemia and was aware that the journey back to full form would be an arduous one. Having struggled with the same health issue for most of my own rookie season, I was noticing that it was taking her a longer time to overcome the illness. Visibly frustrated with the pace of her progress, she seemed to be daydreaming too much about her prospective rank on the team to worry about anyone else's.

"Leah, you awake?" asked Scott.

"Yeah, I'm fine. I'm just thinking about this year. It's going to be crazy, man. You guys are all graduating by its end," she said, in her recognizable, pre-nostalgic tone. Leah would only be graduating the year after us. She looked around the room. "It won't be the same without this group. Scott. Cal, Cyr, Neuffer, O'Regan, Ellen, Heidi, Liz, Nic, Matt, Jeffs, Ferg...oh my God! Just thinking about it makes me sad."

"I can't believe this is our last year," said Neuffer. "We need to actually pull something off. Like, with the team we have, it would be ridiculous to be any lower than fifth at CIS."

"Favero is going to be on," I said. "He's been looking good all summer. He ran a 15:35 back in June by himself off base, and he looked smooth doing it," I added. "Boom, six solid guys."

"Don't forget about Paul," interjected Angus. "He's going to have to step it up this year to make the top seven. Remember when he just forgot to run during last Christmas break?" Angus liked to poke fun at Paul. As co-rookies last year, they had gotten to know each other decently well.

"How's this rookie, Addison something?" asked Cal.

"He has a 15:55. Not bad for a seventeen-year-old," I said. "How's Fuller feeling?"

Cal chuckled. "Ol' Fulldaddy has been logging serious miles this summer. "He looks FIT."

"What about Matt Eliot, what's he been up to?" asked Ellen.

"He was in Norway, so I have no idea," said Scott. "Heard Jeffs is in shape, though."

"Jeffs is back?" asked Heidi. "Good, I like him. I feel like I haven't seen him in years."

"One thing is for sure, Ferg trained very hard," I said, imitating Warren Ferguson's slight British accent and proper dialect. Another senior, he was once quoted saying that he only participated in cross-country "because it's hard," so jokes were often made at his expense. The thought that he enjoyed the terrible, gut-wrenching feeling almost unique to distance running only worked to estrange Warren from the rest of us even more than he already was. But, we loved Warren for it – he was weird despite himself, but too proud to change. His headstrong personality and consistency was refreshing in the milieu of constant entropy that was undergraduate school.

"Here is another sure thing: DJ is ready to go," said Scott, shifting the focus onto Ryan O'Regan.

"Yup, been around here all summer getting ready. I'm finally going to grab that travel team spot. Time trial could be a good race. It could be hard, I guess," said O'Regan, between yawns.

"Only a week to go. Better start catching up on your sleep now, DJ," said Cal, who seemed certain that O'Regan would have to work harder than expected to earn his spot.

"Ok, well. It'll be hard, but not THAT hard. Like, I'll likely be ninth. No way Matt or Fuller touch me."

"Can't be cocky, O'Regan," joked Heidi. "Those boys have run more XC than you over the years." Ellen contented herself with an eye roll at his expense. O'Regan's confidence was overwhelming, for someone who had yet to make the travel team, let alone run a fast 10k. He often overestimated his fitness and relied a bit too much on his natural ability, which seemed to help him a lot more over 800 metres than over ten kilometres.

"Well DJ, you better let the ol' legs do the talking." Neuffer whacked his roommate on the thigh. "I have faith in ya this year."

"Yeah, well, I feel fit," said O'Regan, rubbing his flat stomach. "Summer's been good...I think I got this." His current level of fitness was perhaps the least predictable among all team members, and the girls knew this fact as well as did we. Our running gossip continued until ten p.m., when Ellen and Leah grew tired, and left with Heidi in the latter's Mazda 3. Most of us were also tired, and almost ready to call it a night. I stayed in the living room with Scott to play a game of NHL 2016 on Cal's Xbox One. O'Regan passively watched from the couch, scrolling through his Instagram feed.

"Wow, I'm excited for this season to start," said Scott.

"Me too. I think we're going to be dominant in the conference. We get to host AUS too, on our own course. What a way to finish a career, here."

"Yeah, I've never run an AUS championship on the St. FX course, and this one, we're pretty much guaranteed the win," said Scott. "A cool thing about it too, Cyr, is that an X-Man will likely take the individual title."

"Yeah. I guess." I began thinking ahead. "That race will be hot. I have no idea which one of us will become conference champ." Although I thought

Scott was the perennial favourite to win the individual title, I refused to admit it to him.

Scott was humble enough to go along with my statement. "It's not like in McGuire's days. When I was a rookie, we just would all assume he'd win."

Connor McGuire had graduated the year before my arrival. From Prince Edward Island, like me, he had played a big part in my decision to attend St. FX. He had left the Island a mediocre runner, and then returned, four years later, as a multiple-time AUS champion. He had seven AUS gold medals to his name across cross-country and track and field disciplines. Confident, dominant, and bordering on cocky, he had become the face of St. FX's cross-country program when he won multiple consecutive conference championships between 2011 and 2013. Since his departure, however, top-dog status had been up for grabs, leading to somewhat of a power struggle between the team's top runners of each year. This year, as St. FX now had the supposed four best cross-country runners in the conference in Cal Dewolfe, Alex Neuffer, Scott Donald, and me, I anticipated this struggle to intensify. Of course, those were matters for the course, rather than for the living room.

One game of NHL 2017 was all we had time for, as tomorrow was an important day: the first day of training camp. It was the first occasion for the 2016 edition of the X-Men and X-Women to meet up, and also the first opportunity for us to come up with answers to the hot topics of the night. Tomorrow, we would begin to find out who had done their summer homework.

First Encounters

September 1st

"Neuffer, you're going to scare the rookies away with those calves!" said Angus. He was watching the skinny, orange-haired runner spring down the Greening hill, his leg muscles dancing underneath a razor-thin layer of pale skin. Following him closely, along with Scott, Angus, and Cal, we were jogging towards the Oland Centre to meet the rest of the team for the year's first practice. I was anxious to see the group, wondering if there would be many new faces. Dodging raindrops, we passed the sequence of fast food restaurants on James Street, and made it to the traffic lights signalling the start of Convocation Boulevard and the St. FX residences. A sign reading, "Welcome back, students!" was placed between Somers and Governors hall, but the campus was still quiet. Students only came in a few days later. Varsity athletes were required to report to school early for training camps. Passing the sign and circumventing the Charles V. Keating Millenium Centre, we joined a group of runners – some familiar, some new – standing at our perpetual meeting spot: the wooden Oland Centre bleachers overlooking the orange St. FX track.

The gloomy weather did nothing to dampen the spirits of the sea of runners excitedly stretching and tying their shoes. A contagious energy filled the air. The rookies, all sporting their best running attire, were silently sizing each other up, while the seniors were throwing playful jabs at each other in a nonchalant manner. We were expected to lead the practice today, as Bernie and Kevin, our head and assistant coaches, could only begin coaching two weeks prior to the first meet as per Atlantic University Sport (AUS) regulation.

That official training camp start-up date was on Saturday, September 3rd. Today's purpose was simply to log a few miles together and get to know each other while doing so.

Nic Favero loved every minute of these first encounters. As he observed the few nervous freshmen, he became nostalgic. "Ahh I remember when I was a rookie, boys. Coolest feeling ever! Running alongside a bunch of faster guys, just trying to hold on every day. You gotta love that grind, man."

"Yeah, if you CAN hold on." Cal was throwing a jab at O'Regan, who'd had to stop to walk a few times in his freshman-year training camp, four years prior, blaming meal hall pizza-induced stomach aches. Little did Cal know, the intended receiver of his jeers was still not among the group of skinny, shirtless runners.

Favero took charge of the situation once again. "Where do we want to go?"

"Landing Bethany?" suggested Neuffer. He was a fan of the soft dirt surface of the Antigonish Landing trail.

"Man, there is no way we're running the Bethany loop today," said Favero. We want to show the rooks the Landing when it's nice outside."

Nathan Jeffs moved towards our circle. "I don't know, Nic, I think I hear Bethany calling my name right now." A group of seniors cracked a laugh, acknowledging that Nic's girlfriend's name was also Bethany. Jeffs may have had the sense of humour of a wise twelve-year old, but he had perfected his style over the years. He was always good for a few laughs.

I looked around me. Like a middle-school dance party, the boys and girls teams were intensely segregated at the starting point of the run, with the pack of boys standing slightly ahead. The rookies were mostly standing at the back and making polite conversation with each other. Standing with Neuffer in front of the herd of backwards caps and split-shorts, I felt the urge to get going. I figured that if I began my run, the others would follow. But, as soon as I engaged in a slow hobble, I was called down by a few of the guys, as we had a late arrival.

"Wait! Guys. Wait up!" Warren Ferguson, not unlike a disoriented surgeon scurrying around a hospital looking for his operating tools, speed-walked past the group to reach the change room. His large satchel-style school bag made him seem professional, but his undone polo shirt worked well to counter the effect. Ferg always looked like he was in a hurry, and in most instances, the physics/economics major and medical school hopeful was not faking it. Knowing that Warren always made his best effort to be on time despite his fiendish schedule, the team usually tolerated his tardiness. But, classes had not yet started, so I suspected that his lateness was a product of one too many games of Halo 3 on his Xbox. "Ferg you have two minutes!" I yelled.

"Uhh, I'll be quick. Yes, just hold on one second I just need to..." BOOM! The Oland Centre door shut behind him. He threw all his belongings into the change room and awkwardly slid into the same running shirt and shorts he had been wearing for a week. I used this extra time to introduce myself to a few of the new guys. Addison Derhak, the undisputed class of this rookie crew, stood out. His running shorts were just as flamboyant as those of the seniors, and they intersected an upright, skinny frame. A consistent summer of training had brought him to a time of 15:55 in the 5000m. In this fitness, he would serve as a strong seventh to ninth runner, which on a regular year would send him to the CIS championship – a respectable feat for a rookie. The smile on his face suggested that he had been waiting a long time for this day.

He stood awkwardly in front of me, rubbing his arm. "So, you're the guy? The Alex guy from Facebook?"

"Yeah, that's me. You look a lot faster in person." A few of us had been in charge of reaching out to Addison to entice him to choose St. FX over a rival school.

"Thanks! I just bought these shorts. I have five other pairs!"

Warren stumbled out of the locker room. "Ok, I'm ready." His three words sounded like a single, incomprehensible one, but he had gotten his point across. "Where are we taking the rookies?"

"West River loop," replied Neuffer.

"Hmm... ok," said Warren. "As long as we're not taking them up Brown's Mountain, like Riley Johnston did to me when I was a rookie. That mountain was so steep. You guys have no idea how close I was to quitting on the spot!"

"As if you would have quit," I said. Warren was more stubborn than an English bulldog.

"Cyr, I am serious! I was dangerously close to walking away from Bernie and never coming back."

"Yeah, yeah, yeah."

Addison was giddy. "Oh man, my first run with the X-Men. This is so cool!" Finally, our group was moving. But, like clockwork, we were called back once more.

"Hey guys, wait up!" This time, it was Ryan O'Regan, running towards us in his sandals.

"O'Regan, where were you?" I asked. The question was rhetorical. No matter the answer we were getting, there was no way we were waiting for him to change into his running clothes. At his pace, it at least would have been a ten-minute ordeal. Unfortunately for O'Regan, his lack of punctuality had become commonplace, and teammates and coaches alike had come to expect it. So, without thinking twice about it, the boys took off, chasing the pavement for the first time of the season.

As per usual for the first run of the fall, the tempo was fast. Rookies took their turns showing their fitness by pushing the pace up front. The veterans, not to be outdone, kept up and made sure the pace did not get out of hand. The plan for today was, after all, an easy run. Not everyone, however, felt at ease. As it was every year, a few rookies fell off the back of the pack. One pulled up and started walking. This angered me. We were running at a leisurely pace.

I turned to Scott. "A hockey player who can't skate doesn't show up to the X-Men hockey tryouts. So why the hell do we have these guys come to ours? This is embarrassing." Despite being on the run, Scott spoke calmly, and lowered his voice. "Think of Newf though." He was referring to Melissa Hardy, an X-Women runner who had come in very unfit and had gone on to become the AUS champion after three years of consistent hard work. "What if one of these guys turns out to be really good in a few years and helps us in his junior or senior year? You never know."

"I guess." I replied. "But they had at least a summer to get ready, they should be able to handle 4:30 kilometres. Like, come on!" Scott and I then inched towards the front to join into other conversations. Warren, however, was tagging along near the back. Not particularly blessed with natural ability, but rather with a willingness to work hard and to hurt, he had been in the shoes of these unfit rookies and was living proof for the legitimacy of Scott's countering argument. There was a slight chance that one of these rookies could become as strong as Warren, and perhaps contribute to the team's success. But, I thought to myself, landing a rookie with half of Warren's outlandish ability to grind was more than unlikely.

Near the front of the pack, our speed began to increase. Addison was the main catalyst of the pace change – he nervously ran near the front. "What pace should I be running for my easy runs? I like 4:15 per kilometre, but should I be hitting closer to 4:10s? What do you guys usually run?"

The nature of the question worried me. Easy runs to us had one criterion: they had to feel easy. As a senior, I felt it to be my duty to ensure that Addison would not get caught up in impressive-sounding numbers of paces and mileage. Running with consistency was far more important.

Cal beat me to my answer. "Here's what I think. You should ditch the watch, run by feel," he challenged him.

"This watch? But it was like, 300 dollars! And it's new!" he said, with noticeable concern in his voice.

"Well maybe stick a piece of black tape on top of it," suggested Matt Eliot. "You can still wear it!"

"But then it ruins the look!" whined Addison. "It's the top of the line Garmin watch and it's shiny!" Indeed, his watch did not look cheap.

Steadily, with the group, we comfortably made our way back to campus, knowing that the harder runs and workouts would soon be coming. I looked around and made note of the impressive breadth of the pack and hoped that it would remain this hefty until November. If other years could serve as indicators, it probably wouldn't. Charles Darwin could have just as well been talking about a cross-country season at St. FX University when he refined his theory of evolution and natural selection. Only the strong would survive.

Morrison Hall

September 1st

Our group trotted back onto campus after finishing up fifty minutes around the West River loop. Somehow, O'Regan had gone for his own run, and had beaten us back to campus. The run had been scheduled for 3:30, so suppertime was nearing. We were sitting in a circle on the St. FX turf, doing core exercises.

Scott stood in the middle of the circle to capture our attention. "Ok, guys. So here is what I understand. Diana, our favourite meal hall lady, is working the door today and will let us in, even if we don't have meal tickets right now. They have a list of the names for all the varsity athletes who have permission to be on campus early, and we're all on it. We can go as soon as 4:30 hits."

The news triggered a cheer from the upperclassmen. We had somewhat missed the food served at St. FX's Morrison Hall – the venue we called meal hall – over the summer, but we were especially excited to regain the cherished social aspect of our supper hour (or hours). It was not uncommon for our group to grab a table and keep it for two hours or more while people came and went. Those of us most willing to avoid our studies would stay seated for the whole time. The time we spent there permitted us to get closer with the girls' team, and with each other. I could not wait to catch up with some friends I had not yet spoken with.

As a group, we changed out of our running clothes, and walked past Bishops hall, up the stairs around the Physical Sciences Building, and through the Bishops parking lot. Our first meal was awaiting us.

Addison glared at the cafeteria food and started whining. "Eww...what is this? Like, is that tofu in there?"

"That's the vegetarian option, Addison. I'm going to get stir fry if you'd like that."

"Uhh, yeah. Cause there is no way I'm eating that mush. It looks like puke!" The seventeen-year-old was wearing a backwards cap, a thick, silver chain over a white beater, and sweat pants. He surely would not be mistaken for anything other than a freshman, except for maybe a drug dealer. "Where do we sit?" he asked, still mesmerized by the size of the cafeteria.

"Yellow room," I said, as I led him towards the rest of the team. Three years ago, our group had congregated from the main sitting area and its rectangular tables to the Yellow room – ingeniously named for its yellow walls – at the back of the cafeteria, for its round, group conversation-friendly tables. With Addison, I joined our group of thirty runners who had already merged three big round tables together.

I barely had the time to sit. "Okay, Cyr. Spill the beans on this French guy!" said Neuffer. Our rowdy group suddenly went silent. There had been talk of another recruit joining our team, even though he had not come to practice today. The French guy was Leo Jusiak, an exchange student from France.

"Ok, well, I met him in the Schwartz building yesterday. The Student Union president introduced me to him and said that the guy was French and wanted to run."

"Is he good?" asked Matt.

"He is a miler. He apparently has run 3:56 for 1500 metres. So he'd be in the mix. Not sure about his cross wheels, though."

"So where is he, why was he not at practice?" asked Warren.

"He has a lot of international student initiation activities, apparently. But he is coming out tomorrow. He's already met Bernie."

Cal chuckled. "Oh great! Bernie doesn't speak a lick of French and this guy probably can't speak English. How did that go?"

"It was pretty awkward," I said. "I did most of the translating. Bernie couldn't believe that Leo did not know who Eric Gillis was."

"Bad move by the new kid!" said Scott. "I don't care where you're from. You need to know of Gillis around here." Indeed, knowing of the most successful athlete ever to run for Bernie and the X-Men was a must in Antigonish.

"So… is this guy coming to the rookie party tomorrow?" asked Jeffs.

"Maybe, I guess I'll ask him. I don't know if he likes to drink."

"Cyr, he's from France! Obviously, he drinks!" said Favero. We could buy him a housewarming bottle of wine!"

Scott rose from his chair. "Yeah, we'll see tomorrow, I guess. Anyway, I'm headed back to the house to get some rest. Tomorrow's a big day. Run in the afternoon, then the rookie party. If anyone wants to stop by Greening to lose in a game of NHL 2017, be my guest."

Favero followed him. "Yeah, I'm leaving too. I have some reading to catch up on."

"Reading?" asked Warren. "Nic, I am not sure if you are aware of this, but school has not started yet."

"Actually, Ferg, school never ends," replied the sociology student.

"Of course it ends! Every night at five and every Friday morning," said Cal. He could not be bothered with extraneous readings.

Scott's departure had triggered a chain reaction. The table finally dispersed. It had been two hours and fifteen minutes.

Quiet Giant

September 2nd

"Cyr and I are doing old school for seventy minutes if anyone wants in," boomed Neuffer, as he walked into the change room.

I knew that not many people would be enticed by this idea. When you agreed to run with Alex Neuffer, you were agreeing to run quickly. To him, an easy run could be no slower than 4:10 per kilometre. No matter how much physiological junk would accumulate in his legs from past workouts, he would stay true to his one gear: fast. I felt fresh on the overcast and unusually cold morning, so I made the pledge to keep him company. To me, an easy run had no correct pace. For that reason, I alternated between clusters of running partners within the team on easy run days. On that day, I had come to terms with running on the fast side. Bernie and Kevin still could not be in contact with the team during practice, so once again, the seniors had decided on a meeting time. I had told Leo that we would meet at 4:00. I hoped he could find his way.

"Are we missing anyone?" asked O'Regan.

"Well if you're here we're probably good to go," said Angus.

"Wait, one sec. Leo is coming!"

Wearing long sweat pants and a purple Asics T-shirt, the slender Frenchman was jogging from his house to campus. He was cruising around the Physical Sciences building and picking up the pace, noticing he was late. Excited, I pointed him out to the guys as he jogged up to us, short of breath.

I introduced him to the team. "Guys, this is Leo, the guy I have been telling you about. We met a few days ago in the Schwartz building. "

"Hey Leo!" the group belted.

"Hello. It is, uhm, nice to meet you. Are we doing the footing or it is workout?"

"Just an easy run today, if that's what you mean by 'footing.'"

"How long?"

I pointed to Neuffer. "He and I are doing seventy minutes. I think most people are doing the same, or maybe a bit shorter."

"Wow! Seventy minute! That is a long big run. Oh! I do thirty or forty. I am not ready for this now."

"It's ok," I said. "Some rookies will be doing just about that."

"All right, let's go!" Angus was growing impatient. Our group, one man stronger, began shuffling away from the Oland Centre. As expected, twenty minutes into our run, Neuffer and I started to separate from most of the group, eliciting a few heckles from those left behind.

Cal taunted us from the back of our herd. "Aaaaand the lead group is about to crash and burn and fall to the hands of the hungry and more diligent chase pack!"

"The wiser men at the back are biding their time and will soon gobble them up at once!" added Angus in a faked British accent to mimic the IAAF commentators at Diamond League meets. Nobody wanted the reputation of the Easy Run Hero.

Neuffer grew annoyed. "They don't even run that much slower than we do, and yet they're calling us out for hammering easy runs," he said, frustrated at hearing the other guys make wise cracks to his expense, thirty metres back. Apparently, a certain member of that chase pack was not content with the leisurely pace. As soon as Neuffer and I thought we had pulled away from the entire group, a set of large, clumsy-sounding feet stomping on the pavement began to resonate between our slighter, more synchronized steps.

"Fuller, you decided to join the big boys I see?" said Neuffer.

"Yeah," said Fuller, a man of few words.

The joke was somewhat ironic, as Fuller himself stood on top of a six foot five inch, 215 lbs. frame. The giant from Nova Scotia's Annapolis Valley was often misunderstood – probably because he said very little. With his actions rather than his words, however, he constantly communicated his fascination and love for the sport of running. He knew the ins and outs of Nova

Scotia's distance running history like no other. His passion for the activity was obvious, but one could have inferred that running did not love him back. Aside from being blessed with an overly tall frame and a musculature akin to a basketball player or bodybuilder, his greatest defect of all was his infamous sweet tooth. After a stellar summer of training following his grade twelve year in 2014, Fuller had accomplished a lifelong dream of his; he had earned his spot on the travel team at St. FX University. He had barely made it as the twelfth runner, but that did not matter. He was able to wear the same jacket worn by Riley Johnston, Lee Wesselius, and other runners he had placed in his mind on top of the grandest pedestal. By wearing the blue jacket with the large letter "X" crested on its backside, the young giant could now, in his eyes, consider himself an equal.

Soon enough, however, Ryan Fuller's bad habits at the school cafeteria caught up to him on the racecourse. He had gained weight. His legs grew heavy and unable to handle the extra load, and he soon got injured. Being injured made him less careful of his nutritional habits and every time he tried to return to running, the ordeal would be more arduous. He would say goodbye to his beloved cafeteria desserts when returning home in April, and then return to us in September having dropped the extra weight and looking shockingly lean. This was a yearly occurrence. His problems did not stop there. On top of this imbalance, he also had the tendency to overestimate his fitness and push the pace on easy days. These fast, easy runs were usually his fast track to burnout if injuries did not take care of him first.

"Fuller, are you sure you're good with this pace? Do you remember how these fast, easy runs sunk you last year, and the year before that one?" I said, becoming increasingly annoyed about his habits by the year.

"Yeah I feel good."

That was all I was going to get out of him, so I did not push my luck with the friendly giant. For seventy minutes, Neuffer and I chatted constantly, and Fuller stayed on our heels, quietly listening through huffs and puffs.

Rookie Party

September 2nd

We were the last ones back to campus. All the others had run shorter. We arrived to a determined Nic Favero, methodically planning the night to come. "Ok, so let's go eat now, and we'll meet at my house in forty-five minutes. Then, we will have thirty minutes to plan the final activities before the girls and the rookies come over. That should be enough. Cyr, bring the list of activities."

This list of activities had been created a few days ago, as we did not leave an event of such history and importance to the last minute. Tonight was the rookie party, and the topic of this social gathering had been taboo until now. Part of the magic of the rookie party stemmed from its mystery to its very subjects, the rookies. To them, it represented a rite of passage. To us, the most senior members of the team, it represented the last time until the CIS championship that we would place our commitment to running on the back burner for a night of good old-fashioned college fun.

"I have the list. We'll be over by six," I said.

"Addison, Cullen, Colin, do you guys need anything? I'm going to make a trip to the liquor store," called Cal. Most rookies took him up on the offer, leaving Cal with a list of beer orders. Cal's list held types of beer that were drunk for their effect, rather than for their taste. The rookies looked no further than what was cheap, bulk, and effective. I could tell that none of them were new to the party scene. Although cross-country running seemed to consistently attract a peculiar ensemble of awkward, reserved individuals, our rookie class of this year did not seem as such. For many of the rookies over the years, drinking and partying were foreign concepts. For Addison Derhak and Cullen MacInnis, however, university would not teach them many new tricks. Cullen was from a small country community, and Addison had apparently been given his first sip of alcohol by the age of eleven, so he had said. In their cases, at least, we would not have to be wary of first-time mistakes, such as consuming too much. In the case of other potential rookies, such as Colin Glencross, David Parker, and Spencer Virtue, however, they would be exposed to alcohol for the first time, and we knew to keep a watchful eye out for them. In planning this event, its purpose – to facilitate first encounters and to have fun – could not be forgotten. Bernie had always been half-aware of the rookie party, and his demands were for us to not make fools of ourselves – at least not in public – and for nobody to get hurt or in trouble. He discouraged it but realized that the onus was ultimately on us to act responsibly. I hoped we could give the rookies a similar experience to the ones I had already lived. During my years as rookie (being a red shirt runner in my first year made me a rookie for two years as far as the rookie party committee was concerned), I had given a few seniors lap dances, had competed in lip sync contests, and had competed in a rap battle (which I had handily won against O'Regan, in my opinion). Now, it was our time to have a little fun at the rookies' expense. Excited, the senior members of 18 Greening grabbed the drinks from the fridge and the list of activities and headed towards Acadia Street to our destination for the night.

"Welcome to our humble abode, seniors! Please, take your shoes off and look around. We are honoured to host you all!" Nathan Jeffs was speaking as if we had not spent countless afternoons and nights sitting around their living room and on their deck over the summer months. The house, to us seniors especially, was no new sight – 25 Acadia had character. The address that had become synonymous with our cross-country team seemed to roll off the tongue. In my grade twelve year, I had visited Antigonish on a recruit trip. At the time, three senior runners had inhabited the house. Since then, it had been passed down to new teammates. Connor McGuire had lived between these walls. As did Riley Johnston, the only X-Man to be a part of five consecutive AUS cross-country championship teams. Presently, it was occupied by Nathan Jeffs, Matt Eliot, and returning resident, Nic Favero.

If the word college were an adjective, it would have perfectly described this place. Bob Marley posters were overlooking a beat-up couch, which was placed in front of a vacant area supposed to be occupied by a television. The TV had unfortunately been stolen from the household a few days ago. In its place was a jar with the words "new TV fund" written on its contour. The jar contained around three dollars in quarters. Christmas lights decorated the living room ceiling – they were a quick fix to replace a broken light bulb. The kitchen was decorated with empty beer bottles abandoned by their consumers and left to collect dust, and the fridge was smeared with Scrabble-style magnets with the words "Frisky Warren Ferguson" spelled out. To the left of the entranceway were piles of old shoes. I suspected that some belonged to former residents. A pair of old New Balance flats, which had lost all structural integrity, were kept upright by beer cans shoved in their insides. The guys had not hosted many parties in the summer, so I wondered whether remnants of parties past remained in plain sight because the hosts treasured them as souvenirs, or simply because they cared little to clean up after themselves. The refrigerator seemed to contain more food than three university students could ever need – yet I could not seem to find a combination of ingredients that would go together to make a meal. But, despite it all, the home was our traditional and primary refuge, and we had all grown attached to it.

We did not have much time before the rookies' arrival, so Favero took control of the situation. "Yo man, let's get this show on the road, I was thinking we could start the party with house rules. Like, don't drink with your St. FX gear on, make sure you show up to practice tomorrow morning... that kind of stuff, you know?" He had led us all upstairs to his room, so that we could privately tie together the last strings.

"No help from the seniors in any competition, that's a rule," said Neuffer.

The format of the party was similar to last year's. We would divide the rookies up into three teams of four. There would be a number of challenges, some for teams and some for individuals, all meant to move the rookies away from their comfort zones. It was the ultimate icebreaker. Scott, Neuffer, Cal, Favero and I would each get to lead and describe a challenge or two. They ranged from push-up contests to relay races to rap battles.

O'Regan, late once again, rushed up the stairs, and ran into the room, winded. "Ok guys, what are we doing? How are we going to separate everything, like who says what?" Also a senior, he was just as entitled to the organization of this party as we were, but he had been left behind due to his tardiness. Knowing how much O'Regan wanted to make his mark on the party, Neuffer and Scott each gave him one of their activities for him to lead. "Ok, we all know our events. Do we need anything else?" asked Cal.

"I think we're good," said Scott, as he led us out of the room. "We may as well get started because the girls are here too now. They're waiting for us." Our group of seniors descended from Favero's room together to get the party started.

"Rookies! Sophomores! Everybody who isn't a senior, please pay attention!" Scott was speaking to a group of about thirty boys and girls, dispersed around the living room. "Welcome to Rookie Party 2016!"

"Oh this is going to be great!" shrieked Addison, from the crowd.

"Frosh, silence!" joked Scott. "Tonight, you have been divided into teams. In those teams, you will be facing each other in various challenges meant to get you out of your comfort zone and meet each other. So don't be scared! The main goal of this night is to have fun. Favero, as a host of 25 Acadia House, do you have anything to add?"

"Well, I think you've said it all, Scott. Don't feel pressured to do anything you don't want to do. If Warren offers you a shot of gin, you probably should not take it. Other than that, let's have a good night! Let the challenges begin!"

The push-up contest saw a battle between Emily MacKay of the girls' team and Spencer Virtue. The crowd favourite, Emily, won by a hair. Paul MacLellan led a team of rookies to a relay-race win, while Mary MacDonald, the fifth year student coming from the soccer team and rookie to our team, easily won the Name the Seniors game. The rap battle saw Leo Jusiak spit rhymes in English for the first time in his life. His rhymes were lacklustre, but his accent wooed the crowd – especially the girls.

When Paul saw the positive reaction to the Frenchman's rapping, he wanted in. "Ok! Everyone listen to me. I have a rap too! It's about Cyr. I hope that everyone is ready." Like that, he had everyone's attention. Amused, I sat down and waited to get dissed. "Cyr. You are a little MOUSE. Living inside a little HOUSE." He was emphasizing the last word of each sentence. "You think you can BALL? But you can't keep up with PAUL. At the MALL! I am faster than YOU. You can't even keep up with STU." Looking satisfied, he sat back down. Confused, but amused, everyone roared.

"CYR YOU JUST GOT ROASTEDDD!" shouted Cal. Paul's lyrical genius had put an end to the challenges. Scott cranked up the music and the living room transformed into a dance party. The kitchen would become grounds for a game of flip cup. We seniors were having a lot of fun, but in a controlled manner. We wanted to make it to practice the next morning, and we felt it our duty to make sure the rookies were experiencing their first college party without any hiccups.

"Hey, Cyr, would you mind taking my spot for this game of flip cup?" asked Colin Glencross, a first-year runner from Maine, USA.

"Yeah, sure man. Are you not feeling well?"

"No, I'm just not much of a drinker." I did not consider myself much of a drinker, either, but I quickly accepted the offer. Colin seemed to fit that distance runner mould; calm, reserved, and collected. He had, however, a long way to go before challenging for a roster spot. He had been left behind on the first few easy runs.

As I was finishing up as Colin's substitute in the flip cup game, I spotted another freshman, Cullen MacInnis. Wearing a floral-patterned button-up shirt, he had decided to take control of our dance floor. Normally quiet, it was obvious that he had consumed a few beverages. The young runner from Cape Breton, NS was not a sought-after recruit, but his athleticism and drive had made him a dark horse in Bernie's eyes. Lots could happen in four years, I thought to myself when I had observed his athletic build throw itself around the track with less ease than it was now oscillating around the 25 Acadia living room. His running stride was oddly laborious and steady at the same time. Similar to O'Regan, he was blessed with a Vitruvian mesomorph body, which is indeed a blessing in mostly all areas of life save distance running. The extra muscle was a lot to carry for 10 kilometres. Clearly, he needed more mileage, but he was steady and had potential. On that night, however, there was nothing too steady about any movement he was making.

"Cullen, 7:30 am tomorrow, you'll be there right?" I said, smirking.

"Yeah... I'm fine I just... I just love to dance. I'll make to practice, Alex... don't you worry."

I believed him.

"Yo, this French guy is awesome!" said Addison, pointing into the kitchen. In there was Leo, speaking to a crowd of girls, using his limited repertoire of English words.

"So, I come from France this month. I here for the full school year, then leave again."

"Wow, so are you going to be faster than all the boys?" asked Heidi.

"I meet a friend and he tell me about the running team here. I do a lot of running in France, but I party too much in summer, so no. I'm not fast right now, no," said Leo. He loved the attention from the girls' team – they were mesmerized by his French accent.

"Well who knows, Leo. Maybe you can teach our boys a lesson, they're getting too cocky, I think," said Heidi, shooting me a glance.

Favero came to my rescue. "It's not being cocky if you're good."

"Oh my God this Leo is so CUTE!" whispered Leah to Ellen.

"So, like, he's actually from France? That is so random…but cool!" said Liz.

Leo was a hit, and with reason. The confidence he radiated despite being in a new country and speaking in a different tongue was remarkable. He was already more comfortable with the girls than he had been in his meeting with Bernie. Of course, the former group aroused him more than the latter.

After getting enough of Leo's mesmerizing of our entire senior girls' class, I moved rooms. I felt it important to go introduce myself to the new members of the girls' team whom I had not yet met. In my first year, this part had been incredibly exciting, but now as a senior, it had somewhat lost its novelty. Regardless, I made it a point to go introduce myself. I approached them, smiling. "Are you guys having fun?"

"Yeah, we are," said Paige Chisholm, one of the rookies. To my confusion, her tone, her demeanour, and her facial expression suggested otherwise. Ashley Robson, another first-year recruit, did not look much more enthused. I realized it was not my place to ask if something was wrong, as I did not yet know them very well. I hoped they would come around, and I had faith.

"Yeah Cyr, don't bother with those girls. We've been trying all night. They're not talking," concluded Neuffer. They must be scared of us."

"Why would they be scared of us?" I asked.

"I don't know. It could have something to do with O'Regan looking like he's straight off the set of *The Walking Dead*." Our roommate was sitting on the couch gazing into the open, his mouth agape. He was attempting to open a bottle of Stella Artois, his usual fix.

Neuffer gave him a few taps on the cheek. "O'Regan come on man, give me that. Go drink some water, you're in rough shape." Bouncing back from his melancholic gaze at nothing, O'Regan came back to life.

"I need to stop...I know. But Neuffer, I want to go to the pub." He was slurring. By his demeanour, I could tell that no great adventures were to come his way at Piper's Pub.

"Buddy, we have seven hours before practice, do you think that's a good call?" I asked him. He did not answer. Thankfully, that was the end of his night. He soon made the kilometre-and-a-half walk back home to 18 Greening with Angus. It took him half an hour.

As the challenges ended, a few seniors walked over to Piper's Pub together. I ambled home, knowing that this night would be my last appearance on the party scene until November 12th, the date of the CIS championship. The gathering had been successful. People had fun, the ice was broken, and everything had been kept under control. I was satisfied. Tired, I barely got to set an alarm for 7:15 am before plunging into a deep slumber.

Coach Bern

September 3rd

Bernie Chisholm was standing outside of the back entrance of the Oland centre under the bleachers, arms crossed. He quietly contemplated his new purchase: New Balance Vazee Pace running shoes. At the age of seventy, he knew very well when buying them that they would strictly serve as walking shoes. He donned a quarter-zip St. FX baby blue sweater – the sweater all official team members would receive in a week's time. It dropped over black denim pants, which were hugging his still-slender runner's legs. An avid runner back in the day, Bernie had been through many pairs of running shoes. He had fallen in love with the sport as a young teenager, and had found success in the distance races, competing in the marathon in the Canada Games. It was coaching, however, that eventually inducted him into the Nova Scotia and St. FX Halls of Fame. The one nicknamed Bo had amassed impressive coaching credentials over the years. He had seventeen AUS cross-country championships to his name (nine men's, eight women's). His men's team in 2008 had won a silver medal at the CIS championship, and returned to capture bronze in 2009, while the X-Women had as well nabbed bronze in 2007 – all impressive feats for a school of barely 4000 students. Moreover, his prowess as a coach had earned him trips to a few international cross-country championships with Team Canada, earlier in his career.

He kept those facts to himself – along with many other nuggets of information. No athlete of his knew his personal bests or his favourite distance. Few knew that he had been on national team coaching staffs. We knew even less of what had caused him to retire from the sport. We knew he had suffered an accident that had hampered his running career, but nobody knew of its nature, severity, or timeline. He read a lot of running books, went to church on Sundays, and was a retired English teacher (or was it history), but just about everything else about the septuagenarian was kept under wraps. Yet, despite his discretion, his name had become synonymous with distance-running excellence in the province of Nova Scotia – even more so around these parts. Telling someone you were an athlete of Bernie Bo's was the equivalent of being given the key to the town of Antigonish. He was admired, revered and respected by most members of the community.

Despite these accolades, it was rumoured that Bernie refused any salary St. FX would offer him. It was not about the money. It was about development. Developing great athletes – developing great people. That was the job, as far as he was concerned. The reward could not be cash, but rather empirical proof that athletes entering his program experienced personal growth during their time with the blue and white. The glory of being a winning coach was a side bonus.

Alas, he would witness no glory on this morning. As he knew too well, the hangover that followed the rookie party would take a few casualties. Year after year, the spotty attendance for this run reminded Bernie that his runners were still, to the core, eighteen to twenty-two-year-old young men and women occasionally looking for a good time. This year, 7:30 am had come particularly fast. For Paul MacLellan and Ryan O'Regan, too fast. They were the only team members missing from practice. Even Dancing Cullen was present, looking far less sure of himself than he had in 25 Acadia's living room barely twelve hours prior. Twenty-five minutes were prescribed for the morning run, and as Bernie knew well, their purpose was to gauge dedication rather than fitness level. I picked up my heavy legs and ran around town with Favero at a pitiful pace. He felt and looked no better than I did.

After slogging out twenty-five laborious minutes, it was back to bed for most of us. Since we were a dedicated and competitive bunch, alcohol consumption was not overly commonplace. As few of us were inclined to hit the bars at this time of year, we rarely pressured each other to go out at night. This penchant for clean living, however, came at a price. On the few occasions that we would go out, we would make up for the nights we missed all at once, and the morning after would usually hurt. It doesn't take an overly rowdy party to inebriate a group of 140-pounders.

* * *

The second run of the day at three p.m. was when Bernie addressed the team and officially kicked off training camp. The same long faces that had showed up in the morning returned sharper, and the dragging feet now had a spring in their steps. More rested, the guys and girls teams were also more conditioned to retain information than they had been seven hours ago. Bernie took no time before singling out the morning's absentees.

"Paul and O'Regan, nice to see you're back alive. Could we have a chat?" He motioned to the far bleachers. Nobody was surprised. Bernie usually was lenient about those kinds of things with rookies, but not as much with returning runners. Missing practice was unacceptable for a sophomore and senior team member.

Bernie let out a long sigh before addressing the two runners. "O'Regan, you're in your fourth year here. Can you tell me where you were this morning?"

"I would have been there I swear, but I had to work this morning at the campus tour guide office, and I couldn't get in contact with you because my phone died when I was already at work and I forgot my charger."

Other seniors shared a look of amusement. His long, messy excuse was expected. Something always seemed to happen to complicate his day and interfere with his duties. I had two conflicting theories about Ryan O'Regan. The first was that he did not know how to manage his time properly. The second was that somehow, he simply was the unluckiest man on planet Earth. Bernie shook his head and let out a sigh. Kevin, the assistant coach, chuckled silently.

Bernie turned towards the younger of the two runners. "Paul, what about you?"

"Well Bernie, I was very tired because I drank alcohol at the party we had last night. I had set up my alarm clock to ring at 6:45, and it seems as though I slept through it."

"Uhm... ok. Well, uhh... you know better than that, Paul." Bernie was not even mad, just startled by Paul's ease with the truth.

"Yeah, I do. That is for sure."

We were holding in our laughter, while Kevin was giggling. If O'Regan was the poster boy for questionable stories, Paul was it for mind-numbing, almost comical honesty. Once the pair had finished explaining themselves, on Bernie's orders the boys and girls grabbed a seat on the bleachers. Bernie was about to address the 2016 edition of X-Men and X-Women for the first time.

"All right everyone, welcome to our training camp. I am still a little fuzzy with some of the rookies' names, but hopefully it will come in time. I know there are two Davids and Alexs and Cullens or Colins or something like that and so on, but we will get it soon. I look forward to catching up with you all in the next few days. We will be seeing lots of each other. Two practices are scheduled every day until the beginning of classes. During these days, run within yourselves, and build up your mileage slowly. Seniors, make sure the rookies aren't overdoing it, as we have our time trial next Saturday, September 10th. If some of you have been consistent this summer with your mileage, feel free to organize a small workout amongst yourselves before that time. If you are still building up your fitness, it would be best to stick to easy runs for now.

"Next to me is Kevin Grant, my assistant coach. He is my right-hand man... and often my left hand man as well. He is here to help me with workouts and organization and so on. You will be seeing as much of him as you will of me this year. Another individual you will be acquainted with is my wife, Brenda. When Kevin screws up, she's the third line of defence. She will be coming to most meets – she does some of the administrative stuff for the team, so you will be meeting her in the next few weeks. Anyway, during this week, we are just observing and letting the captains lead practices and tell the young guys and girls what to do. So, don't worry about impressing anyone just yet. Eventually, a travel team of nine to twelve guys and nine to twelve girls will be selected. Later, seven out of these twelve on each team will represent us at the AUS conference championship, and hopefully at the CIS Nationals. But, that's a long ways away. We're going to take it one day at a time, so let's get running. Boys' captains, girls' captains, you already know who you are."

We had no idea. The boys looked around, slightly confused, and presumed he was talking about Scott, and... Cal? Me? Neuffer? Whatever. He would tell us eventually. Maybe. "Where are the boys going today?" asked Bernie.

"Landing Bethany," said Cal.

"See you in an hour!" On those words, we were off.

Bernie watched the group scurry away with enthusiasm. He loved this time of year. He knew that this talented group of runners had the potential to challenge many bigger schools. Scott had just missed a Second Team All-Canadian spot at the CIS championship in 2015. Cal had become a force on the cross-country course with a podium finish at last year's conference championship as a junior. Neuffer had, for the first time in a while, been healthy for the entire summer and looked incredibly fit. Angus was now a junior national bronze medallist in the 5000 metres with a personal best of 14:53. I had experienced a breakthrough in the 1500 metres in the last year and now held times of 3:52 and 4:09 for the mile. Nic and Paul would likely be worth 32:30-33:00 over 10 km by CIS weekend. Then, the likes of Addison, Edward, Warren, and others were on the verge of a breakthrough. The 2016-17 X-Men were full of potential. Bernie also was aware, however, that potential could easily be spoiled, and that we were not entitled to any success simply because of the names on our roster. Our pedigrees and past accomplishments meant close to nothing. Injuries, burnout, academics, social life, and everything in between would threaten to tarnish a successful season. Bernie knew that our way of coping with these possible distractions and mishaps would ultimately determine our success as a team. Years of experience had taught him to never assume anything. Especially after learning that a few seniors were out at Piper's Pub last night.

He turned towards Kevin. "Heard from MacKinnon that the guys were out late. Not the way we want to start the year."

"I know, but it was their first weekend back. It won't last. I think it's tradition to have a get together on the first Saturday, Bernie."

Bernie sighed. "Yeah, well, I suppose."

"The good thing," said Kevin, "is that most of them showed up for the run this morning without complaint. That's the culture we want to foster."

"Yeah, I guess you're right. No excuses from now on, though. I can't have seniors missing practice like that," said Bernie. "It is a long year... still lots to be done before the big day." He paused and gazed at the track. "Is this a winning team, Kevin? What do you think?"

"Too soon to tell, Bernie. Nothing gets decided in September."

Host Fabio

September 4th

"Ahh, come on, Stralman! You're garbage!" screamed Angus Rawling at the virtual hockey player he was manipulating from the comfort of our stained, red three-seater. Addison Derhak had brought his Xbox One controllers over to 18 Greening, so we were engaged in a battle of NHL 2017. Scott and I were taking on the two young guns, and their style of play was quite reckless. "Another penalty? Come on, ref!!"

"Angus, you can't hit my guy when he doesn't have the puck, that's interference," I said, laughing.

Due to their lack of on-ice discipline, Scott and I were constantly on the power play, and won handily. A game of NHL was just what we needed after such a long day. It was Sunday, so our longest run of the week had been done on that morning. Later, we had gathered ten of the guys to play a game of Ultimate Frisbee. All tired, we were content with drinking our orange juice and yelling at small, shockingly real-looking, fictitious hockey players. Angus tackled video games with the same intensity level as he did distance running, and that level was one to behold. Hailing from Calgary, AB, he was one of those runners who, as casual observers would often say, "came out of nowhere." A few breakout years in his grade twelve and freshman seasons had made people aware of his arrival onto the CIS distance running scene, and then he had emerged from the shadows of his training partners and become a force to be reckoned with. Blessed with a slender frame and long legs akin to those of a Kenyan, the genetic lottery had undoubtedly guided him towards our sport.

On top of his physical gifts, he was equipped with a unique mind – one tailored for an elite distance runner. Angus was not afraid to hurt. The thought of hitting a glycolytic wall five kilometres into a 10k did not faze him. He had one effort level, and it was maximal. Though that mindset sometimes backfired (he had suffered a harrowing experience during the 2015 CIS championship), it gave him a chance to win any race. No matter the competitors, the climate, or the stakes, Angus would fearlessly chase the leader. It was almost as if he was too young to the sport to be apprehensive about the possible consequences of not pacing oneself. More often than not, it helped him. His intensity level was not only present in races but was also in every practice. It was rumoured that he had replicated a Saturday morning workout in the middle of one of his Saturday nights in his rookie year, simply because he was upset with his paces in his previous try. His intensity would often entice him to chase high-mileage totals and to work out in an overaggressive fashion, rendering his healthy status rather volatile.

I noticed he was icing his ankle while playing NHL. "Yo Beef, what's up with the ice?"

"It's just my ankle. It's screwed up. I've been dealing with it since the eighth grade. I think it has something to do with the growth plates. It's supposed to stop hurting once I'm done growing, according to the doctor." Since he was already 6'1, growing more would hardly permit him to make a sharp turn on a cross-country course.

"Man, take care of that," said Scott. "It's September 4th, we haven't even started school yet. You'll be happy in a week when you're running fine if you nip it in the bud. Take a few days." Taking a few days off was easier said than done for Rawling, who would go on to play with the idea, before running sixty minutes on the next day. He might have felt like he still had something to prove. He had been recruited on a whim – he had not yet run very fast over any distance.

I remembered Bernie pulling us aside on a bus ride home from Montreal after a track meet at McGill University in the winter of 2015 to fire us up about Angus' arrival.

"Cal, Cyr, you guys better be on your game next year because we have a stellar recruit coming in. He will be top three on the team." We laughed and thought he was being a tad optimistic in his judgement of Angus' fitness.

Prior to his visit, the only time we could find linked to his name was a 17:30 5k. When hearing that Bernie was paying for this kid's flight to Antigonish to have him visit campus, we figured our coach had lost his mind. He could have found better runners in his backyard. But, Bernie's investment was fruitful after all. He liked what he had seen in the lanky Calgarian, and the chance he took on him paid dividends. The one we now call Beef proved to be much stronger than the Internet track and field databases made him seem to be, and he was ready to make his presence felt. The only thing now standing between Angus Rawling and a scoring spot on our team was his broken body, and the only thing standing between him and a clean bill of health was his restless mind.

Save for the NHL game, however, he seemed at peace tonight, as was everyone. We were aware that classes were starting in two days, and we wanted to make the most of this awkward but glorious limbo phase between school and summer employment.

All of us who had stayed in Antigonish had managed to land mundane but financially sufficient jobs. Favero was still working at the Main Street Cafe, a classy restaurant at the far end of Main Street. It was approaching suppertime, so we decided as a group to go test out his competencies as a waiter.

When we arrived, Scott waved at the nearest waitress. "Hi, we would like to get served by Fabio, please!"

"Who?"

"Nic Favero," Neuffer clarified.

The waitress looked slightly less puzzled. "Uhh, yes, of course! Right this way." As she set our table, we spied on our friend, currently waiting on an elderly couple. Dressed in all black with his hair slicked to the side, he looked flawless. Well-dressed, polite and courteous, he seemed as though he could have waited tables at the Bellagio. We eventually caught his attention and, after wishing his customers a good day, and realizing we would refuse that any other waiter or waitress take our order, he ambled towards us, grimacing.

"Ughh, I hoped I would never have to see you guys here. What can I get you guys started with?"

"Uhh, I will have the most complicated three items on the menu, and I want them brought to me all at once, please," requested Angus.

"Ok, if you're willing to pay ninety dollars. But seriously, I can take your orders."

"Wait!" I said. "We have one more joining."

Angus, Neuffer, Jeffs, O'Regan, and I all moved down a place in our half-booth to make room for another. A giant sixth member eagerly walked towards our table. His gait was awkward; he walked as if someone else was squeezing his butt cheeks together. Ryan Fuller, dressed in khaki shorts and a Toronto Raptors hat, had come late.

"Fuller, you're late, can I get you something as well?" asked Favero.

"Yeah I walked, I want fish and chips and a large coke. Will you come back for dessert?" No food item seemed to be too unhealthy for Ryan Fuller.

Breaking out of his character of svelte waiter, Favero shook his head and laughed. "I sure will. Coming right up."

"Went lactic, felt sweet."

September 7th

The high mileage of training camp was taking its toll. Since ordering spaghetti at the Main Street Café, I had covered more than forty kilometres in the last two days. My calves were angry – my back, resistant. But, it was the best feeling in the world. I could feel my quads thinning, and my gluteus muscles strengthening. All the miles run were money in the bank for future races, provided we stayed healthy.

Drowsy, I woke up on Wednesday morning with my bed sheets stuck to my stomach. The calefaction of the summer sun had made 18 Greening sweat from every corner. Even the dust bunnies were feeling its effects, and our quiet cohabitants, the fruit flies, were thriving. It was hot. Professors installed fans by their desks, knowing the attention spans of students would melt away within minutes of entering their sweltering classrooms.

The 2016-17 school year would inaugurate today, and the timing was egregious. Instead of managing this weather with the help of an ocean and sinking sand, we were instead held captive in the world of academia, learning through our sweat drops. I religiously drank out of my water bottle throughout the day to avoid the effects of dehydration before I started to work out. No mandatory hard practice was on the schedule for tonight, but for those who had trained all summer and were ready to slowly tack on intensity to their weekly load, the opportunity was timely. We were three days away from our team time trial. Favero, Cal, Neuffer, Angus, and I had agreed on a fartlek run of 1,2,3,4,5,5,4,3,2,1 in minutes, with the recovery consisting of half the time it would take to run the previous interval. Since the conception of the workout, however, Cal had come down with a cold, Angus' ankle injury had flared up, and Favero had opted for a tempo run in the morning due to an evening commitment. This would leave only Neuffer and me to dread what was to come.

I finished my last class at 4:30, which left me thirty minutes to roll out and do activation exercises in the change room. As I rolled out my quads, my workout partner walked in wearing a sweat-stained, blue, sporty Lulu Lemon shirt and khakis. Somehow, Neuffer seemed to have tanned throughout the day. I thought that if the sun was strong enough to give a tan to my pasty and skinny redhead roommate, then we had our work cut out for us.

"This is going to suck. I started sweating when walking here from class," he said. "We're going to have to run this one smart," I warned him.

We both knew we wouldn't. Neuffer would attack the workout with eagerness and grit, and I would be too stubborn to let him distance me – that was how our workouts usually played out.

"Any others working out with us?" I asked.

"Nah," said Neuffer. "Cal, Angus, and Favero cancelled and I didn't bother asking anyone else. They'd just get dropped like a sack of potatoes. And most would probably just want to run straight tempo, rather than break it up and go faster."

Alex Neuffer always brought a positive vibe to the change room, but there was no hiding the sole reason he ran: to get fast. Any teammate slowing him down was simply in the way. Any workout he judged to be bad for his injury-prone body, he would refuse to do, regardless of how it impacted team morale. He knew his body, and Bernie had come to terms with foregoing team unison to keep one of his stars healthy and happy. Neuffer's at-times rogue behaviour did not convey the right example to rookies, but he could not be convinced to completely give in to the high volume of the team's plan – as it would likely get him injured. His way of helping the team was simple: to get as fit as possible in his own way.

I peeked outside, and quickly stripped down. "I'm going shirtless. Shortest shorts I own, low socks. I don't care what they have to say." I was no longer intimidated by the slurs of crews of local loiterers who hung out by The Wheel and Piper's Pub as we would run by. The sarcastic screams of "nice legs" and "Run, Forrest, Run" had lost their sting. Neuffer put on his backwards cap and took one last gulp of water, and I finished my hip stretches. We slowly walked into the inferno.

With my long-time training partner, I began my trek to the Brierly Brook. The winding road that could be looped for twenty kilometres was a frequent destination for team workouts for its flatness. Tradition played a big part in our strong adherence to this loop as well, as we had all been fondly introduced to it by past team veterans on the day of our first workout as rookies. The Brook, as we called it, was a staple in the cross-country season. That was where, as Bernie often reminded us, "Gillis got fast." Twenty minutes would take us to the Magic Tree – a supposedly mythical oak tree overlooking a large dairy farm that had seen the beginning of many X-Men and X-Women workouts over the years. Tempos could only begin once we had reached the tree. A shorter or longer warm up was sacrilegious. Riley Johnston, who had become acquainted with it through Dennis Kayumba and Zach MacDonald on his own recruitment trip, introduced me to the tree. It had conveniently sprouted twenty minutes away from the Oland Centre doors, making it the perfect warm-up end point. Today, however, the blazing heat made even twenty minutes of running seem too long for a simple warm up.

"How much time do you need?" Neuffer asked. Knowing that every second I wasted doing warm-up drills was driving me closer to the brink of dehydration, I told him that I was ready to start, and I reciprocated with the same question. "I was born ready," said my confident, ginger friend. His clichéd answer was in fact not clichéd at all. Alex Neuffer was an interesting specimen, and a pure grinder. A native of Stratford, PEI, his running ability had skyrocketed as soon as he was introduced to triathlons in his sophomore year of high school. The many hours of aerobic training seemed to form a good match with his disciplined, if not obsessive, personality. Hours of swimming and biking tacked onto his running training regime had morphed the frail, red-haired runner into an aerobic machine. He still covered some of his running mileage on the bike and in the pool, and five years removed from the birth of this new approach to his sport, his confidence in his own athletic ability had dramatically increased.

I liked to think that this unwavering assurance in himself as an athlete came from his conquering of the fear of pain. He had learned how to torture his body while keeping his mind in check. That skill made it difficult to outperform him in the many workouts we shared over the years. It had also brought him unusual success coming off his numerous injuries. Every current runner on the team had witnessed or heard of the momentous track meet of February 2015 – the one in which Neuffer stopped the clock at eight minutes and twenty-eight seconds in his first 3000-metre race of his sophomore year, shortly after taking months off running. He had beaten Cal, John Kuto of Saint Mary's, Matt McNeil of Dalhousie, and others while leaving Bernie and Kevin flabbergasted. It still stood as the fastest 3000 run by any current team member, and he had run it while doing most of his training on the bike and in the pool. Whether he ran that time out of fitness or frustration was still a mystery. Regardless, on that day we had learned that Neuffer was a grinder, and a perennial force to be reckoned with. He was the closest thing to an archrival that I had. Our so-called rivalry, however, was overshadowed by a mutual respect for one another on top of a very strong friendship. I considered him a more brother than an opponent. He kept me on my toes; he made me better.

As the workout approached, I was growing apprehensive. "All right, so we don't need to push this. The conditions are ridiculous. We said 10k pace, but for today, 3:10-3:12 should do." I was in the middle of a large training week, and the legs were out of bounce.

"Three, two, one, go."

Like that, we were off. The first two intervals were the shortest and easiest to knock down, but I quickly found out that no fitness gains on that day would be handed to me for free. From the start, we were huffing and puffing. The air was so humid that we could taste it on our tongues, and so dense that it clogged up our tracheas.

"Wow, this feels harder than it should. Do you want to cut one of the five-minuters?" asked Neuffer, almost out of character.

I did not object. My eyes were already engorged in sweat, and I could feel parts of my body tingling from dehydration. The three-minute interval was worse than the first two. While the other ones had awoken my sudorific glands, this interval made me struggle to clear lactate in my quadriceps and hamstrings. I was approaching oxygen debt six minutes into a supposedly twenty-five-minute-long workout. Ninety seconds were all I had to recover for the upcoming four-minute interval. Neuffer was breathing just as hard as I was, and his face colour had changed from a slightly tan, off-white colour, to a scarlet red. "All right, number four," he said, before striding into the next interval. As soon as we began running hard again, I started playing mental games with myself. Telling myself that I was feeling great was becoming more of a lie by the second. Hearing Neuffer breathe heavily next to me reassured me, as it solidified my theory that it was the heat, and not my lack of fitness, that was the culprit behind my struggle. Three-ten per kilometre had never felt so laborious.

During this fourth interval, we passed Cal and Angus, who were easy running. "Yeah boys, beat that heat! Working hard, chop chop!" yelled Cal, half in encouragement, half in mockery of our effort level for this early in the season. He could tell that we were grinding much too hard for a workout, let alone a pre-season one. After replying with half-hearted thumbs up, we heard him and Angus snickering in the background. We figured they were right, but it was the only way Neuffer and I knew how to run together.

Between breaths, Neuffer tried to get himself ready for the five-minute interval. "Ok... this... is... the longest one. Then... it gets better." Thankfully, we switched directions and gained a tailwind for the long, five-minute interval. Remaining silent, we braced ourselves in solidarity. Though we knew it would hurt, neither of us was willing to ease off the gas pedal, as we led each other to a 4:55 mile. I let out a cry of exasperation that was representative of my elation for finishing the longest interval, but also of my disdain, as we still had ten hard minutes to cover. My mental strength was challenged. I was hurting, so was he. We encouraged each other to carry on, while regulating our own biological feedback.

After 2:30 of rest, we were off again. The second four-minute interval had begun, and my body had not recovered. My legs had become bankrupt of oxygen, my chest hopelessly gasping for air. We were running 3:00 kilometres. I lost form, swinging my arms across my body. This is where I snapped. Barely done of the rep, I had had enough. "That's it for me. Wheels are gone," I panted through my sweat-beaded lips.

I pulled up on the side of the road with one minute to go in the second four-minute interval, and folded into a heap of disappointment, hands on my knees. Neuffer kept going. I listened to his footsteps slowly escaping me; producing a slighter sound each time they struck the pavement. Lightheaded and beat down, I sat on the curb and waited for him to come back. He completed the three-minute, the two-minute, and then powered back to our starting point while completing his last minute of the workout. His arms were flailing and he was gasping as he sported a ghoulish grimace. He was in pain.

"AHHHHH" he shouted. "That was awful. Way too hard. Oh my God." He sat next to me, and without a word, we inhaled more oxygen per unit time than our lungs could ever handle.

"Feeling all right?" he finally asked.

"Yeah, just didn't have any gas left in the tank," I replied, sheepishly. "How were your last three?"

"Oh, went lactic. Felt sweet." Neuffer embraced pain so well that I suspected him to be a closet masochist. "I was cookin.' Like, we're not going to have another day like this one all year. This heat was crazy."

"Yeah, we should get home. I need some water." The threat of dehydration was very real, as our shorts were soaked in the concoction of bodily fluids only known to the exerted runner. We strolled back home talking little, using most of our breath to supply our muscles.

Once he had caught his breath, Neuffer began thinking out loud. "I don't think this will happen, but I'm scared that this workout will have hammered me to the ground for time trial. I went to the well."

"Well, we can't give Cal the satisfaction of knowing we buried ourselves. He was cackling about how hard we were working. Told Angus it was stupid of us. I hope he isn't right."

Running home, I could not help but curse myself for ending the workout early. A half-hearted decision to cut the run short had been fuelled by my fear of burying myself too deep. I had rationalized my quitting as a cautious way to begin workouts. In reality, it was my mental game that needed more work. Fresh off a few weeks of nagging soreness, I had forgotten how to hurt. As I gathered my thoughts, one came to the forefront. *Why did I not continue? Am I not strong enough? Not fit enough? Is this mental?* The answer I would not find on that day, but one realization towered above the rest. I wanted the title of AUS champion, and I wanted to be as high up as possible come CIS, but those merits would not be given to me. Four other roommates of mine wanted them too, as much as I did. If I wanted to emerge victorious, I needed to want it as much as all of them combined. There was a long road ahead of me, and the amount of pain I would allow myself to tolerate would partly dictate how far I would travel.

The Odds Game

September 7th

"Guys, where are you sitting?" Cullen MacInnis was walking towards Scott and me with a plate full of meal-hall food in one hand, and two glasses of chocolate milk in the other. He was balancing another plate of fruit between his elbow and his chest and looked like an overwhelmed waiter.

"Yellow room, as usual. Big crew there already." Because regular practice hours were now implemented, all of our schedules had synchronized. The men and women practiced at five, and would walk over to meal hall to have supper as a group. I led Cullen to the back of the cafeteria and plopped myself on one of the last available chairs, beat and dehydrated from my workout.

Addison sat next to me and was giggling. "Cyr, what are the odds you do it?"

"Do what?"

"Scream as loudly as you can, 'O'Regan kissed a mom!'" said Addison.

I laughed. O'Regan had endured ample taunting in consequence to a particular summer night during which he was allegedly seen leaving Piper's Pub locking arms (and perhaps lips) with a lady nearly twenty years his senior.

"Oh my God, guys. I didn't do it! None of this happened. This is seriously the last time I should say this. Come on," pleaded O'Regan, uncharacteristically bothered.

Feeling bad for him, I refused. "Addi, I can't take the odds, poor guy has gone through enough."

"Cyr, you know better than that. You HAVE to take the odds. That's the game!" the rookie continued.

"Ughh, what is this odds game you guys always play?" asked Hana.

Warren hastily answered. "It's a stupid, stupid game. So, when a challenger asks you what the odds are that you would do a certain thing, you are obliged to play and you must give the challenger your odds. It is you, the player, who decides these odds. The less you want to do the required challenge, the higher odds you may call. So if, for example, the challenger asks you, 'what are the odds you finish your glass of chocolate milk?' and you say one in ten, then a third party counts down from three, and both the player and the challenger scream out a number between one and ten. If the number is the same, then the player must perform what was asked."

"It's a game for the feeble minded, who have no sense of pride," said Favero. "The thing is, there is a loophole to the game. When someone asks you for odds on a challenge you don't want to do – SURPRISE – you just refuse."

"Yeah but then you're a wimp," said Addison.

Favero rolled his eyes. "Better than an idiot."

"Further," Warren cut in, "if the player loses the odds, and fails to perform the task imposed on them by the challenger, they then get a notch."

"What's a notch?" asked Hana.

David pointed at the multiple slits in his eyebrows. "One of these! I always lose odds and never accept the challenges!"

Hana laughed. "David, what the heck? You barely have any eyebrows left!"

"Ahh, it doesn't matter. You can barely notice! I'm seeing this girl and she doesn't care!" We collectively wondered what girl could possibly be interested in an eyebrow-less David.

Cullen, sitting at the other end of the table, looked confident. "I'll do the odds, one in eight."

Excited, Addison turned towards Cullen. "OK. Cal, count us down!"

"Three, two, one."

"FIVE" they screamed in unison.

"YES!" shrieked Addison.

"Ahh man. Sorry O'Regan! I gotta do it."

"Cullen, you don't have to do this. Come on. This room is filled with people!" pleaded O'Regan.

"Sorry man, I know, but it's the game. I don't want to disrespect the rules," said the rookie. "I also don't want my eyebrow to look like David's."

O'Regan was desperate. "Look Cullen, you're a rookie, so maybe we can let you off and find some alternat…"

"OREEEEEGAN KISSED A MOOOOOOM!!!" Cullen used his loudest voice. Our table roared. The rest of the room went silent and turned to see what the unusual ruckus was about.

"Ugh, guys, what if one of my sisters is in here? This sucks! It didn't even happen," pouted O'Regan, avoiding stares.

"Sorry O'Regan, rules are rules. I'm not going into my first week of classes with a huge notch. Had to do it."

"Yeah, I guess. Just, like… pick a higher number next time, Cullen. Ahhh this sucks! I'm leaving."

Addison was red in the face, laughing. "Hey Favero, what are the odds you scream the same thing, but about Warren this time?"

"Zero, kid. I got some real-person work to do. I'm taking off."

"Yes, I believe that it's also my time to dissociate myself from this bunch," said Warren, who had been hiding in the other room for the duration of the fiasco. "No way I'm getting into trouble with Janet, the meal hall lady again. She has had enough of my antics already."

Last year, when Warren had tried to leave meal hall with four bananas, Janet had reminded him of the meal hall rules. One could only take one piece of fruit with them after a meal. Cross, Warren stood in front of her, put one banana in his pocket, looked her in the eye, and proceeded to peel the other three bananas and engulfed them one by one as she watched, confused. "Whether I eat your food here or there, it amounts to the same, damn it!" he said, before storming out, uncomfortably full. Since the banana incident, he and Janet had not exactly seen eye to eye.

"Bye Ferg! I love you!" Addison was relentless. With a collective eye roll, Warren and Nic were fast off, seeking higher, more sophisticated pursuits. "Cal, what are you doing tomorrow night?"

"Going to sleep, Addison. Time trial is Saturday."

"Yeah, I know. I was wondering if I could come sleep at your place. Lane Hall is getting pretty rowdy. I won't sleep if I stay in there."

"Yeah, for sure! You can take one of our couches. I'm taking off now if you need a ride."

"Sweet! Sleepover with the Greening boys!! Woooooo!"

Time Trial

September 10th

I woke up to the sound of a 140-pound runner's pacing steps. The kitchen was right above my room in the basement of 18 Greening, and due to the house's worn-out insulation, the slight prance sounded like the stomping of a giant. By the pattern of quick, efficient floor strikes, I could tell that Neuffer was making his pre-race oatmeal. A set of louder, dragging footsteps belonging to Cal soon joined him in the kitchen. The house was buzzing in the midst of our intra-squad time trial.

Before the official beginning of the season's races, Bernie held an eight-kilometre tryout race, in order to gauge all runners' fitness levels. It also served as a way of making obvious cuts to the travel roster. For our senior gang, the contest presented no real challenge. It was instead a simple group workout opportunity. For most rookies and some upperclassmen and women battling for a spot, this was nearly a matter of life or death. A poor performance at the time trial would lead to one's omission from the roster traveling to Brunswick, Maine, to race the following weekend. Further, though not consistently, Bernie had been known to name ten to twelve men and ten to twelve women to the travel team based on time trial results alone. So, unless a runner had established him or herself as a scoring team member, a bad time trial often led to one's cutting from the travel team. A non-member of the travel team would not be attending away meets, they would not receive gear, and they would not even earn the luxurious title of varsity athlete for the shallow satisfaction of tacking those words onto a resume. For some team members, even the third reason was a big deal.

"Hey Angus, what are the odds you begin the race standing in a three-point start, and take off before the gun?" said Cal.

Angus was rubbing his lower leg. "Ha ha! I'll go one in ten, but I'm a game time decision as to whether I will even line up at all." Suffering a sore ankle, he would attempt to run the warm up, and then decide to race or sit out. An established scorer, he would have no issue with Bernie in negotiating a day off. Cal loved turning serious matters into jokes. His strong opinions and his penchant for challenging authority and establishment – in this case, Bernie's time trial – along with his rank on the team, prompted him to inject some humour in an otherwise serious event.

"Cyr what are the odds you do it?" Cal asked.

"Well, decently high. I want to be in the front. By the looks of things, I'm not conceding the lead to Neuffer. I don't feel like running 24:30 for a workout." If history was any indicator, Neuffer would set a fast pace no matter the day. He shot us a confident grin between spoonsful of oatmeal.

"Three-fifteen per-k, guys. I'm going no faster."

His goal, as was ours, was to not let our egos get in the way of our plan to run the "race" at a controlled pace. As seniors, we were finally becoming able to control our efforts when working out together, but the occasional competitive slip-up still happened from time to time.

Even this early in the day, it was obvious that there was a divide in the household. Scott, Cal, Neuffer, Angus, and I would in some order constitute the top five unless Favero were to niche himself between us. However, it was a different story for our sixth roommate, Ryan O'Regan. He had something to prove. Though also a native of Prince Edward Island, O'Regan had little resemblance to Neuffer or me when it came to running. While we were both uptight and meticulous in our training methods, he seemed carefree and almost too optimistic. I had met him in my grade-nine year, when he had given me a good race over 1500 metres at the Charlottetown track on the University of Prince Edward Island campus. I had beaten him that day and had had the upper hand ever since. His odd approaches to training, in my opinion, hindered him at times. Genetically inclined to be a middle-distance runner of 800 and 1500 metres, O'Regan had thrown himself into the world of cross-country running when he transferred to St. FX from the University of Prince Edward Island. I had a hunch that learning about Neuffer's and my commitment to the X-Men had played a part in his decision to transfer. Though he was one year older than us, the transfer had placed him one year behind in schooling, so he would be slated to graduate with us. Even if we did not share many of the same views in terms of training, O'Regan had become one of my closest friends. I had faith that he would succeed today, despite appearances. In his expensive designer sunglasses and flip-flops, racing could have been the last thing on his mind. He looked more like someone coming home from the beach.

"Cyr, can we make a stop at Tim's on the way there? I'm out of food," he asked.

"Yeah sure, just hurry, the rest of the guys are already gone to the Oland Centre." Five minutes in front of the mirror later, O'Regan hopped in my car. Looking good was a necessity. We zipped over to the Tim Horton's drive-thru, and O'Regan ordered his breakfast: one small coffee. He sipped on his nutritional first meal of the day to the beat of Jay-Z's "No Church in the Wild" as we parked by the track. Turning my radio off, I stepped out of the car and gazed at the infield. The slight silhouette of Addison Derhak was down on the turf doing leg swings. As were most rookies, he was very nervous for the trial. Uncertainty about everyone else's fitness as well as his own fuelled his anxiety – and the pace of his leg swings.

"Hey Addison, feeling good?" I asked.

He was pacing back and forth. "Uhm, I don't know. I'll see when the race starts. I don't want to kill myself today – just finish near the front I guess." It was a far cry from the plan he had proposed last night at meal hall: to gap everyone in the field and win. O'Regan and I calmly walked into the change room. Favero must have taken control of the sound system, as it was between the lyrics of Kendrick Lamar that I heard few murmurs. People were focused.

Most rookies stared at their shoes in concentration, but none were deploying quite as much intense energy as Warren Ferguson. Also attempting to earn his spot on the travel team roster for the first time, Warren swore on hard work rather than talent. Describing himself as "built to drag heavy things through fields," he was well aware that his physique was that of a traditional Scot – sturdy, scrappy, and not conducive to fast running. Luckily, he also had to stubbornness of a Scot. Warren found out at a young age that he would have to work for every second he would eventually chop off his five-kilometre time. Nothing would be handed to him. But, being behind the eight-ball appealed to him. He ran to feel pain. He ran because it was hard. He flirted with his biological limits during workouts so intimately that his ability to work hard sometimes served as a curse. He had experienced injuries, burnout, or some combination of both in his first three years at St. FX. But he had vowed to come back wiser, and the fact that it was September and that he was not yet injured at least put him ahead of last year. Dressed in a collared shirt, black suit pants, and polished black shoes, Warren could just as well have been going to a funeral if you took away his ratty headphones blaring music by AC/DC. Everyone in his vicinity could hear the chorus to "Highway to Hell." Without looking up, he rushed to the back of the change room, and swiftly sat down on the end of a wooden bench. Sitting next to O'Regan, who was taking an impressive amount of time to take off his sunglasses, their contrast was an amusing sight. Yet, it was common thought that they would have to battle each other to the final lap to decide a victor, and possible ninth or tenth place finisher.

* * *

"Guys, the girls are out there doing drills! Remember, you start at 9:30, get going!" urged Bernie. We strolled outside to begin our warm up on the campus cross-country course. Running in front of the pack, I felt an unusual presence on my right shoulder. Warren was silently striding next to me. Usually the first to shame those who ran fast on easy runs or warm ups, something had possessed him. He was silent and running in a straight line – two oddities for him.

The opportunity was too good for Cal. The jokester in him was revelling. This tense moment was the perfect opportunity for a little fun as far as he was concerned. "Hey Fuller, it's time for you to talk some trash to Warren if you want to beat him."

Fuller, owner of a rather malleable judgement, wasted no time. "Hey Ferg, better look out in that last K when I start grinding and DROP you."

We laughed at his uncreative attempt at throwing Warren off his game. As expected, Warren did not respond.

Cal ran in the middle of the group, stirring the pot. "Aha! Hear that, Fuller? That is the sound of focus and concentration. Ferg knows what he's going to do with you, and he doesn't have to say it. He will hunt you down like a wild gazelle and leave you in his dust!" "Uhm, we will see. This time trial will be interesting." That's all we would get from Warren this morning. That had become his catch phrase over the last week. When I had asked him about his strategy a few days prior, he simply told me that he "wouldn't let the person in front of him go, come hell or high water." He would push himself to faint on the track before losing to the runners in his training group. This group included Matt Eliot, Ryan Fuller, and, of course, O'Regan.

At the back of the pack, Ryan O'Regan was running happily. He was a bit more quiet than usual; the angst was present but not overshadowing his easygoingness. Catching some of the dialogue between Fuller, Cal, and Warren, he laughed periodically. He was confident, partly because he had spent the summer in Antigonish running with a group of us, and partly because confidence was niched inside his genetic makeup. He truly did not see the possible consequence of poor performance. If someone of his rank on the team totem pole had a bad performance, Bernie would be ruthless and have him cut – but O'Regan did not seem to realize it. Often, this peace of mind would be misinterpreted as apathy by the rest of us. I believed that he cared about running; he could just not be bothered to overthink.

As I jogged back to the track, where the time trial was taking place, I spotted Angus speaking with Bernie. His ankle had been giving him grief, and he had decided to sit out the run. He joined us to cheer on the girls.

"Not good?" I asked.

"It's a bit wonky. If I had anything to prove today I'd power through but there is no point. It hurts when I push off the..."

"Ellen, pick it up!!" We were interrupted by Cal's hasty scream. The girls had started their 5k time trial, and they were dangerously slow. Bernie had established a travel team standard of twenty minutes for the girls' 5k and twenty-eight minutes for the guys' 8k. The girls ran in one pack and were almost on twenty-one minute pace after their first kilometre. If none of them were to break twenty minutes due to tactics, Bernie obviously would not cut everyone. He could, however, decide to only take a smaller number of girls if they seemed unfit as a group. The savvy girls in the pack knew this, so they began to pick up the pace in solidarity.

"Ok man, see THAT's my problem with the girls." Favero had a frustrated look on his face and his hands high up in front of him. "Why do they have to run in a pack? Man, if I were Liz I'd be gone and the other girls can chase me if they want. This is not a tempo run!"

I did agree with him that it was strange to see our top girl run no farther than five metres in front of our twelfth girl. Their pace needed to pick up fast.

Eventually, things fell in place, and the strongest girls pulled away. Liz MacDonald made the win seem effortless, and Mary MacDonald, the newcomer from the soccer team, followed her closely. Hana Marmura, last year's AUS rookie of the year, came in eighth. Usually up with Liz, she had just recovered from surgery for compartment syndrome, and was fresh off a six-month break. Seeing her running again was relieving, and everyone knew she would be back up in her spot in no time.

As the last few girls crossed the line, we finished up our warm-up drills. I gazed over at the track and saw O'Regan and Warren, doing strides. Here again, their contrast was mesmerizing. O'Regan, athletic and fast-twitched, had sprung off the track like a springbok in Nike spikes. His strongly defined quadriceps muscles gave him more the allure of a professional cyclist than that of a runner. His calves coiled underneath him; he looked primed. Warren, conversely, was moving clumsily, trying to throw down a few strides. His arms looked heavy and disproportionately large for the rest of his body, and his legs slammed down on the track as if he was attempting to exterminate an intrusion of cockroaches. Needless to say, the only pretty thing about Warren's running was his perseverance.

"All right men, it's time!" The final strides were done and we lined up. Bernie asked all the runners to gather by the start line. "Ok guys, so it's an 8k. I don't want you guys cutting in all hasty and so on, it's a long race. How many laps, Kevin?"

"Twenty, Bernie."

"There you have it. Don't worry about counting them. Kevin and I will take care of it. Brenda is here for backup as well. Oh! For you rookies, this is my wife Brenda, in case you haven't had the pleasure of meeting her. She graciously accepted to help us out with the timing today."

"What else would I want to do at nine in the morning?" she joked. "Nice to meet all of you. Work hard today, and good luck!"

Bernie took over again. "Push yourself and try to stick to your goal pace. You have some groups here who can work together and push each other. Remember, though, that this is a chance to demark yourself from your competitors. There is not a spot for everyone on the team, and today is my first chance at seeing who's done the homework. Good luck everyone. Line up."

Like that, eighteen runners, some more nervous than others, toed the start line.

"On your mark, go!" said Bernie. He was calm, and his tone did little to awaken me from my gaze. I had none of the usual race-day jitters, and that was a good sign. Mentally, I was treating this as a workout. I inched to the front and began running directly behind Neuffer. Cal and Favero ran effortlessly behind me, as Scott, the other eventual member of our five-man clan started way back to fulfill the requirements of a lost odds bet imposed on him by none other than Cal. I expected us to break away from the pack immediately, but our group was accompanied by one surprising presence. O'Regan had decided to spring off the line and attack the first 200 metres. The fast start, I concluded, was just a by-product of his muscular push off and fast-twitch fibres itching to go fast. Thankfully, he settled into his pace after another 200 metres. It was not a day for risks, and he knew that. Too much was at stake for him.

Once Scott caught up to our lead pack, we settled into a steady, almost boring, rhythm. We had agreed to alternate leads by the kilometer, and to run the race between 26:00 and 26:30. Nobody deviated from the plan, and the pseudo-race was uneventful. We ran 26:04 together and drew sticks to determine the trivial placing positions. Favero drew the winning stick, followed by myself, Scott, Neuffer, and Cal. Giving each other high-fives, we acknowledged that the most exciting storylines of today were yet to come. Collectively, we turned around to face the finish line to see which teammates of ours would prove themselves worthy of a spot on the travel team to Maine. Paul MacLellan, barely thirty seconds behind us, came in sixth place.

"Ahh, phew, happy that's over," said Paul, not even winded.

"Way to go Paul! The wheels are there! Well done!"

"Yes. The wheels are there. I did not know the wheels were there, but as it turns out, they are," said Paul. Paul's matter-of-fact way of expressing himself was something to behold. The mystery of his current level of fitness had been a hot topic in the past days. Accepting a summer office job had obliged him to run alone at nights, and sceptics had questioned his consistency. In twenty-six minutes and thirty-four seconds, he had managed to silence them all. We high-fived him, relieved that he had done his homework.

Paul's moment in our limelight was cut short, though, as we only had to wait ten seconds for the next finisher to arrive. Addison Derhak and Ryan O'Regan were approaching the finish line. They crossed together, and my first reaction was to stand in silence. A time of 26:44 for Addison Derhak was expected. He was taking the ordeal seriously, and we expected him to only get faster as races went by. What shocked me, however, was seeing O'Regan's cramped body muscling itself through the line a split second behind him. Was it possible? Had Ryan O'Regan achieved a breakthrough performance on the day that it mattered most? We all stood at the finish line, flabbergasted but cheerful, until Addison hastily set us straight.

"Yes! I lapped O'Regan! Hahaha! WOOO!" yelled the rookie, fist pumping past the finish line. The excitement had caused him to forget the importance of this trial for his older teammate. O'Regan still had a full lap to run, but his body had other plans. In his last attempt to round the track, he began to wobble, and collapsed with one lap to go. Edward MacDonald, who had already dropped out to a bad case of turf toe, and Paul, fresh off his own race, were the first two to the rescue, and began carrying him to the therapy room. It was game over. O'Regan had not finished the race. As he was helped off the track, he was semi-conscious.

"I'm ok, but kinda not. My cells hurt...like...nucleuses hurt. It's ok. It's ok. I'm just gonna roll to the side and stretch my cells." He was talking nonsense. He was rushed inside, clearly needing oxygen. Shaken, but still anxious to learn the positions of other teammates, we turned our heads from the infield just fast enough to see the eighth-place finisher cross the line. Fists clenched and gazing to the sky with his eyes almost shut, a triumphant Warren Ferguson had just silenced his demons of time-trial day, which followed him from year to year. For the first time, he had clinched a definite spot on the roster, notching a time of 27:23 – good for eighth place.

Usually one to talk down his own running, he was ecstatic. Covered in sweat, he immediately provided a race analysis. "I felt great. I could have given more. I think on a good day I can run close to twenty-seven minutes. I am so happy with this!" Everyone was happy for him, recognizing that he had wanted such a performance for a long time.

Next to finish the trial was Matt Eliot in ninth, also a fourth year student looking to solidify his spot on the travel team roster for the first time. He was closely followed by Ryan Fuller, who crossed with a wincing smile demonstrative of the unique combination of pain and elation that can only be felt by an endurance athlete testing his limits. Their times were 27:28 and 27:29, respectively. Nathan Jeffs was next, crossing in 28:04. A sportsman of honour, he acknowledged that he had unfortunately missed a lap, and that his estimated 8k time would equate to something closer to twenty-nine minutes. He had finished next to last, in front of David MacDonald, but he had actually outperformed five other runners. O'Regan, Edward Macdonald, and rookies Cullen MacInnis and Colin Glenncross had all bowed out early. Both new runners cited mental collapses as the reason for their dropout. They acknowledged that they would have a long way to go before contributing to the team. The fifth dropout was Leo Jusiak, the French 1500 metre specialist. He had not expected to run in Canada and was not in the fitness to compete.

"Oh, Alex. This feel no good. I think I have enough, but then the 5k come and I just lose the energies. I need, uhh, weeks to do training before I am good."

"Don't worry Leo, you've only had a week to get ready for this. Bernie will understand," I reassured him in his mother tongue. The coaches waited for everyone to cross the line to address the entire men's team.

"All right guys, good work!" said Bernie. "I know some of you are happy with your times, and then some not so much, but that's how it goes. Remember that it's early in the season. If you really underperformed today, however, make it a lesson. I always say that championships are won in the offseason, and there is some truth to that. You should be coming into the season in good shape. Not peaking, but fit. Some guys demonstrated that they've done the work. That's what we like to see. Now, go for your cool down, and give your body a good stretch. Therapy is open with ice bags and ice baths and so on. Great work!" On Bernie's orders, we trotted away.

On the cool down, I began thinking about what I had just seen happen on the track. The episode reminded me that running is a sport of decisions. There are the big obvious ones, such as which spikes to wear and which races to run, but beneath those decisions are the little ones. When should one go to sleep? What is best to eat on the morning of competition? For how long should one stretch after runs? The answers to these questions are usually what separate struggling runners from moderately successful runners, and then moderately successful runners from the great ones who live on the fringe. What I could take away from this thought was that wherever an athlete is located on this spectrum of dedication will influence the decisions they make from day to day. Lifestyle differences could eventually separate two individuals of the same talent, or better yet, make a less talented individual reach higher than a more talented counterpart out of sheer will and consistency.

Warren had wanted this breakthrough for a long time. He had admitted that this year's time trial had been on his mind since getting cut last year. It had influenced some of his decisions off the track, and eventually, knowing that he needed to emerge as the best runner within his training group on September 10th. 2016 had made him a better runner. In contrast, O'Regan's heightened confidence may not have urged him to make these small day-to-day decisions that would lead to him improving. It may not have let him consciously remind himself of what kind of lifestyle was needed to attain the required level, and he now had to deal with the consequence. Whether bad pacing, nutrient depletion, or lack of training was the culprit, the result was the same: O'Regan had failed to prove himself and would not be travelling to Maine with the rest of us.

At the townhouse

September 10th

Once the sun came down and the heavy, humid air was broken by a brisk wind, the outdoors became more tolerable. Showered from the day's work, I accompanied several teammates to the local brewpub. Many of us recognized that this Saturday night was valuable. We would not have many more free nights once the season began, and once our academic schedules skyrocketed in rigour. The first few weeks of a university term were nice. Professors would do nothing but announce the perils we were to face in the next few months, without urging us to begin preparing until late September to early October. All we could do was brace ourselves and wait for the harder times to come. The same could be said about our cross-country season. Harder weeks were ahead. Not now. Ahead. September 10th was meant to let loose and enjoy food and a drink with friends. September 10th was a day to remind us what exactly life was without stress, deadlines, and upcoming races. September 10th was the Yin to the chaotic Yang of mid-October. Cal, Neuffer, Angus, Scott, Ed, Favero, Warren, Addison, and I recognized this. In two vehicles, we followed each other down Main Street, and turned left on College Street. Dinner was awaiting us at The Townhouse.

    The quaint and charming brewpub was a fan favourite amongst the team. Its menu consisted of mostly traditional maritime meals, and their beer hailed from nearby maritime breweries. Its occasional soft live music, dimmer lighting, and old, traditional Scottish aura made the locale toe the line between sophistication and pretention. It was a hit in Antigonish, for it served as a popular watering hole for the academic community of St. FX, and it provided an alternative for students and locals who eventually grew tired of Boston Pizza.

We had barely taken a seat when a slightly monotonous and familiar voice was heard. "Oh, uhm, hey guys." The address came from a tall frame with a mess of hair. Stephen Deering walked with his hands in his pockets towards our table.

"Hey Steve!" we said.

Warren jumped out of his seat. "Stephen! How are you? Ah... it has been a while!" We were all excited to see Stephen again. He had been a member of the team in my first year, before graduating and moving on to Carleton University to pursue a master's degree in physics. Though often injured, Stephen had been a hugely respected presence among the cross-country team. He was level-headed, knowledgeable about running, and had a quick sense of humour. What made him remarkable, however, was his intelligence. Stephen was brilliant. He had graduated with the highest academic ranking at the university, while studying physics. His mathematical capacities and his ability to grasp complex concepts set him apart from other students of high standing. Professors in the physics department still marvelled at his abilities to this day. He was a quick thinker and sporadic conversationalist; his eccentricities could spice up any conversation. This was especially true if Warren was around. The current physics student was a not-so-secret admirer of Stephen. The former X-Man's recent application to medical school further enticed Warren to pick his brain. "So, Stephen, you...you're in town just for a few days?" he eagerly asked.

"Yeah," replied Stephen, putting his hands in his pockets and looking to the ground. "I'm heading back to Ottawa in a bit. Just here for an interview."

Warren was mesmerized.

"Who's this new guy at the end?" asked Stephen.

"Hey I'm Addison! I'm in first year. It's nice to meet you," Addison said, in the respectful tone someone would use when meeting a great uncle for the first time.

This made Stephen laugh. "Yeah, same to you. How old are you anyway?"

"I'm seventeen! Uhm, guys, speaking of that. What if the waitress IDs me? What do I say? I look way too young...I should probably just lea..."

"Addi, relax," interrupted Favero. "You just don't order a beer and you'll be fine. Here, we could get a pitcher and sneak you a beer. Just be quiet about it."

"Ha ha ok! Thanks guys, this is unreal! I bet they have no idea a seventeen-year-old is at this table. Hey Cyr, think I can pass for nineteen? If I take the hat off, maybe? I bet we can make them believe you're younger than me!"

Addison's zeal and enthusiasm for virtually any situation could be tiring at times, but he had gotten me amused. "Addi, you have a weird amount of chest hair for how young you look. Just unbutton your first two and they won't ask any questions," I said.

"So, I hear your big time trial was today, eh?" asked Stephen.

"Yeah, real big race WENT DOWN on the track today, and there were some casualties" said Cal.

"Who?"

"Well," said Warren, "there were multiple. Edward's foot was hurting so he dropped out. Colin and Cullen, who are both in first year, did not finish the race either. They were both getting lapped and got discouraged. We had dropped them. Then, Leo, an international student from France had a bad day. He is fast, but apparently he had not been training in the summer. I do not know much about him. And then there was O'Regan."

"What about O'Regan?"

"His 'nucleuses' were falling apart in his cells," said Angus.

"Wait, what?" asked Stephen, confused.

"Ok, so let's start from the beginning" said Cal. "So, O'Regan thought it would be a good idea to run 132 k the week before time trial, after averaging, like, 60 k per week all summer." Stephen shook his head. "Come time trial, he was dead set on being the ninth guy. He had Scott, Neuffer, Cyr, Angus, Addison, Favero, Paul, and myself pegged as top eight, and then he was set on taking ninth place. So, he went out too hard. His body was tired, and it gave out with a lap to go. He blacked out just short of the finish line and started babbling. It was scary."

"What? Come on O'Regan. He should know not to double his training load randomly like that," replied Stephen. "No way he usually runs anything close to 132k in a week."

"Yeah well, he probably came to his senses in the therapy room where they took care of him for at least an hour, feeding him food," continued Cal.

"That's the other thing. He rarely ate in the summer. He had no job, so he really watched his rations. He just ate enough to survive… for sustenance."

"Oh, ok. So that explains why he's not here with us then; he's resting," said Stephen. "Uhm, not exactly," said Scott. "He's with Fuller and the boys in The Village. He's probably going out tonight."

"Going out? Like, drinking?"

"Yup," said Angus. "Just drowning his sorrows in good old liquid gold," he said, in his classic, taunting tone.

"Wow. Does he not understand how dangerous that is? Stupid move, O'Regan." Stephen was incredulous. As fourth-year students, we knew there were times where partying was appropriate. The hours following a maximum effort and a fainting spell were not one of those times.

"Well, he will have some work to do if he wants to be ninth on the team," said Ferg, still riding on a bit of a high from his race. "All I knew was that I was not letting the people in my group get ahead. I would stick to them until I, literally, could not hold any longer. I…well…I think I would probably have passed out on the track before letting a gap open up between myself and Matt or O'Regan. Indeed, come hell or high water I would stick with…" Warren's claim was cut short. "Sir, a gin and tonic for you."

"Uhm, for me? Well, uhm, ok. Thank you. Who did this?" asked Warren, slightly flustered.

"Sorry, it was sent anonymously," whispered the waitress, with a wink.

"What in the…? It was one of you. Edward? Cal?"

"Sorry Fergie, I would have gotten you straight gin if it were me," joked Ed.

"Not me either," said Cal.

"Ok, I wonder who did this. What if it was someone from another table? Wh…who do we know here?" Now, Warren was turning his head in all directions, as if one anonymous stranger had just granted him a million dollars instead of a simple gin and tonic. He had to know where the drink came from, because he had to avenge it. It was improper to accept a drink and not reciprocate. Warren currently owed someone something, and it was making him direly uncomfortable.

"Ok well, so for the rest of you guys, the season looks good," continued Stephen. "If five of you cruised to low twenty-six, that's pretty promising, you guys obviously won't have much trouble with the other AUS teams."

"Probably not," I said, "but Dalhousie might be decent. They have Will Russell, Jake Wing, Angus MacIntosh, and Graeme Wach, among others. I just don't think they have the depth. Besides, a strong CIS finish is what we're shooting for."

"Yeah, we really can't peak for AUS this year to try and beat each other. Like I know we're going to want to, but we can't do it," said Neuffer.

"Easier said than done for this group. You guys would do anything to take home the individual AUS glory," half-joked Stephen. "But, that's where the maturity kicks in. You really need to know what you want, and that should be a CIS medal."

"Oh we have tons of maturity," said Addison, sneaking a drink of Edward's beer. Stephen shot a look at Addison and laughed. "Jeeze, think it's past this kid's bedtime. We should go."

"We pay up front, you boys ready?" asked Scott. Our group got up slowly and painfully. Eight kilometres on a track had beaten our bodies to the ground, and a good night's sleep was needed.

"Everyone paid?" asked Ed. "All right, let's roll."

"Five can get in my car and five can get in Cal's," I said. "Wait, who are we missing? I only have four. Where's Ferg?"

Neuffer spotted him. "He's still inside." Walking back into the Townhouse, I found Warren speaking with a girl sitting at a nearby table. "Oh, so it was not you. Are you sure? I could have sworn that drink came from your area of the restaurant."

"Uhm, nope. Ha ha...sorry, not me," said the girl, slightly confused.

"Oh, well I...uhm...it's a shame. Uhm... yes. Well, uh... very well. You have a good night."

"Ferg, come on man, the drink will remain a mystery."

"But Cyr, don't you wonder where this gin came from? Perhaps someone was trying to get my attention for something!" Perplexed, Warren followed me out and grabbed his seat on my passenger side. We followed Cal's car out to Main Street as I dropped the guys off at their respective homes around campus.

"That was fun, I hope we can do this again before things ramp up," said Cal, in the other car.

"Yeah, good time," said Edward, settling into the passenger seat. "But Ferg got way too worked up in there. That's the last time I'm buying that guy a drink."

Straight Shooter

September 11th

The morning after time trial represented our entrance into a new realm. We were slowly becoming familiar with the faces we would see at away races and in team pictures, and which ones we would strictly see at practice and social settings. A long run was on the schedule, like every other Sunday. Our crew slowly cleared campus and jogged down towards Main Street. Even though yesterday's effort was not a race for some, everyone was feeling the track-induced soreness in their calves, shins, and hip flexors. Probably for that reason, our group was moving at a lacklustre pace, chatting. After running past the Brierly Brook, we turned left towards Pleasant Valley. The dirt road was relatively flat with only a few rolling hills. I ran with Leo, Neuffer, and Favero, and our pace was uncharacteristically slow for a group involving Alex Neuffer, who was running stiffly. "Wow I am so sore everywhere. Why did Bernie have to have this time trial on a track?"

"Nah, man," said Favero. "The track was great! Like, everyone is dissing the track but I think it was badass, man! Just a group of guys clicking seventy-eight seconds for twenty straight laps. Ah, there's just something about hitting the same time lap after lap. It makes me feel skinny and fit, like you know what I mean?"

I silently concluded that the compelled cross-country-relishing version of Nic Favero was being reborn. Everything he would do from here on out would be conducive to running fast and looking faster."

Leo changed the subject. "How long do you guys run today?"

"Most of us are doing 22-23k," I said.

"What? Wow. This is so much. You are crazy in Canada!"

Neuffer laughed and reassured him. "We're not expecting you to jump into huge mileage right now, don't worry,"

"Yes. I know. I wanted to say to you guys, I am going to do training with the track team two times this week. I can do speed, just not so much long run."

"Whatever works for you. You'll be ready to rip some 1500s in the winter," I said. "Good. I talk to Bernie and he is ok with it. I want to focus on track." Leo changed the subject again. "You know I, uhh, I see O'Regan last night at Piper's Pub. Ha ha... he look ok. Better than yesterday after race. He is there dancing, and with a girl!"

"Ha ha! Of course. When the night comes, O'Regan comes back to life. It's almost like he – ARGH!" My dig at O'Regan was interrupted.

"What is it, Cyr?" asked Neuffer.

"I think I strained a muscle in my lower leg again. It's like the third one since the summer. This is ridiculous." Dull aches were shooting up my right calf. It was manageable, but likely to get worse. My lower legs had been giving me grief since early August, and I was growing frustrated. I realized quickly that my run would be cut short. The sudden tightness and soreness around my Achilles tendon caused me to turn from the run after only half an hour. I let them go and turned to begin the sheepish trek back to campus, angry. Feeling the pain getting worse, I muttered periodic swear words under my breath. I had expected setbacks here and there, but a fourth minor injury since early August had killed any consistency I had hoped of having thus far. I was now behind the eight ball, and I knew it. A great season would still be possible but was becoming increasingly improbable by the day. I could not attain my desired fitness running eighty kilometres per week.

I tried to ignore the pain for a while. But, at forty minutes, the pain had intensified. I knew the nature of the injury was minor. A strained soleus muscle would be the diagnosis, and I was so familiar with this sort of injury that I might as well have diagnosed it myself. Luckily, these pesky setbacks usually healed in two to three days if taken care of properly. If I continued running now, however, it would probably be a week.

I slowed to a walk with twenty minutes left to run to reach campus. It would take me over an hour to walk back in the wind and rain on this uncharacteristically cold September morning. Dreading the trek, I threw my thumb in the air, in the hopes that at least one driver would be kind enough to pull over for a shirtless, skinny guy wearing multi-coloured, galaxy-patterned running shorts. After I walked for five minutes, luck came my way. Mary-Catherine Thompson was driving by and picked me up. She was a jumper on the track team and the girlfriend of Mike Tate, a standout runner from the Antigonish area and a good friend of mine. He had taken his talents to Southern Utah University and competed in Division I of the NCAA. Mary-Catherine was a St. FX student whom I had met through Mike.

"What the heck happened to you?" she screamed out of her car window.

"Achilles problems. Now I'm freezing…so happy you were driving by!" I said. "Any chance you're going towards campus?"

"I can take you wherever you need to go, you look like you need shelter," she said with a laugh.

I eagerly hopped in the backseat, freezing. In less than ten minutes, I would be inside getting ice from the therapy room. I thought to myself that I was lucky to know a good number of people around Antigonish. An hour-long walk in the rain and wind on a strained right leg would have been pitiful. Now, thanks to Mary Catherine, the road to recovery could at least begin one hour faster.

After thanking her, I hobbled into the main doors of the Oland Centre, and came face to face with Edward MacDonald, working the welcome desk. The third-year runner from Arisaig, Nova Scotia had also earned himself a hall pass from today's run after yesterday's drop out – he needed to rest his foot. He asked me why I was back so early, and I proceeded to explain my fate. "Some strain in my leg. What about you? How's the foot today?"

"Well, she ain't great," he replied in his heavy slang. "Been throwin' some ice on her every few hours or so. They seem to think it'll at least be a few days I guess." Though diminutive in size, Edward may have had the largest heart on the team. He was empathetic and helpful to all, and nobody liked to see misfortune come his way. He was talented, but since he spent part of his summers fishing, we knew he needed a spotless bill of health to access and exhibit this talent. With a DNF at time trial, he needed to find an alternative way to prove himself, and he already seemed to be on top of things. While those who had proven themselves on Saturday had punched their tickets to the race in Maine, nothing restricted the ones who would stay behind to run the first conference open meet at Acadia University. "I think if I feel better by tomorrow or Tuesday, I'll ask Bernie if he'd let me drive the truck over to Acadia and take a few of the boys to the race... would be a good way to prove ourselves. I know Cullen and David would want to run it."

"Good idea. It'll be a good way to gauge your fitness compared to other runners, too. Just get that foot thing figured out, we'll need you down the road."

"Get that Achilles looked at Cyr, we need you too!"

I walked down the hallway of the Oland Centre and turned left to walk into the therapy room.

"Cyr, what's going on?" asked our team athletic therapist, Laura Sevigny, as I limped towards the ice tub.

"Just a strain or something, I don't know," I replied, without much thought.

She sighed while digging into the ice machine. "Ah! You runners! Why are injuries such a thing with you guys?"

"I just need one of your magic ice bags, please."

"Ughhh... coming right up," she said, pretending to be annoyed by our daily complaints. At least, I thought she was pretending. "Take care of it, buddy!" she encouraged me, as I left towards our changing room, ice wrapped around my right ankle.

Annoyed with my failing body, I stormed into the change room with an ice bag strapped around my lower calf. Cullen MacInnis was stretching nearby, just finishing up his run. Still relatively new to the sport, he was not prescribed as much mileage as the older guys. His muscular legs injected power into every one of his strides, but he still lacked the smoothness and efficiency of a seasoned runner. He was visibly focused and determined to improve, and those skills as a varsity runner were indispensable.

"What's up Cullen, how was the run?" I asked.

"Not too bad. Legs were a little sore." His defeated tone and demeanour were uncharacteristic of Cullen, who was usually upbeat and positive. I suspected it had something to do with his DNF in yesterday's tryout.

"Everything all right, man?" I asked.

"Yeah. I'm just realizing how far back I am. Getting lapped by you guys at 5k wasn't really motivating. Then again, it's crazy watching your group run. X has definitely never had this much depth. Like, five or six of you have run in the 8:30s, 8:20s even for 3k. That's ridiculous." His words were those of a startled freshman from the back roads of Cape Breton. He had never seen much competition growing up. Being one of the slowest runners in a training group had knocked him out of his element. He might as well have been thrown to the wolves.

"What about you Cyr, why are you back so early?" Cullen asked.

I was growing tired of explaining myself for cutting the run early. "I messed up something in my leg, probably a muscle strain... nothing serious, just annoying. It's like, every time I try to increase my mileage past 130k, something bad happens. It's like my limit, or something."

Cullen tilted his head to the side. "Hmm, you're probably just running too much. Duhh! That's why you're injured all the time. See you at meal hall." Before I had a chance to reply, Cullen was gone. It had been made evident that he said exactly what was on his mind. Though this quality could vex people from time to time, I respected it, for there wasn't a straighter shooter than Cullen MacInnis.

14- Teeter Totter – September 15th

A few days passed, and before I knew it, I was back running, though being cautious. It was not the time of year to worsen an injury. I walked to practice after a long session of rolling and stretching in the basement of 18 Greening. Bernie was ready to get us on our way at 5:10.

"All right here, can everyone listen up? Just a few quick things before we head out on our run." Bernie was leaning on the railing of the Oland Centre stands, clipboard in hand. Kevin Grant had assumed his typical position on Bernie's left, wearing his short-billed ball cap. He would let his elder do most of the talking but would be aware if Bernie were to slip up in his delivery of information. We joked that Kevin was secretly the mastermind of all team operations. "Ok, so just a few quick things," said Bernie. "We are going to cross the border between Canada and the United States tomorrow, so make sure you have your ID cards and passports and so on. I don't want anyone saying they forgot their spikes or shorts or anything like this here so make sure you're all packed up and we will see you in front of the Oland Centre at 5:45 am tomorrow!"

The boys left for a leisurely sixty minutes, and I went down to stretch on the turf. I had done my workout in the morning to maximize my recovery time before the race in Maine. Thankfully, the workout had gone smoothly, and I felt ready to race. I joined Angus on the turf.

"Cyr why aren't you running?" he asked.

"I did this morning instead. Are you still hurting?"

"Yeah. It's not perfect. Like, I could race on it, it's just it would get pretty sore. No point in making it worse, I guess." I could tell by the look on his face that taking the day off required much self-restraint. "That being said, if it still hurts by the Moncton meet, I may just say screw it and run through the pain. I have some Advil and I'm not afraid to use it," said Angus.

"Ahh, the Ferguson special. Apparently, it works!" I said, referring to the fact that Warren relied on monstrous quantities of Ibuprofen to get him through his cross-country seasons in once piece, according to the man himself.

"Yeah, I just don't want to let the boys down. I don't just want to be fifth on the team by AUS, but I want to be a strong fifth, possibly even higher. That's what we need if we want to do well on the national stage."

I wanted to offer my advice, and suggest that he play it safe but, in a way, he was right. Angus was instrumental in our pursuit for a medal. September was early, but not early enough for someone not be affected by an extended period away from running. Negotiating with our bodies was a part of training, and decisions on training volume were always difficult to take.

"Like, I could just take two weeks completely off now and be fine," said the sophomore runner, "but then I'm undertrained. Or I can train hard through the pain, and risk being injured." He had read my mind. "Cross-country season is like a teeter totter. Too much of one thing tips the scale, and it's near impossible to balance at the sweet spot," concluded Angus. For not even being nineteen yet, he approached the sport with remarkable maturity. He understood how to push hard but was also learning how to hold back when needed. He routinely made everyone forget that he himself had probably still played with teeter-totters a mere ten years ago.

"You going to meal hall?" I asked, changing the subject.

"Nah... I still haven't gotten a meal plan, yet. I'm living fine off my frozen lasagnas for now. I'll see you at the house."

"All right, later Beef."

***

By ten p.m., I was at the house as well, and Angus was already asleep. O'Regan had assumed his usual position on the couch, flicking his finger up and down his phone screen, scrolling through his Instagram feed. "Sup?" he asked, still looking at his phone.

"Not much, just got back from the library. Had a good run today. What are you up to?"

"Not much. Man, I just don't get it. I don't know how my sister has so many Instagram followers. Like, it's so much easier if you're a girl. All the guys will just follow them to make them think they're into them. I'm sure if we were girls, we'd have way more followers than we do right now." I chuckled and turned on the X-Box for one quick game of NHL 2017 before bed. Now I knew what had been preoccupying O'Regan for the last hour. Interestingly, it had nothing to do with sending off his five roommates to race in another country while he stayed at home. He would go on to stay awake until two in the morning like most other nights to view and like pictures on his social media, compose rap lyrics, or finish an assignment. The latter would only be done if necessary, and the former two, out of routine.

The Snowman

September 15th

After a short night's sleep, the five of us groggily left Greening the next morning at 5:45 am. A sign made by O'Regan was glued to our front door. It read: Good luck in Maine Boys! Kick some American Ass! The kind gesture really made me wish that he had gotten it right; that he had taken advantage of the opportunity he had been given and had punched his ticket to Maine with the rest of us. Alas, he would be left behind. We hoped he would be able to turn his season around and eventually capitalize on his supposedly huge summer of training. Many questions had been raised on the topic of his training regime. None of us were aware of all the facets of each other's running schedules in the summer, but given O'Regan's propensity for organizational chaos, we could not imagine that his training plan had been overly structured.

"Ok, so when is he going to wake up and take care of himself? His chance to make this team is slipping away, here," said Neuffer, concerned.

"If he buckled down and really performed, there would still be time to bump someone out of the top nine by Interlock," figured Angus.

Cal snickered. "Well, he has not been running much, and has gone out several times since the time trial. He's not headed in the right direction. He will need to run very well to get Bernie to take him on the team now. Actually, I don't think Bernie will take him under any circumstance."

"I was under the impression that the team was already picked," I said.

"Well, not for sure. Ed is driving to the Acadia meet, and is taking anyone wanting to race with him. I think if people run well there, Bernie would consider taking them," said Cal. "I think Bernie will give the boys who are not coming to Maine another chance at proving themselves.

"But has O'Regan told Ed that he wanted a spot in the truck?" I asked.

"Probably not," said Neuffer.

He hadn't.

Scott hastily walked towards the car, losing patience. "Guys, just quit talking about this." He was tired of our speculations. "O'Regan will do whatever O'Regan will do, and it's not up to us to babysit him. Let's just go." Like that, we silently drove to campus.

We rolled onto Convocation Boulevard in Cal's Volkswagon Golf. One by one, we threw our bags underneath the bus and soon grabbed our seats. The eight-hour bus trip to Bangor, Maine would soon begin. I quickly remarked that the inside of the bus was spacious, as I was used to travelling with greater numbers. A few of the girls had no passports and would not be granted permission across the border, so they were forced to stay in Antigonish for the weekend. On the boys' side, we were down by two. Paul MacLellan had been sidelined with a mysterious calf injury. Though he was convinced that his "calf cramp" had manifested because he "wasn't drinking enough water," we were pretty certain that he had experienced some sort of muscle strain. But nobody had the heart to tell him that his elaborate theory was wrong. He had elected to take the weekend off in order to sit down and "drink a whole lot of water." Though the absence of Paul and his kid-like curiosity would leave a lull in the team dynamic, the individual most conspicuous by his absence was Nic Favero. A last-minute retreat from the trip due to unspecified scholastic endeavours had left the team questioning his decision. Usually one to take pride in his loyalty to the team and in his commitment level, his way of handling his predicament was out of character.

"Ok, so why is Nic not coming?" asked Neuffer, still confused about his friend's decision.

Warren quickly defended him. "Uhh, Nic had things to do. He's under a great deal of pressure with his thesis proposal."

Cal did not like the nature of the excuse. "Come on Ferg, give me a break! Almost all of the fourth years have theses to write! That's no excuse for missing out on the first meet of the year. Oh when I see him, he's gonna get it!"

"Also, it's September 15th," said Neuffer. "Like, how busy can you be this early in the year? This whole thing is weird."

Nic's absence was shooting down the team morale. But, even though he was our perennial fifth to sixth runner, we would likely not need him to win this Division III level meet. We expected to win easily, and that could have explained the almost nonexistent level of stress present on the bus. Boys and girls had merged and were now chatting with each other, playing games to pass the time. Before we knew it, we had driven all the way to the US border.

Kevin rose from the front of the bus, and made the chatter dissipate. "Ok, guys! We are entering a new country. Could you please take out your passports? They don't like any nonsense here, especially when dealing with a large vehicle of people. So let's get this done quickly."

The border crossing was characteristically American: traditional and uncongenial. An officer wearing aviators was standing in such a way that would suggest someone had inserted a straight metal rod up his backside. I had a strong distaste for superfluous authority, and Officer Dix was the personification of just that. He looked at us as if we were members of a gang fresh out of jail.

"All right line it up! Get your passports ready," he barked. At the far back of the line, Cal was doing his thing.

"Hey Fuller, what are the odds that you start screaming and run across the border without passing through customs?"

"Uhm... one in twenty." I eyed Fuller in a stupor. Come to think of it, his thinking that this stunt was futile enough to allocate himself a one in twenty chance to be coerced into doing it was not too surprising. Fuller had a knack for bad decisions. He trained sporadically, fed himself a consistently poor diet, and he was rumoured to have threatened a bar bouncer with defecating on his shoes if the door worker would not grant him entrance into his bar. Cal, on the other hand, was clever, and could sometimes manipulate others of lesser wit with the grace of a puppeteer for the sake of his own enjoyment. Though always entertaining, Fuller and he often made a bad combination. They said together, "Three, two, one."

"Seventeen!" yelled Cal.

"Three!" shouted Fuller. Though usually clever, Cal had missed his shot. Fuller always chose three.

"Next! Passport. Are you carrying any illegal substances or weapons today?" spat officer Dix in my direction.

"No sir," I said. I figured he would like to be called "sir." After scanning my face for an awkward five seconds, he almost regretfully let me into his beloved country. Had Fuller tried to pull a stunt with him, he likely would have been tazed… or shot, on a bad day. I chuckled at the useless brutality of Dix's demeanour, moved along forward, and hopped on the bus to join the rest of the team. We would find out that this trip required patience, as another four hours separated us from Bowdoin College, where we would go shake out our legs on tomorrow's cross-country course. I got up to go to the washroom and left my seat next to Heidi MacDonald in the middle of the bus. I was gone for barely a minute, and in that short amount of time, Addison managed to steal my seat. I was greeted with the embarrassed yet self-righteous grin only a seventeen-year-old rookie could produce.

"Hey Cyr, looking for something? Heidi likes it better with me sitting here." I rolled my eyes and smiled.

"Well I'll just cuddle with Ashley," I joked, making reference to the completely platonic slumber session enjoyed by the two first-year runners a few hours prior at the front of the bus. I proceeded to sit next to Ashley and hug her. It was a bold move on my part, as I may have talked to the rookie twice at this point of the season. She did not play along. Instead, she looked at me, petrified. This was my cue to not let the joke linger on too much. Awkwardly, I apologized and walked back towards my seat. I searched for Addison in the back, and he was still grinning.

He had, however, already shifted his focus from my antics to his own. He was now poking Neuffer on the arm. "Neuffer really thinks he's going to beat all you guys tomorrow but he has no idea that I'm coming for him. He's going to be surprised when he sees me on his shoulder with one kilometer to go." Nobody knew Addison enough to tell whether he was seriously threatening to beat one of our established top runners, or whether he was joking.

Neuffer, overhearing this banter and unfazed, contently answered by exhaling nonchalantly out of his nose. His confidence may have been at an all-time high. As far as he was concerned, no seventeen-year-old could hold a candle to him, and perhaps, neither could anybody on this bus, given his current level of fitness.

As if out of nowhere, our travel bus slowed, and came to a stop. We were rolling into the athletic headquarters of Bowdoin College. The grassy campus was crowded with various sports teams practicing. Frisbee players were occupying the baseball field, and a few different groups were playing soccer. We descended from the bus and headed for the field house.

"Canadians! Welcome to Bowdoin College!" A short and slender man who presented himself as the Bowdoin cross-country coach greeted us. He undoubtedly had been a runner in his day. "Follow me, I'll show you where to place your stuff, and then we can jog over to the start line and you can familiarize yourselves with the course." He led us to a state of the art indoor track, like those we had seen on the Flotrack website. I was shocked. The school competed in Division III, and their top runners were supposedly slower than ours. Yet, we would never be able to afford facilities of that calibre. The track was bouncy, and the whole facility was covered in Mondo rubber. The infield was clean and held all the gear needed for the field events. We dropped off our bags in one corner of the room and excitely, we got our shoes on to explore the course. The Bowdoin coach jogged to the start line with us and showed us a map of the course. We followed his instructions and began jogging on the flat and fast terrain, scoping it out. Most of it was run on grass, with a gravel part. There wasn't a hill.

Neuffer, confident about his past workouts, was running at a breakneck pace for having just finished a ten-hour bus ride. "Oh man I'm just gonna be flyin' tomorrow, this is insane!"

Angus Rawling was just as excited, running alongside him. His ankle did not seem to bother him. We pranced along for half an hour before stopping in front of the field house.

"Is that the team from Canada?" I heard someone ask. A few students of Bowdoin College were staring at us in amazement and confusion.

"Yeah, that's us!" I said.

"Why did you guys come... you wanted to escape the snow?" one of them asked, clearly puzzled.

Another piped in, "You guys know you're going to destroy everyone here, right? We saw your times online; this race won't even be competitive for you."

Cal turned to me and lowered his tone around the Bowdoin runners. "There we go, just what I thought. We have no business here and we're going to make a huge joke of everyone else for no reason at all. Does Bernie know that we could drive an hour from here and race against Division I schools?"

"Hey this isn't so bad," said Neuffer. "I can win here! Uhh... I mean, one of us can win here." He laced his spikes and confidently strode away. The pre-race shakeout was done, and Kevin gathered the crew in the field house. A friend of Kevin and Bernie's had passed away earlier this week, and Bernie had been asked to be a pallbearer at her funeral. He would only arrive on Saturday morning. This made Kevin in charge of a crew of twenty-one runners. Luckily, our team was loaded with seniors, and did not need much adult supervision.

Amidst our noise, Kevin spoke up. "Ok guys, I have just made reservations at Applebee's for us. It's a five-minute drive. Grab your spikes and don't forget anything here. We will be heading for the hotel in Portland soon after supper." Without hesitation, we grabbed our spikes and warm ups, and left the impressive field house. Kevin had a way of speaking that could silence an entire crowd. He was so soft-spoken that we sometimes needed just that, complete silence, to grasp his message. He swore he cheered us on during races, and we believed him, but none of us – other than Scott, once he would break away from the lead pack of runners in the late stages of races – could remember hearing Kevin's voice on the racecourse. Bernie's entertaining digs may have overshadowed his cheers. "You're not tired!" and "it's all in your head!" now resonated within our subconscious so direly that we no longer questioned the scientific validity behind his claims. As far as intensity levels went, Bernie and Kevin balanced each other remarkably well.

* * *

A good meal at Applebee's got us fuelled for tomorrow's battle – whether the race would solely be disputed amongst ourselves or not. Bellies full, we retreated to the hotel to rest up. Angus was looking at me, smirking, as we got off the bus.

"What is it?" I asked.

"Look at Warren," said Angus. The physics major was clothed in a full retro blue and white Adidas tracksuit and a backwards all-white ball cap. He was still wearing his running shoes: old, beat up and bulky Asics Gel Cumulus. He had forgotten to bring any casual clothing with him on the trip – forcing him to wear warm up gear around the clock. Juxtaposed with his usual business-like and formal attire, this get-up really changed his style. "He looks like a crack dealer," continued Angus.

I burst out laughing at the thought of Warren selling drugs to thugs in his awkward style.

He caught me staring at him and laughing, he inquired, annoyed, "Cyr, I can tell you are mocking me by your impish grin. What is it now?"

"Ferg, you look like there are a few grams of coke in your back pocket that you're trying to get rid of." The whole team understood what Angus and I saw and burst out laughing.

Warren, in his new wardrobe, just smirked and went along with the joke. Placing his index and middle fingers in a peace sign and waving them up and down, he began mocking himself. "Yo... uhm... man. I am the snowman. Do you want some drugs? Some white cocaine powder, perhaps? I believe I know a guy who has drugs," he uttered in his still proper and articulate dialect. "I will give my, uhm, homie a call, and I will hook you up. In fact, I can hook you up really well!"

The contrast between his straight edge personality and the character he had taken on was too much for all of us. We spent the next ten minutes laughing with him. Warren had no problem accepting friendly jabs and was improving at dishing them back. The graceless and confused kid I had met three years ago in front of the Oland Centre had become an integral part of the social core of the cross-country team. He had no choice but to learn how to think on his feet around us; we loved to joke around.

"Yo man, I am the snowman! I will give you some drugs in exchange for a reasonable lump of cash!" He had singlehandedly lightened the mood after a long day of bussing.

After a good laugh, we dispersed into our respective hotel rooms. We were divided in threes – I shared a room with Scott and Angus. In excitement, we set our alarm clock for 7:30 a.m.; the first race of the year was approaching. I ingested the one drug I regularly consumed – a Ferramax iron pill – and went to sleep.

Bowdoin Invitational

September 17th

"Tell you what. Carbs are all you need before a race. You'll see." Cal DeWolfe was convincing himself and others around him that his breakfast of cereal, a cinnamon raisin bagel, and oatmeal would bring him to victory today. I was not one to get caught up in eating habits, but I had noticed that an almost dangerous portion of Cal's diet consisted of breads and cereals. At 6'2" and 150 lbs., he did not spend much time consciously thinking about his waistline.

"This food sucks," said Addison, as he picked at his oatmeal. "The only thing I eat before a race is a Subway flatbread sandwich with roast beef, cheddar cheese, and cucumbers. I wish I had one right now." The look on his face suggested that he needed his mother's embrace more than a sandwich.

"Buddy, are you all right?" I asked.

"I'm just nervous, this is my first university race – the first time I run with the St. FX singlet! I don't want to go out with you guys and then blow up." The way he romanticized the university experience constantly triggered my nostalgia. I would later try to make him snap out of his constant daze. His affinity for his new surroundings reminded me of the way I had approached my first year, inflating the importance of everything to the point where my angst would crush me.

"You've looked great in practices. Don't worry about this – it's just another race," I said, remembering how I'd anxiously dreaded races in my rookie year. Cal, Addison, and I retreated to the former two's room. Angus and Scott had left for a nearby Tim Hortons, which had apparently spilled over from the Canadian side, and I had forgotten my key inside my locked hotel room.

95

"Where is Neuffer?" asked Addison.

"Probably buying nuts at the grocery store," said Cal. Neuffer's caloric intake was largely dependent on nuts. "Hey Addison, what are the odds that you tell Neuffer that you're going to destroy him on the racecourse today?"

"Ha! I should do that! It will throw him off his game. I'm going to keep a serious face when I say it." The easily influenced Addison was candy for Cal. I was controlling the sound system, and played one of Kanye West's new songs, in an attempt at getting me into the zone. In the middle of the first verse of "Famous," however, Neuffer walked in with a bag of almonds from the grocery store.

"Hey Neuffer, guess who's going to be breathing down your neck today?" said Addison. "Once you've dropped all the other guys, you'll see me creeping on your left shoulder. It'll come down to a kick, and your legs will be rubber. It's going to be game over real quick. Hope you like second place!" Those taunts could have been taken more seriously had they not been accompanied by the rookie's permanently goofy-looking grin.

Neuffer, confident to the bone, just snickered. "You can think that all you want. I know Cal is trying to get you under my skin, but it is hilarious how unafraid I am of you right now. Start the race with me, and you will not be able to finish it." One should have known better than to disturb him on race day.

To add fuel to Addison's fire, Cal jumped in. "Hey man I don't know, Addison has been looking great in workouts, and if you go out too fast you may have a rough time by the end. Perfect time for little Addi to reel you right in like a..."

Slam! The closing of the bathroom door interrupted our spectacle. Neuffer would not stand for it this morning, and it was clear. On that note, we left the room and hopped on the bus, dressed in our St. FX attire from top to bottom.

As soon as we touched foot on the course, all eyes were on us. Word had spread about the Canadian school travelling across the border to attend a Division III race. It made me realize that this meet would be no different from all the AUS meets that we had dominated over the years. A runner warming up in basketball shorts stopped making me assume an easy victory, and instead made me presume it. I didn't mind. I hadn't raced in two months, and my last 8k race had happened a full year ago.

We had been able to gauge what kind of competition we would be up against by watching the girls' race. Our girls were beaten by the hosts, Bowdoin, but had a strong showing. After running around the course to cheer on our teammates, we finished up and began doing drills on a soccer field by the starting area. During this window of high tension – the minutes leading up to race time – I enjoyed observing my teammates' differing ways of trying to achieve mental readiness. Neuffer was striding up and down the soccer field. Cal, Matt, and Angus were doing dynamic drills. Warren was pacing around, muttering to himself. Scott was lying down on the ground, eyes closed, in perfect peace. A lot of my warm up consisted of positive self-talk. I was predisposed to negative thoughts on race day, and to enter a race with a positive mindset was something I worked on incessantly. I had gotten better at it with age. I remembered the times when my parents had driven me to track meets wondering why I would even bother signing up if racing made me so nervous and insufferable. Thankfully, those days were long gone.

Upon meeting Cal, I immediately envied his apparent race-day carelessness. In reality, it was just a means for escape. Cal was a perfectionist who cared deeply about his performance. He paid attention to the most minute of detail in his training, to the point where some would think he was making things up. A rationalist by nature and a realist by choice, he believed that his performance would not be optimal if he were to make the slightest mistake. A mindset of this sort inevitably brought him a great deal of anxiety on race day. In addition, he was coming off a six-month bout with burnout and staleness that had seen him massively under-perform. But, cross-country had always seemed to bring out the best of Cal, and he hoped that this season could help spark his dormant progression.

"Ok guys, let's go, and get in here!" Bernie had recently touched down in Maine and was ready to deliver his pre-race talk. I had heard so many of these talks over the years that I knew all that he would say, but a reminder never hurt. "All right, so guys, first race of the year. I don't want everyone getting anxious and nervous and so on. Today is a day to go out there, work hard, and show them what X is about. You know who you should be running with and make sure you're running on their shoulders like this here, I don't want one guy leading the whole time and so on. Share the workload. Scott, take it away."

Our team captain and only fifth-year runner took the reins. "All right guys, time to get our feet wet. Don't put too much importance on this one. It's only the first meet of the year, and we're probably going to win. Get out there, work hard, have fun. Let's get a cheer going."

Last year, we had borrowed a historic mantra from the anthem of St. FX's athletics program: "Hail and Health." It was the name of a poem that had been chanted by our varsity football teams since the 1950s. The poem's title served as a popular cheer for our teams. To add our own twist to the tune, we had exchanged the word "health" for "hell," to reference the pain and suffering we endured while racing. It had become catchy. Scott would boom "HAIL AND HELL!" to which we would answer: "WHITE AND BLUE!" We would repeat this sequence three times, before screaming in unison, "One, two, three, X!" I had not heard the hearty cheer in months. It made me hungry to race.

We retreated to the start line. The boxes were large, allowing room for four abreast. Scott, Neuffer, Cal, and I assumed the front positions. It was time to break the ice.

"On your mark," announced the race starter.

POW! The two-command start triggered an avalanche of skinny, flailing legs. I made sure I was near the front pack, consisting of about fifteen runners.

"Hey guys," said Addison between strides, "my watch says we're going 2:55 per kilometer. I think that's too fast. Oh wait! Now it says 3:15. We're good. I think it's because the GPS doesn't..."

"Shut up," muttered Scott, annoyed. If one more word was to come out of Addison's mouth, he was going to stop running and slap him. Nobody cared about the pace after only 400 metres run in an 8-kilometre race. Rookie move. Cross-country was not about time and pace. Every course was different, so time meant little. It was all about effort and placement.

Luckily for us, Addison did not stick with the lead pack for long. Neither did most of the Americans. Soon, five X-Men surrounded a single runner from Bowdoin College in the lead pack. We ran through the first mile in 5:02. Running in two files, Neuffer and Cal were leading. I ran alongside Scott. The terrain switched from gravel to grass, back to gravel, and then we would enter a trail surrounded by forest. Soon after finishing our first loop, our two-mile split came at 10:03. We had not eased off the pace. I began hearing one less set of spikes flinging dirt behind me. Angus had already fallen off the lead pack. The hope for a perfect score – sweeping the first five places – was likely lost. I was running alongside Cal, Neuffer and Scott – my perennial rivals. Nobody was giving an inch. At three miles, we split 15:05. Cal had surged to the front and had taken control of the race with Neuffer, Scott, and me chasing. The pace stayed constant, and the Bowdoin runner dropped off our pack of four. Coming all this way to race, and I was battling with my roommates once again; it felt like practice. But, I was beginning to feel something I had not felt in a while: the burning pain of cross-country running. Unlike the sharp, stinging burn I had learned to tolerate on the track this summer, this feeling was insidious. It snuck up on you until you suddenly found yourself in oxygen debt, gasping for air, dragging your feet under your tired quads.

Six kilometres into the race, it was Scott's turn to show his hand. Injecting pace, he dragged Neuffer along with him. Cal and I stayed behind. Soon, they assumed a twenty-meter gap. Without warning, we had now entered the final stage of the race, and the real burn settled in. Struggling, I fell off Cal's pace and eventually got caught by the Bowdoin runner, and could not fight him off. I was not ready for the last kilometre and slowed considerably. Working for every stride, I lost ground to my three teammates, and ended up finishing fifth in 25:29.

Ahead of me, Scott had accelerated once more, and broke Neuffer with barely one kilometre to go. The diminutive Ontarian charged to the end, arms red and pumping. He looked dominant, crossing the finish line with an air of ease in a time of 25:08. Behind him by six seconds was Cal, who had overtaken Neuffer. Surprisingly, he had gained a lot of ground on Scott, and a strong last two kilometres had propelled him to second place. With a clear view of what was happening in front of me, I could see Neuffer faltering in the final 500 metres of the race. I was surprised. The gingerly runner crossed the finish line, disappointed, in 25:19 for third place. The runner from Bowdoin had finished between him and me and grabbed fourth.

Angus had held on for sixth place, but watching him limp back to our bags after finishing was a troubling sight. His ankle had caused him some problems, but it was his knee that had become the main concern. Icing it immediately, he sported a grim look on his face. Nobody wanted to be dealing with an injury this early in the season. We decided to leave him with his demons, and only offer our words of encouragement after the dust settled.

Once I had replenished my stores of oxygen, I turned and joined the guys at the finish line to see what would happen next. At 27:05, Addison Derhak cruised to the finish. After running his first few kilometres at a torrid pace, he had barely held it together. Today, he was our sixth man. Warren Ferguson crossed the finish almost a minute after Addison, and the dissatisfied look on his face showed that he had wanted to place higher in the final rankings. His 27:59 did not please him. He had, however, distanced Matt Eliot, who had run 28:41, looking sluggish by the end of the race. A wave of sympathy overtook me when I realized that a time that slow would perhaps make Bernie think twice about sending him to the next travelling meet. Matt apparently had shared my thought. He looked distraught. He had, however, secured his ranking of tenth man on the team depth chart. If Bernie would perhaps reconsider Matt's spot on the team, he would most definitely do so for Ryan Fuller. The tall, orange-haired giant crossed the finish line in 30:03. He had seen many better days. Once all our runners had crossed the line, we walked back towards our bags to meet the girls.

"Cal you looked great out there today! That's awesome!" said Hana Marmura.

Cal took off his spikes, indifferent. "Thanks, but today doesn't really mean anything. Still a long way to go." His mindset was the right one, as nobody would remember who had finished where in the first meet of the season. Nonetheless, he had accomplished something today. He had showed everyone that his fitness was where it was supposed to be, and the timing was perfect. Our team would not succeed without Cal. His rekindled fire was good news for team morale. With him running well, the division in speed that had started forming between our top end would shrink, and perhaps disappear.

The five of us who finished in the top seven at the meet were awarded a Bowdoin College tank top. Sporting our new swag, we hopped on the bus that was taking us to Applebee's for the second time this weekend. From there, we would drive to Portland, where we would stay the night, before making the trip back to Antigonish after our Sunday long run.

* * *

At the popular American restaurant, we replenished our stores with greasy food. "Fuller, what did you order this time?" asked Matt Eliot.

"Uhh, a plate of onion rings, a chicken finger and fries platter, and a beef and broccoli stir-fry." The amount the 6'5", 210 lbs. runner could eat was, well, expected. He towered over perhaps every runner in the AUS conference. Always sporting a Toronto Raptors hat, he would have fit in better with the basketball team.

"Fuller don't you get full?" asked Heidi MacDonald.

"No. The food is just all right."

Matt laughed from the other side of the table. "Fuller must have the most ironic name. I don't think he's been full for a minute in his life." He then addressed the giant. "Want dessert, buddy?"

"Can we get dessert?" asked Fuller with the excitement of a child. As none of the other runners were planning on indulging in Applebee's American delicacies of apple pie and chocolate brownies, he sucked it up and resisted the urge. Luckily for him, our bus needed some repairs as we got back outside. We were forced to wait inside a nearby Dunkin Donuts. Sitting at a table with Cal and Scott, I witnessed Fuller walk back from the ordering counter with a bag in his hands.

Angus was eyeing him, incredulous. "How can this guy still eat?"

"What's in the bag buddy?" I asked Fuller.

"Not much. Just three donuts."

Bangor Blues

September 18th

Cyr: Scott, wake up.

Scott: Long-run time?

Cyr: Yup. Angus is in the hallway.

Angus: The guys are waiting for us downstairs.

Scott (groggily): Rrrready.

Cal: Ok, the clerk at the desk said that we could catch a good trail if we pass Stillwater.

Warren: I may ask him for a map just in case.

Neuffer: You don't need a map. I know where I'm going.

Matt: How do you know where you're going? We're in Bangor, Maine.

Neuffer: Pfft. Common sense.

Addison: What if I'm doing less?

Cyr: We could circle back at ninety and do extra.

Addison: No I want to do like sixty minutes.

Fuller: (Chuckles)

Addison: Are you making fun of me, Fuller?

Fuller: Sixty minutes is nothing Addison. You're not a real grinder.

Addison: I don't want to get injured.

Cyr: Let's go. I'm falling asleep again. Girls have been gone for a while.

Cal: All right speedsters, if anyone is going faster than five minutes per kilometre, they will lose me in their dust. I am going to PUTT [go slowly].

Neuffer: Yeah, me too.

Warren: Aha, I would love to see this. Neuffer running easily on an easy day. God forbid.

Scott: Neuffer, your definition of "putting" is, like, 4:20 k's.

Neuffer: Yeah well, I'll make an effort to go slowly.

Matt: Pretty sure Stillwater is this way.

Neuffer: Yeah, I know. Just follow me. It's simple.

Addison: My calves are so tight. Maybe I should turn back.

Cyr: You're fine. We're not even fifteen minutes into the run. Take some time to warm up.

Cal: When is Neuffer going to pull away from us?

Matt: Within the next ten minutes. He won't be able to resist.

Scott: Yo guys, this is a dead end.

Warren: This map indicates that we would have more room to run if we turn to the left.

Matt: How far are we in this run?

Neuffer: About four kilometres.

Cal: And here it comes: the Neuffer surge.

Matt: Aaaand Fuller goes with him.

Scott: Well I'm not running that fast. It's not worth it at this point of the season. We'll have to separate soon.

Warren: It would be best to stay as a pack.

Addison: Ok guys, I'm going to turn back.

Scott: How long are you running, thirty minutes?

Addison: I want to do sixty, but I don't want to get lost.

Neuffer: Jeeze guys, nobody's going to get lost. Addison, just follow your steps back.

Addison: I have a bad feeling about this, boys. We're in the States.

Cal: Yeah careful. Anyone could literally have a gun in their pockets.

Addison (nervously chuckles): Oh God.

Scott: Oh come on...you'll be fine. See you back there.

Cyr: Crazy how cautious that guy is.

Cal: Maybe he'll be the first X rookie to make it through a season without injury or burnout.

Warren: Another left here.

Neuffer: The run goes by so much slower when I don't know where I'm going.

Warren: Aha! So now you admit to it. You're just as lost as the rest of us without this map.

Neuffer: I'm not lost.

Cyr: Wait, you don't know where you're going?

Neuffer: Well yeah. Kind of. Not really. Can't be that hard to find our way back.

Scott: Ok, Neuffer is going too quick. Cyr and Fuller can go if they want. I'm sticking right here in the back.

Cal: Agreed!

Cyr: Why did I pick the fast pack? Jeeze, nobody is following us.

Neuffer: Cyr how slow do you think these guys are going?

Cyr: Just fast enough to call it running, but I'd be with them if I didn't feel this fresh. March of the penguins.

Fuller: (chuckles)

Neuffer: Let's go up this way; they can follow us if they want.

Cyr: Yeah, like I'm really feeling the uphill right now.

Neuffer: Ok we're at forty. Let's turn around.

Cyr: Pee break.

Neuffer: Wow they're not even coming behind us. They must have been walking.

Cyr: Or they went a different way.

Neuffer: Yeah, I'm pretty sure they turned.

Cyr: Oh God, how the hell are we going to find our way back? I'm lost.
Neuffer: I think you turn right somewhere.

Cyr: Great help.

Scott: HEY! GUYS!

Cal: You guys missed out! There are a bunch of trails in the woods up there. It's like a cross-country course.

Matt: It was like Point Pleasant Park in Halifax!

Cyr: Why did you guys turn in there?

Warren: Cyr, do you see the hill ahead of you? There was no way I was doing that after race day. Ever since Riley took me up Brown's mountain in my rookie year I've avoided hills like the plague. Oh, you have no idea but I was THIS close to quitti...

Cyr: I know Ferg. I heard about your wrestle with that bloody mountain at least ten times.

Warren: No, I don't think you know how close I actually was to quitting!

Neuffer: Yeah, yeah, yeah.

Cal: How about we try to stick together on this way back, I'm kind of fuzzy on how we got here.

Warren: I have it on this map. Keep going straight.

Neuffer: Don't need a map. The way back is obvious.

Scott: Well at least Neuffer sounds confident.

Cyr: What are the odds that Addison made it back?

Scott: I can see that kid getting way lost in these streets.

Fuller: (chuckles)

Matt: This is embarrassing, guys, but I already have no clue how to get back.

Warren: We will turn to the right soon.

Neuffer: I know the street.

Matt: I feel like I've been running for three hours. What's our time?

Neuffer: Just over sixty.

Scott: This hotel breakfast is going to be great.

Cyr: I'm still full from my Applebee's ribs.

Cal: That's what happens when you have a small stomach.

Scott: That's what they call him: Small Stomach Cyr.

Fuller: (chuckles)

Warren: Little meals for a little boy.

Cyr: All right, all right.

Cal: Oh no, an intersection. Screw it, I'm running around in circles to not let my legs get cramped.

Car (at Cal): BEEEEEP

Cal: Hey! I'm off the road, idiot!

Warren: Shut up, Cal. Right after this intersection, we turn right.

Neuffer: Yep, got it. Knew it all along.

Scott: Finally, green light. Go.

Matt: Wait...this is not it.

Cal: I'm pretty sure it's one street down. Because do you remember? We passed that convenience store down there.

Warren: Yes. Uhm, yes that's right.

Neuffer: Wait, this is not the street either.

Warren: Ok. Let's go straight for a bit. I may be misreading this map.

Matt: All right, Neuffer has no clue what's going on.

Neuffer: Yeah I do, just wait a few seconds.

Warren: And this map is faulty. I swear it's faulty.

Scott: Just keep looking at street names. Which was the one that led us to Stillwater?

Cal: LOOK! PARKVIEW STREET!!

Scott: This is the street?

Cal: No! That's my old high school's name!

Warren: Thanks for sharing, Cal.

Matt: Ok, are we lost here?

Neuffer: No, we're fine.

Warren: We are not lost. I must just take a minute to study this perhaps faulty map.

Cal: Hey, let's stop at a convenience store and ask the way back to the Marriot.

Cyr: There's one right here!

Scott: Excuse me. We are looking for the Marriot hotel.

Cashier: Uhm yeah, it's like a mile away. Just take a left and go up the street. Take a left at the end, and it's just one street over to the right.

Cyr: Perfect, We're at eight minutes. That will get us to about ninety.

Neuffer: Ok, let's go.

Fuller (quietly): Uhm, hey Cyr?

Cyr: Yeah?

Fuller: Can you guys wait, like five minutes?

Cyr: Ughh... why?

Fuller: I have to poop.

Cyr: Fine.

Cal: Ughh... Fuller hurry up!

Neuffer: Can we go? It's raining and I'm getting cold.

Matt: And it smells bad in this store.

Cyr: Wait for Fuller.

Scott: Here he is. Feel better Fuller?

Fuller: (nods)

Warren: Ok, we're following this guy's instructions and nothing seems familiar. Let's stop at this one.

Neuffer: Hang on, I think we're almost there.

Scott: No. You don't know where we are. We're stopping.

Cyr: We'll wait out here. Get more directions.

Cal: OK, as soon as I hit a hundred minutes, I'm starting to walk, no matter where I am.

Matt: It's really starting to rain.

Warren: Ok guys, I got it. Follow me this way.

Cyr: Neuffer's peeing on the side of the road.

Cal: Me and Matt are going with Warren.

Cyr: Neuffer let's go! Will you empty that tiny bladder of yours?

Neuffer: Where are they?

Cyr: Up there, follow them. Come on Fuller.

Scott: Man, I'm dead. This has to be right.

Neuffer: Ok honestly, I don't remember seeing any of this.

Scott: We're almost at ninety-five minutes.

Cyr: Ok, I don't want to get lost here. We should call a cab. I'm tired of this.

Neuffer: Wait! Why does Cal have his hands up, up there?

Scott: Oh my God, the X bus! Right there!

Cyr: RUN!!

Cal: (from a distance) WOOOOO!

Neuffer: Guys pick it up. It's at an intersection.

Scott: Sprint, Fuller, come on! We can't miss it.

Cyr: We're good! We're making it!

Bernie (screaming from the inside): Guys get in here. You had us worried!

Cal: We got lost! We had no idea where we were! Ferg butchered the map and...

Warren: This map is faulty! Nobody could have navigated us back to the Marriott with this map, nobody!

Neuffer: If you just never looked at the map and listened to me...

Scott: Doesn't matter, I just want food.

Matt: Yeah, I'm starving.

Clif (bus driver): Well you're lucky we found you. I was mostly out to get a coffee.

Cal: Thank you so much Clif!!

Bernie: Well, leave them alone for two hours and they manage to get lost in the United States (shakes head). What was I thinking?

Cyr: What about Addison? Have you heard at all from him?

Bernie: He made it back and is eating pancakes as we speak. Looks like he has a better head on his shoulders than the rest of you.

Fuller: (chuckles).

AUS Scout

September 21st

Bernie leaned against the radiator across from our change room by the Oland Centre doors. "Ok guys, listen up. Just a few things and you'll be on your way. We are at Wednesday, and the Moncton meet is Saturday. You've just raced last Saturday in Maine, so I don't want anyone trying to push the pace and going fast on easy runs. Today is an easy effort so you can be ready to go for tomorrow's workout. Got it?" We were back to reality after a ten-hour bus trip back to Antigonish. "Kevin, anything you want to add?"

"Well, Bernie, you were going to mention Trackie, and..."

"Oh right, thanks Kevin. So..." he paused, folding his hands into one big fist, "it has come to my attention that some of you are posting messages and comments on the Trackie forums and message boards and so on. Last night, Kevin went through these web pages and found some pretty childish stuff."

Trackie.com was a growing phenomenon in the world of Canadian distance running – especially in the realm of varsity cross-country. Website visitors ranging from athletes to parents to coaches posted – often anonymously – on the website's popular message boards. It was a networking platform connecting runners from across the country, but it unfortunately doubled, for some, as a perfect way to throw anonymous shade at other athletes.

"Now Kevin noticed that there were people talking themselves up and putting down other teams and things like this here. Now I'm not accusing anyone in particular, because nobody uses their real names on these websites, but many conversations on there talk about St. FX. St. FX is going to win, St. FX is going to lose and so on. What you're doing when you post these things is giving information to other teams that they don't need. What do I always say Angus? When you lose you say little and when you win you say…"

"Less," finished Angus.

"Correct. Now if I catch any of you on the Trackie forums talking about others, or us, there will be consequences. There is one account that is always in the middle of these things and it's AUS Man or AUS runner or something, Kevin what is it again?"

"It's AUS Scout, Bernie."

"Yeah right, AUS Scout. Now if that account tries to start something with someone on this team, I expect you to know better and to not play into their games. He or she is just on the Internet to stir the pot by sending messages and emails and so on. These are distractions, and I will have none of it. Understood?"

We nodded and left for the Landing-Bethany loop.

Running next to Fuller and Leo, Cal flashed me a look and shook his head, smiling. I knew exactly what the look meant.

"So, what did Bernie talk about? The Trackie?" asked Leo, slightly confused.

"He warned us not to post on its forum. People try to get others angry by making fun of them or putting them down on the Trackie message boards."

Ok, I see. And he does not want us to do… uhm… like the AUS Scout? What is AUS Scout?"

Cal started giggling uncontrollably. "Well, Leo, let's just say that you know this AUS Scout better than you think!" he said mischievously.

"Oh! So AUS Scout is a person on the message boards?"

"Yeah," I said. "He always tries to lure strangers into online conversations about the AUS. The topics are of little relevance. Things like 'Who is the best long runner in the AUS?' or 'Who could win in a fight between so and so?' Some posts are just made to put down other runners whom he doesn't like. His posts can be funny, but for the most part, he just attracts unwanted attention."

"And Cal you know who it is?" gasped Leo. "AH! It's you Cal! I can see it. It's you!" "Ha ha! Well, Leo, let me tell you something. Cyr and I have had our fun on Trackie, back in our first and second years. But we've matured."

I jumped in. "We still follow it decently closely, but we don't really contribute to the conversation. Also, AUS Scout makes too many spelling mistakes to be Cal or me. He is on this team, though."

"NO WAY! The person Bernie he talk about? You know who? And he is on the team? Oh! It is Angus!" guessed Leo, in his imperfect English.

"Nope...good guess though. Angus might have an account, but it's not AUS Scout."

"I don't think it is O'Regan. He never use computer. Uhm... Neuffer or Scott?"

"Nah, Scott hates that type of stuff. Neuffer also wouldn't kill hours of his day to post about others. Too busy cross-training," said Cal.

"Well, is it a rookie?"

"No. AUS Scout has been around for a few years."

"I know it is not Nic. And I don't think Warren has time, continued Leo. "Matt?"

"Matt said he hasn't been on Trackie this year," I said. "Try again."

"Ahh! Who else is left? Edward? Paul?"

"Edward and Paul love reading his posts, but as far as we know, neither is the culprit. AUS Scout was still posting in May while Ed was on the fishing boat. Paul doesn't know enough about the conference to keep throwing out names in the posts."

"Jeffs?"

"Nope. Doesn't do much Trackie either."

Leo threw his arms up in the air. "I say everyone! There is nobody left!"

"Well, Leo, you missed one member. A BIG one too!" said Cal. At that moment, the gingerly behemoth striding alongside Leo started smiling, and became hysterical.

"Fuller? It's you!?"

"Hmmmm... hmmm... hmm... no. Probably... Angus," he said unconvincingly, between bursts of laughter.

Cal and I roared. Even though he refused to admit it, we knew that Ryan Fuller, the tall and quiet giant, was absolutely ruthless on the Internet forums. He had challenged the entire Dalhousie cross-country team to a fist-fight, he had mocked high profile university coaches and accused them of "not knowing how to properly coach", and he had called out people from across the country – most of them not knowing who Ryan Fuller was – for being slow. His account was stupid and infantile, but his façade was so transparent that it had become silly.

"Fuller, admit it, man! You're the Internet troll!" yelled Cal. "We found you to be guilty in the mock trial of AUS Scout that we held last year."

Lee Wesselius had served as Fuller's lawyer. They had suffered a harrowing loss to Cal and Nic Favero, the prosecutors.

"Then, we saw you were logged into Trackie as AUS Scout on your phone. Plus, the writing style is the same as all your other Trackie accounts."

Fuller was roaring, despite himself. "No, it's not me," is all he could come up with. One thing was for sure: he was definitely most clever behind a keyboard.

"Wait, Fuller you have other accounts too?" asked Leo, now very amused.

"Uhm, just one or two," said the giant.

"Fuller has six accounts that we know of!" corrected Cal. "But he does most of his dirty work under AUS Scout."

"How do we know it's not you, Leo?" said Fuller.

"Ha ha! Fuller no! Don't try to blame me. I don't know this Trackie. You are, how you say, guilty! Guilty, Fuller! Bad boy!" Leo was loving this. "Now hope Bernie doesn't find out because if yes, Fuller you will be in big, big trouble. No more desserts for you!"

Quarrels and Qualms

September 22nd

"Bernie, something hurts in my leg!"

"Awhhh, Addison. Do you want me to kiss it better?" Bernie's quick wit generated a few laughs in the Oland Centre hallway.

"No, ewww! I just don't know if I should do the workout. The pain is like, around my shin, kind of. It didn't hurt during the Maine trip, but it started being sore yesterday during the easy run. I don't want to make it worse."

"Well, Addison, we're still two days out from our meet in Moncton. It's not really the time to take things down; it's still early. Try it out for the warm up, and then let us know. You can run when you're sore; you can't run when you're injured!"

That line was one of Bernie's favourites. Over his thirty-one years of coaching, he had seen athletes of all sorts. Subsequently, he had heard all the excuses in the book to get out of workouts. Running was hard, the weather got cold, and people got sick, tired, discouraged. Numbers would dwindle down by the end of September, as some runners were beginning to lose the fire that had been burning in them since August. Bernie then made it his duty to encourage toughness and consistency in his athletes – he wanted men and women built to last. Respective to his quote, being "hurt" was to have aches and pains through which it was fine to push.

He addressed the legion of runners pouring out of the guys' and girls' change rooms. "Ok everyone, just a quick word before you go out for your warm up, please!" The giggles and banter faded, and the guys and girls turned to face Bernie and Kevin. Our head coach addressed the crowd. "So, today is our first three-minuter workout. If you are a veteran of this program, you know that this workout is a staple in the cross-country season. If you're a rookie, you're about to be acquainted with our grass loop. For those of you who don't know, the loop is about 600 metres long. We start right behind MacIsaac Hall and run down the grass until we're parallel with the Keating Centre, turn up the hill, and run back. We usually get about 1.5 of these done every three minutes. Today, we do eight, with ninety seconds of recovery between each. Sound good?"

"Yup!" we said.

"All right, get your warm up in!"

"Are we waiting for Cal?" asked Addison.

"No, he's not coming," I said. It was a shame, because Cal was an integral part of our training group up front. Losing a teammate to work out with made this workout harder than it already was.

"Why? Does he have class or something?" asked the rookie.

"Nah," said Neuffer. "He just doesn't want to do this workout today. I guess he felt it would be better to only work out once before the weekend and do the workout on Wednesday."

"Oh... all right," said Addison, disappointed.

"I don't like this," said Scott. "People just go and do whatever they want. How are we supposed to get used to running together when there is always someone missing at the workouts? Not great for team morale, especially with Angus missing." The sophomore runner had managed to heal his ankle, but since the Maine race was now dealing with knee issues.

"Whatever, we're here. Might as well make the most of it," said Neuffer as he turned right on St. Ninian Street.

The thermometer read a frigid six degrees. A cold wind was blowing, knocking down a few yellow leaves. I wore a long-sleeved shirt and half-tights. For the first time this season, I had broken out thin wool gloves. I finished my warm up by running back to the Oland Centre to pick up my spikes, and then ran the 200 metres back to the side of MacIsaac Hall.

"Guys, two minutes?" Favero seemed ready to go.

"Two minutes? I just got here!" I said. I did not like being rushed into workouts.

"It's cold. We don't want to wait too long," said Neuffer.

"Yeah, but we want to loosen our muscles a bit with drills. That's the whole point of a warm up," countered O'Regan, who was attempting his first workout since his time trial mishap.

"Come on guys, pick a start time, let's go," Bernie was growing impatient. "I don't care if it's two minutes or ten minutes, as long as we're all on the same page. Look, the girls have already started."

"Ok, Cyr man, I'll say five minutes tops but we've had plenty of time," said Favero.

I just shook my head and reluctantly rushed through my warm up drills.

O'Regan shared my sentiment. "What's even the point of a warm up jog if they're not willing to stretch properly after?"

"Beats me. Whatever," I said, trying to get myself ready to go.

"Ok guys, it's been five minutes. Are you ready?" We all got on the start line, ready or not. Bernie held a stopwatch that was wrapped around his neck. "Three, two, one, GO! Let's go guys! We will whistle at three minutes!"

We stormed out of the gate. Favero, Paul, Neuffer, Scott, and I ran at the front of the pack, but still chasing an unlikely leader – Fuller. Neuffer flashed a look of confusion in my direction, and I returned it. Fuller did not have the pedigree or fitness to be running the same times as us in workouts, so why did he always have to start out in front? It made him an inconvenient obstacle for the rest of us. Annoyed, we clumsily trotted around him on the first stretch of grass.

The loop consisted of a flat bed of grass stretching for 250 metres, followed by a hairpin turn around a tree and up a foothill. Now up the hill, we would run parallel to the grass bed back towards where we came from, and cruise down a short dirt path back to the start line. We would run around it until the three minutes were up, usually covering anywhere between a loop and a half to a loop and three quarters. By now, I could have run that course with my eyes closed.

The summer had helped the first tree we ran around proliferate. Branches were now long and more tiresome to sidestep. By the time we got to it, we had already overtaken Fuller, and Paul was our new leader. *Great,* I thought. *Another guy to slow us down.* Though he was levels faster than Fuller, Paul usually would finish a few metres behind us in workouts. So, why did he insist on leading? Paul sharply rounded the tree and, without thinking, pushed one of the branches out of his way and its momentum flung it back to whack Scott in the face.

"Paul, what the hell!" screamed our captain. Paul said nothing, and kept running at the front, unfazed about having fed his teammate a mouthful of pine.

"Three, two, one good," said Neuffer, between breaths. He was keeping track of the time.

"Paul, use your head. Come on!" ordered Scott, rubbing his face. Despite the scratches on his left cheek, he led us to consistent splits. The first few reps were run conservatively – around 3:10 per kilometer. Leo Jusiak had joined the lead pack up front. He and Paul would run the first bit with us, and drop back a few metres by the interval's end, unsure how to pace themselves.

"Guys, that's four done," said Bernie. "Switch into your spikes if you want. The last four should be your best four. Time to raise the intensity a bit!" Upon hearing our coach's words, Fuller positioned himself at the front of the start line, right in my way.

"GO!"

Quickly, I sidestepped Fuller and ran in front of him. I was getting angry. He had started at the very front of every single interval. We approached the tree as a group of five. Again, Paul rounded the tree so sharply that he sent the branches flying. This time, Neuffer caught the worst of it.

"F***! Paul, you idiot!" he shouted.

"Oops," said Paul, nonchalant. Rain had started to fall during our fifth interval, making the grass slippery. We ran down the dirt path and rounded left to begin our second round of the loop.

Bernie shouted as we passed. "One-forty-two, one-forty-three, good! HEY! Don't be cutting corners down here!" Leo had cut right in front of Favero, causing Nic to lose his step and trip up on the wet grass. Bernie shook his head.

We finished rep five and six on top of the hill on our second loop, parallel to a street sign on the nearby highway serving as a checkpoint. We were gaining ground on each interval, but still had about 100 metres to go before reaching the dirt path taking us back to the start. The checkpoint ahead signalled the end of the second loop – it was where Scott had tried, year after year, to finish the interval. We were far off. Without a doubt, we had run faster on this loop before.

The seventh, we finished ten metres closer to the path, despite having to sidestep Fuller off the line once again.

I had had enough. "Ok guys," I said as I glared at Fuller. "If you plan on FINISHING at the front of the pack, start in front. If not, get out of our way." Fuller didn't understand. He parked himself directly in front of Neuffer. "Fuller, you plan on finishing near the front?" I asked him, fed up.

"Yeah."

"Three, two, one GO!"

"Ok, now everybody try to stay away from Paul if you don't want to get killed," said Neuffer, before elongating his stride.

"Agreed," said Scott. The three of us took charge of the last rep. We rounded the first loop.

"One-thirty-seven, one-thirty-eight, well done guys!" screamed Bernie.

Behind us, Leo, Favero and Paul ran in a pack.

"Let's go guys," said Neuffer between breaths, pleased to round the tree with Paul out of sight. We finished strongly on top of the grass hill, having covered more distance than in any other interval. On top of the hill, we walked back to find the rest of the guys.

"Hey Fuller, way to finish in front there, big guy," said Angus, mocking the giant. Fuller said nothing.

Scott, still plucking pine from his face, threateningly addressed Paul. "If you ever do that again, I swear it won't be pretty. You could have taken my eye out!"

"I'm sorry, I didn't notice! Jeeze. At least I'm not cutting people off like a certain someone! "Paul glared at Fuller.

"Shut up Paul," said the giant. "I can start where I want."

Neuffer interrupted him. "Well just don't get in front of me next time. You've never beaten me in a rep, and you never will, so... you know, scooch."

Bernie could barely get a word in between the bickering. "Good workout, gentlemen! Get your cool down in and see you tomorrow." He did not feel the need to inject more negativity into the air. Instead, he waited for us to vacate the premises, and turned to Kevin. "Did you feel a bad vibe today? Everybody seemed on edge."

"Well, Bernie, you know how it is. It's almost October. Academics are piling up, people are getting tired; it's a stressful time."

"I don't know if that's it, Kevin. Maybe you're right, but the guys seem to be challenging each other. Cyr and Favero can't agree on a workout start time, Fuller is always cutting everyone off, and Cal should be here!"

"Yes, I know. But give it time. Some of these guys are still learning how to work out as a team. It's going to get better."

"Yeah, well I hope you're right, Kevin. Because once we get to Quebec City for CIS, there's no time for learning anymore. I mean some of these guys have been on the team for years. They should be doing this for each other – encouraging one another – not stepping on each other's toes." Bernie sighed. "We have a long way to go."

Moncton Classic

September 24th

It was 6:30 a.m. when my iPhone began beeping mercilessly. The seven and a half hours of sleep I had strung together were just not enough to make me feel fresh and race-ready, even if nearly two days had passed since we had run the three-minuters. There were many things I would have wanted to do with my day rather than pushing myself to the brink of exhaustion. Comfortably tangled in my bed sheets, one thought came to mind: *I don't want to suffer through the pain of racing today.*

I had always believed that the ability to race was malleable. The more I raced in a season, the more I would become accustomed to its nuances: the early onset of discomfort by three kilometres, the creeping in of self-doubt by five, the fearing of what was to come by six, and finally the acceptance of intense pain by 7.5. No workout could perfectly simulate the last kilometres of an 8k cross-country race. It was only by the end of my seasons when I found myself in the best control of my body and of its signals. By then, I was not afraid to challenge homeostatic conditions one step further and explore new worlds of pain. But it had not always been this easy or straightforward for me.

I stepped out of my bed, popped open one of two little white cylindrical containers on my nightstand and washed down a little brown pill. I brought these travel-sized white bottles with me everywhere I went, for their constituent had made the pain of racing much more bearable. Their inscription read: Ferramax. It was an elemental Iron supplement – the one Dr. Jeremy Beck had prescribed to me in 2014. I had religiously taken two tablets a day ever since being diagnosed with severe iron-deficiency anemia shortly after my first year with the X-Men. A fainting spell during my warm up at a local road race at the end of my rookie year had quickly landed me in the hands of paramedic personnel, who had rushed me to the hospital. Shortly after I'd gotten my vitals taken, a slender, grey haired, middle-aged doctor looked at my chart and gasped, "Holy sh*t, you're anemic!" My weakened body had almost jumped in place out of excitement. I finally could attribute a full year of shortcomings and bad performances to something.

The intervention had been timely – I had been growing impatient. My running had been slowed down for over a year, and I did not really know how to handle adversity. Growing up on Prince Edward Island had done much for my confidence as a child and a teenager. Exposed to a diminutive population of athletes and competitors, I grew accustomed to achieving success despite doing a negligible amount of work. All through my teen years, I felt like I was entitled to the top spot, because more often times than not, I would get it. I had won the elementary school provincial cross-country championship in the sixth grade and had remained undefeated until high school graduation. I was competitive in the province in badminton and soccer, and I had found a way to nestle my diminutive frame onto the provincial hockey team. Oblivious to the fact that more and better athletes existed across the Confederation Bridge that connected our small island to the mainland of Canada, I was perfectly content with thinking that I somehow was an athletic anomaly. Working hard to attain my goals was a quality I only believed I had. Adversity scared me, because it was unknown.

My first obstacle in the sport of running came in the form of Achilles tendonitis in my senior year. While I was preparing myself for the Canada Summer Games as well as for my first year of university, running in the summer of 2013 became difficult when a dull pain emerged in my lower right leg. For the first time in my running career, things were not perfect. Not knowing how to deal with the problem, I had decided to ignore it and stubbornly train harder. Relapses and missed races followed. I eventually developed a stress fracture, missed out on my entire summer of training, and arrived to the St. FX campus unfit and unconfident. Not only was I nowhere near the veterans on the team; I was getting beat by the other rookies. Neuffer, my long-time provincial rival, who had been my perennial runner-up until summer track season, was now leagues ahead of me. Cal, my counterpart from Nova Scotia with whom I shared virtually the same slate of personal bests, was working out with an entirely different – and faster – group within the team. I instantly felt like I was underperforming. I was the recruit who didn't pan out.

Cross-country soon passed, and things just got worse. Unbeknownst to me, I had begun suffering from anemia – probably from the overtraining. This made me struggle immensely in track season, getting beat by virtually everyone. The further I got from becoming a scoring part of St. FX's team and legacy, the more I romanticized the idea of being relevant within it. I became miserable. I thought of quitting the sport and walking away with the negligible amount of dignity I had retained from my high school years. If I could no longer improve and be competitive, I did not see the point in training. I ran to be good, I ran to improve; I ran to win. I spent my long bus rides home from meets, in which I had run terribly, wondering how it would feel to win a race donning the X singlet, or what it would feel like to be admired and looked up to by teammates. There was nothing I wanted more than to become the guy others wanted to chase – wanted to beat. I told myself that if I ever reached that point, I would soak up every minute of my time on top and strive to climb even higher.

Now, thanks to this pill that was replenishing my blood stream with haemoglobin and subsequently, reconciling my muscles with oxygen, the speck of a dream that I could one day be fast had suddenly again become a realistic goal. The pain of racing still hurt, but it was bearable. I felt like myself again. Not even a year after being diagnosed and taking the supplements, I had won the bronze medal in the 1500 metres at the AUS championship. Then in my third year, I was fourth at the conference cross-country championships, and won silver and bronze medals in the AUS 3000 metres and 1500 metres, respectively. As soon as I found success again, the dormant dreamer inside of me was revived. This time, however, there was a difference. I understood what it took to achieve those results at the university level. I recognized how much more I had to work, and it made the end results even more worthwhile. Being less blind to the task at hand, along with seeing improvements in my fitness made me enjoy the grind that much more. I had been in a great mental place in my running for the majority of the last three years.

Today was a good day to remind myself of my journey. I was unsatisfied with my performance in Maine, and the week's workouts did little to reassure me that the weekend was only a fluke. Though this meet held no real meaning, I needed a strong performance to satiate my ego and boost my confidence. I remembered how thankful I was to simply be healthy and racing, and my willingness to race grew stronger. I would run today not as the angry fourth-year needing to prove himself, but rather as the evolved first-year who once had dreamed of simply scoring for his team.

* * *

I walked on the bus to a familiar sight. The girls had congregated towards the front seats, while the guys were talking in the back. The conversation was not yet too animated, as we usually tried to sleep for the first hour of our early trips. I quickly noticed the absence of one of our more prominent pre-race conversationalists. Cal was attending a philosophy department conference and was sitting this one out. Luckily for Ryan Fuller and Warren Ferguson – Cal's two favourite targets to rile up – he would not be up to his antics today.

"Hey where are we stopping to get something to eat? Cause I want to have something before the race," said Addison. The pathetic little bowl of dry Vector cereal he had consumed for breakfast was long gone.

Bernie turned from his seat in the front of the bus. "We're stopping in Oxford, blueberry capital of Canada and home of our beloved Ryan Hatchard."

Hatchard had run for the team a few years back and was now working at a blueberry plant in his hometown, which was conveniently situated between Antigonish and our final destination.

"We're gonna go to Tim Hortons. They have a legit Timmies there," said Neuffer. "The oatmeal with berries is quality stuff."

By the time we arrived to Tim Hortons, I was hungry. My pre-race meal consisted of oatmeal and little fruit. I did not particularly like Tim Horton's oatmeal, but it was tradition.

"Hi there, I'll get a maple brown-sugar oatmeal please."

"Sorry sir, our machine is broken. We can give you oatmeal but it will be cold." There was a limit to my rituals. I wanted to race well, but there was no way I would eat cold, lumpy oatmeal. The thought of it repulsed me to the point where I almost lost my appetite. I settled for a blueberry muffin and juice. Favero ordered after me. Apparently oblivious to my conversation with the cashier, he requested the same thing.

"Yeah hey, I'll have an oatmeal please."

"Absolutely, sir, but we can only serve it to you cold."

"Yep, no worries. I'll take it!"

"Ewww!" said Addison, in line behind him.

Back in the bus, Favero's frigid breakfast had become the talk of the team. One of the girls asked him how his cold oatmeal was.

"Ok man, I don't know how all this oatmeal talk propagated so quickly. It's not even bad! On race day, eating is all about sustenance, man. Hot, cold, it all ends up at the same place." He then sat in silence, sporting an old beat up ball cap to hide his messy hair while enjoying his newfound delicacy. We collectively shook our heads and chuckled. There was no use in trying to understand Nicholas Favero, as one would likely emerge perplexed and frustrated. Headphones were back on, and we were on our way.

A little over an hour later, we were rolling onto the Université de Moncton campus. Gold and blue colors representative of their mascot l'Aigle Bleu (the Blue Eagle) surrounded the leafy headquarters. A beautiful stadium had been added to the campus in 2010, when the fastest-growing city in Atlantic Canada had hosted the World Junior track and field championships. The city of Moncton had a rich history of track and field, having produced multiple Olympians, coaches, and national-calibre athletes. Because the university only offered a French curriculum, however, their team never challenged us. It was difficult for their athletics program to keep up in a predominantly English milieu. Their selection pool was much smaller than that of their rival universities. As a French-Canadian, I had been somewhat expected to attend Université de Moncton, to follow in the footsteps of my parents. Moncton's city lifestyle and its low athlete-to-coach ratio were luxuries, but I had eventually opted for the school with a larger training group of more runners to push me to improve. St. FX also presented the element of mystery that I longed for, as mostly everyone who had previously made it out of my high school had attended U de Moncton. I sometimes caught myself thinking about how my university experience would be different, had I chosen the smaller, francophone school.

We had arrived quite early, and this gave us enough time to get settled under a tree near the start line. I plugged my headphones in and sat down next to Warren, whose focus was so dense you could almost see it in the air surrounding his face. His mouth was moving to the words of the music coming out of the same beat up headphones he'd worn at the time trial. Still two hours before race time, I was scared he would psych himself out.

"CYR! HEY! CYR!"

I was abruptly shaken from my own inner focus by a voice I knew too well. I stood up to accept a handshake from none other than Jérémie Pellerin – U de Moncton's most well-known runner. "Hey Mr. 1500 metres, think you can hold pace with Mr. Marathon man today?" he said in a broken English, sounding more like French. Knowing Jérémie for over five years made me presume that the "Marathon Man" he was referring to was, indeed, himself. Pellerin was known to pull the most dramatic stunts in the entire AUS. Rumours circulated of his running of secret marathons on easy run days, race-walking ten kilometre courses around his neighbourhood and puzzled neighbours, and time trialing extra "races" after his workouts, simply out of enjoyment. He was at best an interesting character and, at worst, down-right crazy. Genuine and kind, he was well respected, but his antics were often questioned.

"Oh guys look, Cyr is talking to Jérémie, let's go see this!" said Neuffer, as he sprung off a picnic table. He brought Favero, Fuller, Scott and Angus along with him. Whatever would come out of Pellerin's mouth would serve as funny long-run chat on the next day.

"Hey Angus Rawling!" said Jérémie. "How you are doing? The one thing I remember with you is your 1k race last track season. Almost beat Jake Wing last year on the indoor. I remember thinking, he is a crazy one that Angus Rawling, oohh! I was in the back saying 'ok I can kick' and then I ran out of gas in the last 200. Russell is running by, I'm screaming NOOOO! Rawling, the rookie, finish second? What? No way, no way, no way! Ah Rawling, I hope you have that extra kick today because I'm practicing my last 200 metres and I don't get outkick by nobody. I remember Stuart MacPherson last year try to outkick me. He have no chance! No chance, Stuart MacPherson!"

We burst into collective, booming laughter. Whether we were laughing with him or at him did not seem to bother Jérémie. The fifth-year runner had a way of bringing stories to life that we all enjoyed. His enthusiasm, coupled with his Acadian French, accent bred a comedy act.

"Ok, now I was thinking, the record for fifty-mile treadmill run is only five hours and fifty-seven minutes. That is easy to do! I think I'm going to try for that in the winter so I can be in the Guinness Book. Me when I hop on the treadmill I can run forever with music in my ears you know? And now I'm marathon man so I have the endurance. Anyway, I'm gonna go warm up with the guys. Bonne Chance, Cyr! Good luck, guys!"

"Man, he is a polarizing little dude." Angus, as only a second year, was still getting used to Jérémie, now a perennial figure in the AUS conference. He had been around for six years, once challenging for the conference title in 2012. Nowadays, he was a tier behind us, but was considered a huge dark horse, holding down a personal best of 31:09 over ten kilometres.

"Talking to Jérémie may be my favourite part of racing in the AUS," said Neuffer. "I don't know where he comes up with these ideas."

Scott and Favero were cramped with laughter. "Why would anyone want to challenge for the fifty-mile treadmill run world record?" said Scott. "That's like, eighty kilometres on a treadmill." He had been racing against Jérémie since 2012, yet, still could not make much sense of him.

Bernie was conscious of time. "Ok guys, let's go. Stop standing around and go run the course! Make sure you're cheering on the girls when they pass and so on!" The boys left in a pack to begin the warm up. We picked up a familiar presence in Lee Wesselius on the way. The former X-Man had graduated with a degree in biology and was now attending Veterinary College at University of Prince Edward Island. A talented runner who always seemed to be dealing with injuries, he had been healthy for three months, a long stretch by his standards.

"Jannes!" I called out. This was his real name.

"Hey," he said. Our team surrounded him as we picked up the pace to a jog.

"Looking fit, ready to throw down?" I asked.

"Hmm, we'll see."

I didn't take his conversational idleness personally. Lee was a man of few words – especially before his races. He was smart, quiet, and analytical, unless the topic of conversation was distance running or the Montreal Canadiens. Then, he would ramble for hours if we'd let him. We figured we could get more words out of him after the race. For now, he was content to simply run amidst our pack of X-Men. It was as if he had never left. Neuffer and he sprung in front of the crew. I settled behind them, alongside Edward MacDonald, who was ambling from leg to leg with his bouncy stride. If anyone had something to prove today, it was he. He had dropped out of time trial with an undiagnosed sore foot, and even though most people assumed he had enough talent to grab one of the travel team's bottom spots, he needed to generate a solid performance.

As we finished our warm up run, we stripped down a layer to run our dynamic drills and strides. The sun was coming out, making the temperature a bit more race-friendly.

"All right, can everyone get in here for a second? Right by the start line, this will not take long." Bernie was ready for his pre-race talk. We huddled in. "Ok guys, we've made it to the second race of the season. For the first time this year, you'll be racing against the conference. Most of you know where you should be. For the newer runners, Moncton is much hillier than Bowdoin's course. Starting off a bit conservatively may not be a bad idea. But, remember that I am still looking to see who will prove themselves. Last week's race was to get the jitters out, now it's time to roll into a bit of momentum. Run hard, but smart."

Bernie had given much more moving speeches than this one. He knew that the race did not mean much for his top end. We were still over a month away from the championship. We assumed our positions on the start line. Standing next to Scott and Neuffer, I planned to take control of this race from the gun. Even if the race meant little, I was unable to completely shake the pre-race angst from my system. Like on any other race day, my coiled legs were shaking under me, ready to bounce off the unforgiving hills of the Université de Moncton campus.

"À vos marques, POW!"

Sixty-seven men were off. Fuelled by my jitters, I led the pack off the start line. I figured someone (likely Neuffer) would challenge my position within the next 100 metres. To my surprise, another X-Man soon blew by me. Nic Favero sprung to my left side, and authoritatively took control of the field of runners. Looking extra bouncy, he gapped the field by a few seconds. It had to be the cold oatmeal. Slapping his leg, he was signalling for me to join him out in front. I sighed and picked it up even more to offer company to my friend. Barely one minute into the race, I pulled equal to him, perplexed as to why he was running so fast.

"Yo man, is this really fast? Cause, like, it feels fine to me" he said in a casual tone. From hearing him, you could not have guessed that he was running close to twenty kilometres per hour. He sounded more like he was having a conversation with a colleague while sitting down in his academic habitat, the fourth floor of the library.

"Yeah we're good, but cool it down a bit," I snapped back.

"Ok man, got a little excited, ho! ho! ho!"

I just shook my head and smiled. Nic Favero was a box of surprises. He eventually conceded his spot to Neuffer and Scott, who were prancing just behind us. Our pack of four quickly distanced itself from the rest of the field. I ran alongside Scott, Neuffer, and Lee. A chase pack of Will Russell from Dalhousie, Josh Shanks from University of New Brunswick, and Favero had been created at our heels by the end of the first loop.

The course consisted of four two-kilometre loops. Most of the loop was spent descending grassy cascades and gravel trails. Then, each loop ended with a big climb up a grass hill, taking us directly back to the starting area. By the end of the first loop, we were all moving comfortably. Running with these three guys had become second nature to me. Scott and Neuffer were my current roommates, and Lee had been a member of the 18 Greening house in the prior year. I could tell who ran by me by simply hearing their breathing pattern. Neuffer's aggressiveness, Scott's calmness, and Lee's smarts on the course were all expected. None of these three runners could take me by surprise with their antics. Or so I thought. By the time we got to the second big climb, and hence, the end of the second loop, Lee decided to spice things up and deployed a bold, ruthless plan. He mounted the hill like a madman, leaving all three of us in his dust. In twenty seconds, what I thought would be a sit and kick affair had become a flat-out goose chase, with Lee assuming a seven to eight second lead on Scott, Neuffer, and me. Quickly, I began to feel tired. His tactic was paying off and had thrown me off my mental game.

Luckily, Neuffer ran up beside me. "Keep this pace, we'll reel him in." His confidence had reassured me, and we began chasing him with Scott trailing our group. Refocused, I watched the blonde, bow-legged runner prance from a distance. He did not have a pretty stride, but he looked fit and strong.

My relationship with Lee had evolved drastically over the last four years. When we had first met, I was star-struck after comparing my high school times to his much faster ones. We had quickly become good friends, but the dynamic of our interactions soon would change when I began catching up to his speed. We had remained close, but I now looked at him as a rival as much as a mentor. Had injuries not slowed him down, I suspected he would have been beating me more often. Today, however, he was healthy, and running away from us. Neuffer and I took turns increasing our pace to haul along our trail pack, and Scott would quietly run behind us. Mounting the large grass hill a third time, I noticed that we had gained some considerable ground on Lee. Injecting more speed into my stride, I led our chase after the hill. Neuffer and Scott followed.

With one lap to go, Lee was growing vulnerable. Increasing his pace that early in the race had generated an insidious lactate buildup in his legs, and he was running out of gas. Our pack of three soon gobbled him up with less than a loop to go. Entering our fourth lap, we were once again a pack of four, with Lee trailing but holding on. I used the downhill that inaugurated the final loop to my advantage by letting my momentum fly me down towards the small patch of gravel terrain. Neuffer and Scott followed me in my surge, and left Lee behind. I did not spend much time leading. Neuffer decided to throw in a surge of his own. He inched past me, teeth clenched. Refusing to let him gain ground, I urged my aching body to run even with him. We cruised up and down a few hills on the back end of the course, and this seemed to tire him out. I took a small lead, and Scott slid next to me. For the first time in the race, our diminutive captain ran at the front. He picked up the pace once more with a kilometre to go. I matched his every stride. We had broken Neuffer. On the fourth and final mounting of the now-sadistic grass hill, I pushed to win. I forcefully pulled away from Scott with three hundred metres left to run. I did my best to maintain form, hoping that my kick would be enough to win the race. Unfortunately, my body began resisting my mental commands. My legs grew heavy and my breathing became shallow. I had kicked too early. Scott sped past me in the final stretch to take top spot. I had finished second, and Neuffer came in shortly afterwards.

Lee was fourth, having slowed after realizing that he would fall out of the medals. As I joined Angus who was holding the long-sleeved shirts we had taken off at the start line, we looked back to see where the others would finish. Our ranking among other schools was unimportant at this time of the year. We were more interested in the rankings within our team, as Bernie had oddly not yet selected the travel team. Favero comfortably came in after Lee, almost a minute behind Scott and me. He had run a solid race, and had gotten the best of Jérémie, gapping him by fifteen seconds. Edward MacDonald was the next X-Man through the finish line, and he had just made a strong case for his admission to the travel team. Warren came in after him, followed by Ryan Fuller and Matt Eliot.

Addison Derhak, running much under his potential, was the last X-Man to cross the finish line, save for Cullen MacInnis. Running by himself, he carried his heaving body across the finish line almost a minute behind Fuller and Eliot. The rookie was looking for answers after feeling tired all week long. A look of disappointment and fear was painted on his face. He did not want to get cut from the travel team. We offered a few words of encouragement, but what he really wanted was a drink of water and granola bars from the food tables.

I slowly walked back to our team table to the chaotic blend of ecstatic and devastated runners. Scott, Neuffer, and I were taking pictures for the Moncton newspaper, while Warren was angrily throwing his spikes back into his spike bag, and Addison was sitting quietly on the end of a bench, glaring at the ground. Mary MacDonald was elated, finishing directly behind our top runner, Liz MacDonald, in her first cross country race for the X-women. Ellen Burnett, on the other hand, was visibly frustrated with her fate, finishing twenty-eighth overall. On a different day, people would swap sides between thrilled and crushed – the beauty of having a good day was that it was never guaranteed.

Robotically, I walked back to the bus and settled in my seat. I stared out the window towards the battlefield we had just conquered. The real adversary when racing in Moncton was, in fact, the course. I had stuffed the silver medal in my bag without thinking much of my accomplishment just yet. It was only in my moments alone that I would indulge in a small amount of self-satisfaction – a dangerous point of view to adopt as an athlete. Barely three years ago, I had been aching to make a difference and to be noticed as a top runner on this St. FX team, and at times, I never thought my goals would materialize. I had come to dread meets and competitions, as I hated the feeling of finishing near the middle or bottom. Now, I was a threat to win the AUS championship. The feeling of dominance was what had made me fall in love with running, and it still was what I longed for. I once again felt like my time training and preparing was well spent. By my own arbitrary standards, I now had a place in the sport of distance running, and by this same judgment, I had become good enough to keep my dreams alive for just a bit longer.

Miles with Eric

September 25th

The three-hour drive from Moncton got us back to Antigonish by suppertime. Without changing out of our running clothes, a group of us walked straight to meal hall.

"Well, I am excited to hit the hay and sleep tonight," said Favero, as he rested his elbows on the table. "I'm pooped."

"Can't sleep too long, we run with Gillis tomorrow!" said Angus. Though he had not raced, he seemed to be almost fully recovered from the knee problems he'd run into in Maine.

"Yeah, I guess. Nine a.m. isn't bad though. Bern's gotten us to get up way earlier than that before."

Leo chimed in: "Who is this Gillis?"

"Leo! Don't you know who Eric Gillis is yet? Don't let Bernie find that out, he'll cut you from the track team," joked Scott.

"Oh, is Gillis the one Bernie was talking about on the first day we meet? I remember!"

"Yeah, Leo. He held a meet and greet with the community on Saturday, and he's coming for the long run with us tomorrow."

"Aha! We are going to meet the big great Gillis! The one on the wall of Bernie's office! We are, how you say, not worthy! Not worthy!" His exclamations brought laughter to the table. He was referring to his first encounter with Bernie, when our coach all but questioned Leo's integrity when the French miler admitted to not knowing of Eric Gillis, a capital sin as far as

Bernie was concerned. "And we are running with him? Wow, I don't think I can uhm, how you say, keep up."

"Nah, word on the street is that he runs his easy runs at almost five minutes per kilometre," said Scott. "What did I say? The best runners take it nice and chill on their easy days." He was alluding to the fact that he was perhaps the slowest easy runner on the team.

"Pfft. That's bullshit. You're not getting anything out of five-minute k's. You may as well go for a leisurely walk to Mini Moes at that pace," said Neuffer. "Waste of time."

"We'll have to ask Eric," I said. "He's thirty-six years old and still improving – he must be doing something right. All right, I'm taking off. See you guys at practice tomorrow!" I hastily left. As we were around mid-term season, the academic workload was rapidly intensifying. Unfortunately, my conversations about running, school, and the meanings of life would be cut short, only to pick up again at tomorrow's meal hall gathering.

* * *

The morning came fast, and it was chilly. The cooling winds of early October were increasingly uncomfortable. Today, six out of the fourteen guys present for the run were wearing tights. I had opted for shorts, even if my breath evaporated in front of my eyes on my walk to the track. It was the arrival of real cross-country weather. The early September races in the sun and summer weather were comfortable, but they did not match up with the ethos of discomfort, toughness, and struggle that defined our sport. Five degrees felt uncomfortable, but somehow, it felt right.

With my five roommates, I anxiously jogged over to the Oland Centre, excited to run with Eric Gillis. We had met him before – a few brief times over the years – and he knew most of us by name already. The three-time Olympian oozed class. Humble, focused, and friendly, he had clearly not let the fame that came with being the first Canadian man to finish in the top-ten in the Olympic marathon since 1976 go to his head. If anything, he almost came across as shy. Native of Antigonish, he now lived in Guelph, where he trained with Dave Scott-Thomas and the Speed River running group – Canada's elite when it came to distance running. He had spent his undergraduate years at St. FX, and then stayed for two more years to complete his bachelor's in education. During that time, he had won the individual gold medal at the 2003 CIS (then CIAU) championship. He was being inducted into the St. FX Hall of Fame this weekend; hence the visit to his Alma Mater.

"Neuffer, if Gillis is running at five-minute k's, are you going to drop him?" Cal asked.

"Hmm, we'll see. If I feel like I want to go faster, I will," he answered. "I don't care. But he won't be running five-minute k's. That's garbage. Eric Gillis doesn't run that slowly on his easy days. Come on."

We rounded the back of the Oland Centre and entered through the doors under the stadium bleachers. Where the girls' team usually stood – to the left of the entranceway – were four men, chatting like old friends. Bernie and Kevin assumed their usual spots, leaning against the heat radiator.

Next to them was the skeletal frame of Eric Gillis. "Hey guys!" he said in a quiet, almost sleepy voice. I was taken aback. I had not seen Eric in running clothes from this close before. His kneecaps were narrow, his calves minuscule, but defined. His shoulder blades looked like they were being yanked away from his body. A man this gaunt in any other setting would have looked out of place. To us, however, he did not look skinny – he looked fast, intimidating. He made me and all of my 135 pounds feel chunky and flabby. This frame was what was required to be among the best on the planet in track and field's most archaic distance – the marathon. It was apparently what it took to own a personal best of 2:11:21. "Bernie told me you guys want to do the Brook? I'm doing about two hours, so we can do the full 20k loop and add on if some of you are willing."

"That sounds great! I think that's what a few of us were thinking," answered Cal. "Lee what are you thinking?"

A fourth man standing next to Eric piped up. "I'll do whatever you guys are doing. As you know, I'm not picky." The answer was typical for Lee McCarron. Another native of Antigonish, Lee was a good friend of Eric's, who was in town for the Olympian's induction into the Hall of Fame. Nicknamed "The General" by the close-by running community, McCarron was a running mogul in his own right. A member of the X-Men cross-country team between 2006 and 2009, he was a leader on St. FX's silver and bronze medal-winning teams at the '08 and '09 CIS championships. He owned strong personal bests in all events from the 1500 metres (3:51) to the marathon (2:27). He was now pushing thirty, and was still hugely present in the Maritime running community, coaching a fast-growing running group in Halifax called the Road Hammers. He consulted with athletes of all ages, offering training and coaching advice to anyone who asked. He was usually up for any type of run; his love for the sport was simply contagious. I suspected that if we told Lee McCarron that today's run of choice would consist of every single running loop in Antigonish in succession, he would comply without question… and probably commit to doing it twice if it meant he could skip Sunday mass.

Addison looked worried. "The Brook loop is 20k; I don't know if I should do 20k. Last time I did that, my calves just started hurting and I couldn't walk for the next two days. I'll just do the short loop if anyone wants to join."

"Look out, Silk. That short loop is still seventy minutes long. You might break something," joked Angus. Addison's apprehension towards mileage had earned him the nickname "Silk."

"I think I'll handle the short loop as long as I chill at the back with Scott."

"That's the key, buddy," I said. "No need to keep up with Neuffer on easy days." My roommate was, once again, taking control of the pace in the front.

"Neuffer, how's it feel to lead an Olympian on an easy run?" said Cal.

"Just keepin' the pace honest, boys," he replied, pumping his arms.

"Ha ha, well I won't challenge you up front. Easy runs don't get much faster than this for me," said Gillis, softly.

I looked down at my watch. We were averaging 4:35 per kilometre.

"Ha! Told you Neuf!" said Cal.

"This feels easy to us, it must feel like you're barely moving," I said.

"Well, maybe I like it slow because my workouts are long when I'm training for the marathon. The one from yesterday was pretty tough."

"What was it??" asked Angus.

Gillis blushed at the sight of fifteen enthralled runners eager to hear his splits. "Ha ha… so I warmed up for thirty minutes. Then I ran three times thirty minutes of tempo pace."

Angus needed to know every detail. "What pace was it at?"

"Well, the first thirty-minute interval was done at 3:04 per k, then 3:03 for the second and third interval."

"Wow!" said O'Regan. "So, you ran at 15:15-15:20 5k pace for an hour and a half?"

Eric's tone made him seem as surprised as the rest of us. "Ha ha... uhm... yeah. I guess so!"

"Well if I'd have run that yesterday I'd be running pretty damn slow on this run too," I said.

"I could probably keep up for 3k of that on a good day!" realized O'Regan.

"More like 2k! Your PB is 9:21," chirped Angus.

"Hey Fuller," Cal whispered, in the middle of our pack. "What are the odds that you go run right next to Gillis, and whisper in his ear, "Hey Gillis, I'm Kipchoge," and start sprinting ahead of him?" Cal was making reference to the fact that Eliud Kipchoge of Kenya had won the Olympic marathon and beaten Eric by nine spots.

"Uhh, one in fifty," said Fuller.

"Three, two, one, three!" both said in unison.

"NO!" screamed Fuller. "I don't want to do that."

"Why not?" asked Cal.

"I'm embarrassed. What if he starts chasing me?"

"Well Fuller, you played the game and you lost! If you don't own up to it, you get a notch!"

"No, I'm not playing. I'm not saying that," said a frustrated Fuller as he surged to the front of the pack with the help of powerful, laborious strides.

Cal turned towards me and giggled. "I don't know what he's so sour about. Worst comes to worst, he gets the notch and nobody notices. His eyebrows are blonde anyway."

Meanwhile, Lee McCarron and Scott were having a chat about one of Lee's favourite topics: training philosophies. I always enjoyed hearing about Lee's opinions on running matters, so I dialled into their conversation.

"So, with Bernie, you're going to run three workouts per week. I prefer two, but if you have to do three, you need to be smart about it. Giving 110% in every workout may backfire after doing it for three straight months. People get tired."

"So what would you suggest?" asked Scott.

"Well, there should be one of these workouts taken as a 'down workout,' so that you don't overdo it. The other two should be run hard, but not insanely hard, where you need a few days to recover from it. Your hardest efforts in the year are your races. I used to tell the guys at Dalhousie to not try to be workout heroes. You should be aiming for B to B+ workouts for most of the year to not burn out, and then throwing in a couple A workouts by the end of October. It's better to work out at ninety percent all year than to work out at a hundred percent for six weeks and then get injured."

Scott was just taking it all in. Lee loved training talk. It was his desire to always learn more about coaching, which was earning him a living. Although he already worked full-time in sales, we suspected that most of his cash flow came from his coaching hobby – he was living the dream. He had always aspired to succeed Bernie and become the head coach at St. FX one day, but his current training group was approaching a hundred members, and new registrations were rolling in at an astounding rate.

"Lee, you'll have to apply for the coaching job once Bernie retires, and test those methods," I said, figuring that Bernie, at seventy years old, was approaching the twilight of his illustrious career as the X-Men and X-Women coach.

"I am tied down, Cyr. You know that. Anyway, I think someone else is think-ing of stepping in. said Lee. "In fact," he lowered his voice, "he's running with us right now." Our eyes shifted towards Gillis, running at the front of the group of nearly twenty.

"Eric?" I asked. "Bernie wants him to take over?"

"Easily. The guy is the new poster boy for Canadian distance running. Do you know how much good publicity he would bring to this school? Plus, "Eric deserves it. He's done wonders for this sport. Nova Scotia has never produced a runner of his calibre, really."

I looked at the marathoner floating effortlessly at the front of the group. He bounced off the ground, never fully extending his legs. Years of miles had eliminated or modified any part of his body that resisted the natural motion of running. He was a machine, tailored to run. At that moment, a black SUV passed us, moving about as smoothly as did Gillis.

"Hey guys, look here! I am taking pictures for my tweeter or twit thing!" It was Bernie on his cell phone. We looked over and smiled between strides, now close to being done the loop. "Eric, are you making them hurt?" Bernie asked.

"No, if anything, I'm the one trying to keep up," Eric said between flaw-less strides.

"Well make sure they keep the pace easy. Hear that guys – Neuffer?"

"Yeah, we're fine." The red-haired senior was still pushing the pace up front.

Bernie snapped a few pictures, offered us some water, with a "Good work guys!" left us alone with the second half of the Brook to cover.

Once Bernie had taken off, I jogged up to the front of our pack and addressed Eric. "So, what are your plans for the next few years? Are you thinking about training hard until the 2020 Olympics?"

"Well, it's hard to know this now. Honestly, I figured I would retire after Rio, but things went so well that I want to keep running. We'll see what happens in the next few years, but I definitely will not rule it out."

"What if a coaching job came at you, would you take it?" I asked. I wasn't teaching him anything new. Apparently, he knew that St. FX had only him on the radar to succeed Bernie.

"Maybe. I think that moving to Antigonish would be great. I would have to get a feel for things, but depending on how my career unfolds, I'd say it's a possibility. But for now, I'm taking it a year at a time. I'm thirty-six, so I have no idea how long I have left as a professional runner. I could have one year left, or I could have five… who knows?" He quickly changed the subject. "Are you guys doing two hours?"

"Scott and I will. So will Lee, I presume."

"If it's not two hours, it's not a real long run!" said Lee, on our heels. We dropped off the rest of the group on campus at one hour and fifty minutes. With Eric and Lee, Scott and I finished up our last ten minutes on the cross-country course. I wondered how many miles these two gentlemen had run in these trails over the years. Representative of two different eras – Gillis, the early 2000s and Lee, the late 2000s – they both had helped shape the program into what it was today. Their leadership and capital in the running world had greatly helped Bernie in his recruiting. Perhaps they had played an indirect role in my landing here. And now, here I was, running the trails they had blazed, over and over again, trying to recreate the success they had both found. Reaching the halfway point of the season, I felt hardened.

"Cyr what's your mileage this week?" asked Scott.

"One thirty-five k. You?"

"About 130k. Feeling fit."

"That's plenty to get you guys fit. But it's about consistency," said Lee. "Keep plugging year after year and you'll get to Eric's totals."

"Eric, what's your mileage this week?" I asked.

"I'll be at 135 by the end of this run."

"Really?" I asked. "We run the same amount of mileage?"

"Ehm, no," said the Olympian. "I count it in miles."

Time Trial (L to R) Alex Neuffer, Scott Donald, Nic Favero, Cal DeWolfe, Alex Cyr

A typical meal hall supper

Bowdoin Invitational (L to R) Addison Derhak, Alex Cyr, Alex Neuffer, Warren Ferguson, Cal DeWolfe, Matt Eliot, Ryan Fuller, Scott Donald, Angus Rawling, and Laura Sevigny (athletic therapist)

Scott Donald winning Classique Université de Moncton

(L to R) Warren Ferguson, Edward MacDonald, Ryan O'Regan

Dalhousie Invitational

Dalhousie Invitational

Leo Jusiak and Cal DeWolfe — Poker Sharks of 18 Greening

Interlock meet at Odell Park

(L to R) Nic Favero, David MacDonald, Alex Cyr, Eric Gillis, Scott Donald, Angus Rawling and Liz MacDonald

Nic Favero and Scott Donald

Captain Scotty D

Pre–AUS huddle

AUS Championships

Cal DeWolfe in the final stretch

2018 AUS champions — St. FX X-Men

Looking onto the CIS battlefield — The Plains of Abraham

CIS huddle

CIS take-off

(L to R) Warren Ferguson, Angus Rawling, Cal DeWolfe

X-Men at the CIS banquet

Warren Ferguson in Acadia house as The Snowman

The Ninth gear bag

September 25th

After thanking Eric for the company, we stretched and putted along to meal hall. There was no better feeling after a 24k run than to walk through the doors of our beloved cafeteria for the Sunday brunch. Though we had thousands of calories to replenish, most of us still found a way to overeat. As usual, the guys and girls set up camp in the yellow room, pulling two round tables together.

"Well I, for one, am glad I missed that Moncton meet. Do you realize what we have coming for us?" said an apprehensive Cal, before taking in a spoonful of meal hall's butternut squash soup. "So, Tuesday is the 1400 metre loop around our course, Thursday is a long tempo, and Saturday is the mile alternation workout. Then, we do 12 x 400m hills next Tuesday, forty minutes of tempo on next Thursday, and then we race at Dal. By then, we are going to be cooked." Bernie was taking advantage of this uneventful time of the season to throw his hardest training block at us, so that we would reap its benefits by the championship races. I had trouble paying attention to what Cal was saying because my gaze was fixed on Addison's frightened facial expression at the other end of the table. The rookie was learning his fate for the next few weeks, and based on his demeanour, it did not excite him.

"What's the Notre Dame workout?" he asked.

"Eight miles of alternating speed. One, three, five, and seven are on the cross-country course, and two, four, six, and eight are on the track. The track ones are at 10k pace, and the course ones at threshold," I said.

Leo's eyes grew wide. "Ouf, Alex. This is a lot of running. What is the recovery between the miles?"

I felt bad for the poor Frenchman. "These are continuous, Leo," I said with a chuckle.

"What? No stop?"

"No stop."

"Oh! I guess this means there is no party for me on Friday night. Last Saturday, I wake up at six. But, in the afternoon! Can't do that this time, oh no no no."

As much as we discouraged drinking among potential team scorers during the season, Leo seemed to have a free pass. The exchange student from France was a lucky find who had not exactly left France to join a bunch of grizzled or crazy young Canadian men in their pursuit of high mileage and personal bests. Chance had brought him to the team, but his wanderlust was what had brought him to Canada. He was here to live the full Canadian University experience – one that was hardly conducive to running fast. For that reason, we felt like we had no authority over him. It almost did not feel right to pressure him to make the same lifestyle decisions as we did – especially because the veterans suspected that only two thirds of the team really respected our "sober season" policy. So, for that reason, we would mostly stay out of Leo's business. We all had heard about what went on inside the walls of the international students' house on 77 Hawthorne Street, and we had judged that in order to preserve the health of our lungs, it would be best to stay far away.

"So, we have to do all these workouts next week? Wow that is going to be painful!" said Addison.

"Yup, this is the part of year where boys become men!" said Cal.

"You've made the travel team, Addi, now you gotta grind to stay on it," said Scott. Although Bernie would not cut anyone after awarding him or her the singlet and gear, it was expected that all travel team members remain fully committed until the CIS championship.

"I'm on the travel team for sure?" said Addison.

"Well, Bernie gave you the gear bag. That means yes," I told him.

"Wait, so who's on the travel team? There is me, Cyr, Cal, Neuffer, Scott, Angus, Paul and Nic. So only eight? And I'm the only rookie? I thought

Bernie was taking more." Addison had brought up a sensitive topic, especially with Warren Ferguson sitting at the other end of the table.

Scott splayed his fingers on the table. "So, sometimes Bernie only admits some people to the team a bit later."

"But, I thought you made the team automatically if you ran standard at time trial! In that case, Fuller, Matt, and Warren would be on it already," said Addison.

"That's what we thought. Bernie needs to get moving with this," said Cal. "I can see him cutting Matt and Fuller even if they hit the standard at time trial, because they haven't performed since then, really, but Ferg? Come on! It's bad enough that he didn't automatically give everyone who ran under twenty-eight minutes at time-trial a spot, like we thought he would, but Ferg has demonstrated that he deserves to be on the team three times now. Moncton was a bit worse than his other races, but he's consistently our ninth guy. He's definitely fitter than Matt and Fuller, and Edward is out because he's decided not to use his year of eligibility. It's clear that Ferg should be on the travel team."

The discussion made Warren uncomfortable. "Uhmm Cal... Cal I'm sure Bernie has a plan. He told me that he had been watching me in workouts and that he will give me a shot in another race."

Cal banged his fist on the table. "Ferg! How can you not be livid right now? You hit time-trial standard, and you're consistently in the top nine in races. Your Maine race was good, you placed fine in Moncton, but Bernie still has not given you gear like he has the rest of us!"

"I'm sure he has a plan. Besides, he cannot only take eight to CIS. He often takes seven plus two alternates. He is probably just waiting to see how things pan out. I don't know. Let's talk about something else. David! How are you enjoying Physics 120?"

"Oh it's great!" said David.

"Ferg!" said Cal. "You better be wanting to prove to Bernie that you belong on this team! Fight for that spot because you more than deserve it now. This is driving me nuts!"

"Uhm, yes ok. Perhaps he wants to give the spot to someone younger, or more talented. After all, I graduate this year. Anyway, it's not important. I have to go. I have a lot of work to do. See you all at practice tomorrow."

I watched him walk swiftly across meal hall, clumsily sidestepping tables. His red jacket contrasted with our blue and white St. FX cross-country ones. I remembered how thrilled he had been to cross the finish line in ninth place at the time trial. I was sure that he never dreamed of having to wait this long to be admitted to the travel team following such a performance. In his shoes, I would have been campaigning for that last team spot, rather than disregarding the issue. But, Warren saw no value in pleading his case. It was not that he did not care to be given the spot; he wanted to make the team more than anything else. Warren, however, knew only one route to take when it came to achieving goals. It did not involve begging to Bernie. It did not involve favours. It did not even involve talking about it. All it involved was working even harder to improve, hoping that Bernie would notice his times and finally grant him the elusive ninth gear bag. Work ethic, leadership, or any other countless intangibles Warren brought to the table should not be factored into Bernie's decision. Like he planned to achieve everything else in his life, Warren wished to make the team the hard way – the fair way. He would have to make it on speed and speed alone. Aimlessly talking about the matter was nothing but a waste of his time – a resource in which he was perpetually short. Off to spend another afternoon tackling the mathematical physics textbook in the basement of the Physical Sciences Centre, Warren Ferguson was gone.

960 telephone poles

September 27th

"Nic, can you believe it? These will be our last hills ever! After these twelve hills, we are done! We do not have to do these next year!" said Warren, excitedly lacing his running shoes, sitting on the bleachers of the change room.

Favero shook his head and exhaled through his nose, unfazed. "Yes Ferg, it's fantastic."

"No, Nic, don't you realize? This workout is big! It's symbolic! This workout has the potential to be one of those workouts we remember for years!"

"Yeah, yeah I know Ferg. It's great." Favero was now smiling, probably not because Warren's spiel was finally sinking in, but rather because he was amused by his teammate's hatred for our hill workouts. A heel striker ungifted in the fast-twitch muscle-fibre compartment, Warren was perhaps the prototype for bad hill runners. To add insult to injury – and sometimes eliciting insults and injuries – he refused to wear lighter shoes for the hill workouts. While most of us would strip down to racing flats, he would remain faithful to his bulky, Asics Gel Cumulus 16 stability shoes. He knew very well that those shoes did little to correct his already woeful form, but he refused to act on the problem. For Warren, hill workouts were a microcosm of his running career; they were approached with great struggle and determination. He did his best to make up for his inherent deficiencies with unparalleled hard work. He would go on about his personal vendetta with hills, but deep down, I suspected he liked them. They were a challenge, after all. To buy lighter shoes was nothing but an easy way out – a sign of weakness. It defeated his purpose to run – to suffer.

"Ok guys are we ready? It's 5:10." Warren was yearning to begin this workout. We joined him and Nic outside and trotted as a group towards William's Point, the site of our notorious 400-metre dirt hill. The hill, overlooking Antigonish's South River, had been a staple in Bernie's training program for years. We ran three workouts on it every year, for three consecutive weeks. The first week was eight reps, the second, ten, and the last one, twelve. As we would be in the middle of racing season by the third workout, but still running high mileage, we would have to muscle up the hill on tired legs and broken-down muscles. But even on rested legs, the hill, assuming a more pronounced grade the higher up you ran, was a killer. As we left the Oland Centre, we ran past Neuffer, only getting in to change now. Because of his history of stress fractures around hill-running season, Bernie and he agreed that it would be best if he sit out the Tuesday hills this year and run some tempo instead.

"Hey Beef, let's do ten hills instead of twelve," said Cal. "These weeks are crazy. We don't need to do twelve hills. It's just overkill at this point." The senior runner was always looking to tweak the training plan to his liking. Some changes that may have seemed insignificant to others made a difference to Cal. These little modifications may have only helped him more or less over the last few years, but perhaps this time, he was on to something. He had only been working out twice per week compared to our three, and the two workouts he would do with us would often be altered. And if he was, in fact, on to something, so was Angus. Cal was often successful in dragging the sophomore runner with him to do the modified workouts. This time was no different.

"Yeah, sure Cal, I'll do ten," agreed Angus. "We could pick it up on the last few."

Conversely, I decided to do the prescribed twelve. I would have Scott and Favero to run with on the last two reps.

"Yo Cyr, I think we should be smart with this workout. Let's not try to destroy ourselves. Remember what Lee said on Sunday? We need to be consistent, rather than be workout heroes," said Scott.

"Yeah, I'm with you." I hastily agreed with his proposal, partly because Lee had warned us of the perils of working too hard in a single workout, but also because it came from Scott. Since I first laid eyes on St. FX in grade 12, Scott had been one of the faces of the franchise. By taking an intelligent and patient approach to training, he often hit his stride at the right time, and performed when it mattered most – late October and early November. If anyone of us had figured out how to peak properly, it was he. It was his fifth season with the X-Men, and he was looking increasingly fit. Occasionally riding on his coattails did not seem like a bad idea.

It was getting cold and dark. Bernie looked to the ground and tucked his arms to his immediate sides. Chilled, he did not want us to waste any more time. "Ok guys and girls. Let's go! Gather round! There is no need for me to tell you guys this, but this is the last hill workout of the year. You've run up this hill eight times, and ten times in the previous weeks. This week, you are doing twelve. It's going to be tough, and you are going to have to dig deep to finish this one on a strong note. But you're ready. Today is a day to put some good work in, and that will translate to the toughness – physical and mental – that you'll need by the championships. Now, when you are going up the hill, keep your eyes up on the person in front of you, and imagine that they are pulling you up with them. Keep your form until the end, and eyes always up. Work together and encourage each other. Make it count!" On those last words, we were sent down the hill, jogging towards the start line.

Warren was bouncing off the hills' downgrade, gazing at the nearby telephone poles. "So, we do eight, ten and twelve hills every year. This totals thirty hills. That means that in four years, we run up this hill 120 times. Unless, of course, we miss a workout due to injury. And then, along the hill there are eight telephone poles. 120 times eight equals 960. Guys, we have run by 960 telephone poles during these hill workouts! And, 1920 if you count the ones going down as well. This is crazy! It really makes me realize how much time was spent on this hill!" Warren was hysterical. The hill workouts had visibly marked him.

"Yes Ferg, this is really important," said Favero, not sharing Warren's zeal. "Everyone, let's congratulate Ferg on his accomplishment."

"Let's get these last ninety-six poles taken care of before celebrating," I said.

"Yes, I know. I'm just so happy it's over after today! I think it's because hills have a special place in my heart since Riley took me up Brown's Mountain when I was a rookie. You can't imagine how close…"

"…You were to quitting! We know Ferg, we know!" finished Favero.

On that note, we had made it to the bottom. The hill ended almost at the doorstep of an old country house, hidden by prolific oak trees. A slight crevice in the packed dirt, dug by many feet over the years, indicated our starting point.

"Ok guys, three by three!" said Scott. As a fifth-year runner, his pole count would reach 1200. "On your mark, go!"

As a group, we attacked the beast. Angus and Cal took control of the first few intervals. They both liked leading workouts. I slipped in right behind them, as did Scott, Favero, and Leo. The first four ascensions were comfortable. We were saving the faster ones for the end. On the fifth climb, Edward joined us in the front. He had been held back with class.

"Time?" asked Bernie.

"Seventy-three," Kevin answered.

Bernie liked to know our pace. We usually averaged seventy-four to seventy-five seconds per 400-metre hill. On the track, that pace would be a cakewalk, but the grade of the dirt made 3:05 per kilometre pace feel quite challenging.

"Addison, are you good?" I asked.

"Yeah, I just need to fix my shoe, I'll join you on the next rep," he said while peeling off to the right of the hill and taking a knee after the fourth rep.

"His shoes seem to often need some fixing," I said.

"Especially during hill workouts," added Scott.

The next few reps were done on autopilot. Between the fourth and eighth interval, it was important to stay mentally focused. If doubt and self-pity crept in at this time, making it to twelve would be unlikely. The collective goal was to keep the intervals at the same pace, and grind hard, but still comfortably. After eight, things would become interesting. "Cal, do you want to pick up our last two?" asked Angus seeing the end of their workout near.

"Sure," said Cal.

Scott noticed a potential danger with this surge from the front. "Boys, let's stick to our own plan. We can pick it up a bit, but let's not get sucked in. They're done before we are."

We all agreed with him, but the inevitable happened. Angus and Cal got up the hill in sixty-nine seconds; this was four seconds faster than our average of seventy-three. In the world of 400-metre intervals, four seconds is a lot. Our group was pulled by the surge in the front and ran a seventy-one - still manageable, but faster. This surge had also ignited a flame in the back group. Warren climbed the hill in seventy-five seconds, his fastest climb yet.

Ryan O'Regan began struggling. Since Bernie had announced that everyone – not just the travel team – would get a chance to run at Dalhousie University on the weekend, he was trying to salvage his season. It was not going so well today. "Oh man, I don't feel great. Maybe I'll just call it right now…"

"O'Regan! You are finishing this. Suck it up! Let's go!" Warren had not even let O'Regan finish his sentence. Warren was at war and wanted to have his soldiers along with him.

O'Regan reluctantly began jogging down the hill to start the tenth interval, to Warren's contentment. He could not quit now.

The tenth one was quicker than the ninth, and the eleventh quicker than the tenth. "Time on that last one?" asked Bernie.

"Sixty-eight. The other one was sixty-nine," I said, feeling my legs grow heavy. "Good. McGuire has a sixty-two to his name. Still got a way to go!"

Addison had dropped back to the second pack since coming back from his shoe fixing. He had left Nic, Scott, and me alone in the front. He had a tendency to save it all for his last rep and was currently running very comfortably. The contrast between his facial expression and O'Regan's after the eleventh interval was comical. While Addison looked fresh and rested, running at a submaximal pace, the senior looked defeated and ready to throw in the towel. A simple glare coming from Warren put O'Regan's ideas of quitting before the last one to rest once again.

"Boys, let's do this. All of us!" said Warren, almost threateningly.

A thought came to my mind that may have simply been the product of an oxygen-depleted brain. I was beginning to understand what Warren had been rambling about before the warm up. This workout was in fact symbolic to us, the fourth-year runners. This last hill would be the last one we would surmount together – most of us much faster and stronger than we had been when climbing our first hill. Suddenly, I wanted to make this last hill a success, perhaps as much as did Warren.

Somehow, he had gotten all of us inspired. Favero, Scott, and I lined up at the front, ready to tackle our last obstacle. In synchrony, we counted down from three, and bolted towards the top. Inspired, I took the lead. I felt like the leader of a troop of wildebeests, running with heart while hearing the masses engaging in the same activity directly behind me. I was jolted with energy. Comfortably uncomfortable. At the halfway mark, the footsteps I was hearing directly behind me caught up. Then, they passed me. But they did not belong to Scott or Favero. To my surprise, Addison shot up beside me and sprinted up the hill. Until now, our efforts had been hard but controlled. He, in contrast, was deliberately destroying himself to surmount the hill. He was expending all the energy he had saved in the last reps. Seeing a rookie put a gap on me on our last-ever hill climb lit a fire under my legs.

Oh no. This is not how this workout ends, I thought to myself. Noticing that Addison was already slowing, I began charging up the hill. Pumping my arms and springing off my toes, I pulled even, and then blew by him. The last hundred metres flew by, as I cruised confidently past Kevin and his stopwatch with Scott on my heels.

"Sixty-four," Kevin called out.

***

Over high-fives and smiles, Warren piped in. "Guys, we are done with hills! This is over! Congrats everyone! This is awesome!" Apparently, a gruelling workout was not enough to strip Warren of his enthusiasm.

"Ferg, good thing you kept me in there, man. I was on the verge of stopping. Happy I didn't!" said O'Regan as we began cooling down. With sore legs and tight backs, we ambled towards campus, happy with the work we had just put in. With Neuffer sitting out the workout, we did not feel guilty for cooling down at a snail's pace. We doubled back towards Main Street, passed the lights, and turned right on St. Ninian Street. As we approached the end point of the cool-down route, we heard someone scream.

"Warren!"

"What? Who said that?"

"Over here!" Bernie was driving by with Kevin. "Come here!"

"Ferg, we'll keep going. See you on campus!" I said, as we ran away from our teammate.

"What do you think he wants to see him for?" asked Favero.

"No clue. Hey let's spy on them!" said Edward, running slightly ahead of us. Slowing our jog to a walk, we kept our eyes behind our backs to figure out what Bernie wanted from Warren. It was unusual for Bernie to invite someone to his SUV, especially parked on the side of the busy street by the university. We rounded the Schwartz building on the edge of campus and hid around its corner. To our amazement, Bernie pulled a bag of St. FX gear out of his car and handed it to Warren.

Elated, Warren grabbed the Adidas backpack. He had never made the team in all his years, and therefore, had never owned his own St. FX jackets, singlets, pants, and shorts. Other members of our training group who had never made the team had bought some older gear of years-past from Kevin at a discount price, but Warren had refused to wear anything branded as "St. FX cross-country," waiting until the day he would earn the right to do so. If finishing the hills was a great moment for him, this had to feel even better. We were too far away to hear the dialogue between him and the coaches, but we could see all three of them smiling and engaging in hearty handshakes.

"Guys, let's jump on him when he runs by!" said Ed. Favero, Edward, and I were anxiously waiting for Warren to run by. Excitedly, he was coming towards the Schwartz building with the big, heavy backpack on his back, smiling, and oblivious to the fact that he was being watched by three eager sets of eyes.

"Ok, three, two, one." At once, we surged towards him.

"YESSS FERG WOOOOO!" We jumped on him, cheering like a novice hockey team around their goalie.

Warren joined the celebration, visibly surprised. "HEYYY! Oh wow. Guys, this is unexpected! Finally."

Like four giddy little kids, we jumped around in the middle of campus, attracting a few confused looks from passers-by.

"Ferg it's about time you get your gear. Long time coming!" said Favero.

"Finally. I am thrilled about this, guys," he said, still riding the high from the workout. Despite carrying the heavy backpack and dealing with a pool of lactate in his quads, Warren bounded all the way to the change room. Favero and Edward arrived at the Oland Centre slightly before Warren and me. We followed them in.

"Ferg, I know the work you put in to earn this. Proud of you, man," I told him. "Thanks," said Warren. "Now we just have to keep it going."

I had no doubt that he would.

Luck of the Draw

October 7th

"All right, the four of you please gather round!" said Matt Eliot. "It is time to conduct the ceremonial drawing of the numbers."

Angus, Cal, Favero, and I crashed down on our meal hall chairs. Hell week was almost over. After Tuesday's hills, we had grinded through forty minutes of tempo running on Thursday. All that was left was Saturday's race. Then, the training volume would slowly begin to simmer, as the championship races were coming. AUS was in three weeks, CIS in five. We would not be tapering yet, but we could rejoice in knowing that the worst of Bernie's wrath was behind us. For now, however, we were two days out of our third race of the year at Dalhousie University, and no top-nine member – with perhaps the exception of Addison, who wanted to prove himself after Moncton's race – had much interest invested in the meet. The third race of the year was somewhat irrelevant. It did not elicit as much surprise and excitement as did the first few races of the year, because, at this point, everyone already knew who the big players would be. But, it was still too far from the championship races to allow for legitimate predictions. Almost paradoxically, the third meet of the year was at a time too early and too late to be of any relevance. With this in mind, we had decided to make things a little more interesting.

"Yo, ok guys. Are we sure we want to do this?" asked Favero. "Like, do we know for sure we are going to be the top-four at the race?" He was addressing the small elephant in the room. With Scott and Neuffer choosing to sit out the race to give their bodies a rest, and Dalhousie's Will Russell taking a breather as well, it simply felt like our race to dominate.

"Favero, there is no way anyone beats any of us on Saturday," said Cal, while pulling up the race start-list from his phone. "If anyone even comes close to the slowest guy out of us four, it will be Paul, and then X will claim the top-five spots!"

"Guys, it's settled," said Matt. "I have your four names on pieces of paper in this hat. "We will pick names in reverse order. Whoever is picked first will be slated to finish fourth in the race. The last picked will receive the honour of winning the race. It is an elimination draw. You four will run at a comfortable pace that is just fast enough to break everyone else in the field. At the end, when only the four of you are left in front, you will then line up in the formation that will have been determined today. Is this clear?"

"Crystal, Matt. Give me the hat," I said, reaching out for the small pieces of paper. Although the race did not mean anything, and the order of finishers would obviously be staged, we all secretly wanted our names to be drawn last. Finishing first in a cross-country race added a feather to one's hat, not to mention the best prize at the race and a shot at the St. FX Athlete of the Week title.

"Wait!" said Cal. "We need some more ground rules. What if one of us falls off pace?"

"Ok man how about this?" suggested Nic. "If anyone falls off the pack, they are forgotten about, and the other three remain in order. The plan stays in effect whether we are all there or not."

"Ok, Favero, good idea. Now I'll pick a na..."

"Oh, Cyr wait," said Angus. "What if someone from another school tries to pick up the pace and gaps our pack?"

"Angus, nobody is going to gap us, come on!" I said, losing patience.

"Hey now, I wouldn't be so sure. There is Jérémie Pellerin and Matt Power, who we know nothing about, really. Andrew Peverill from high school is racing too and he has been running very well!"

"Beef, we wiped the floor with Jérémie two weeks ago. Peverill is like sixteen years old. He can't hang with us for 8k."

"Power is the only one we don't know too much about," said Cal. "He won the Acadia meet that happened while we were at Maine. He beat Angus MacIntosh of Dal pretty easily. Also, he's run in the mid-fifteen minutes for a 5k, and that was a year ago. This kid may be no slouch."

"Well, Cal, that's the last thing we'd need after being hyped up on Trackie by everyone in the AUS, losing to some kid nobody knows anything about," I said, pulling up the website's message boards. The webpage was becoming the Canadian version of Letsrun.com.

"And by 'everyone on Trackie,' you mean Fuller – ehm, I mean, AUS Scout?" asked Matt, poking fun.

"I'm just saying," I said, "there is no way some nineteen-year-old from Memorial University of Newfoundland comes out of the woodwork and hands it to us. Like, could you imagine?"

"Yeah, I agree, it's unlikely. But we need to have a plan in case it happens," said Angus. "I say, if he tries to drop us, we go with him. Whoever is left at the finish line among the four of us gets in order, and if we are really racing Power or whomever until the end, then it's every man for himself."

"Ok fine," said Cal. "If someone passes us, and we judge that we must pick it up in order to catch them before the end, we do so. We can't conceal the win. If some people can't hang with the new pace, we drop them. Whichever ones out of us four are still standing when we drop, the new leaders will get in the formation we determine today. Now, if I can just..."

"Wait!!"

"Ugh... what is it, Favero?"

"Prizes. If we are all willing to accept an arbitrary, random place, we must divide the prizes equally. None of us should have a better fate than another, because we are leaving it to chance. I suggest the winner gives his prize to the fourth-place finisher, because the winner already earns the pleasure of winning. Fourth usually gets no prize."

"Yeah, I like that," I said. "Everyone gets an equal share."

"Typical Marxist thinking from Favero. All right then," joked Cal.

"What if the winner gets Athlete of the Week?" I asked.

"They have to give the nice little Boston Pizza free pizza coupon to the fourth-place guy," said Cal.

"Ok, it's settled. Matt, will you?"

"I will pick the first name out of this hat. The person whose name is written on this piece of paper that I currently hold between my two fingers will be slated to finish fourth. Drum roll please!" We repeatedly rapped our hands on the round table. "Sorry, Angus Rawling. You are runner number-four," said Matt, placing the piece of paper on the table.

"Well, thanks for the pizza, boys! As far as I'm concerned, I lucked out on this one. I'll just be striding comfortably to the finish, looking good."

"Ok, next name to be picked," continued Matt. "Sorry, Alex Cyr, you will be finishing third."

"Ahh no! Third is the worst! Nowhere near the win, and no potential Athlete of the Week coupon. Cal and Favero, you better not falter, because I'll be on your heels."

Two names were left in the hat.

"Ok now, so next one you pick Matt, finishes second?"

"Yes, and that poor soul will have missed out on the glory of crossing the finish line of a cross-country race in first place by one single draw. Ladies and gentlemen, I give you your second-place man... drumroll please!" Matt slowly plunged his hand into the hat to pick out one of the two remaining pieces of paper. "Nic Favero!"

"Woooo!" yelled Cal. "I am the champ!"

"Ahhh man..." pouted Favero. "So close!"

"Ok, this is official," said Matt. "Cal will cross the finish line first. He will be followed by Favero, then Cyr, then Angus. Are we all good here?"

"Yup. Now, to execute!" I said.

"Let's show this Power guy who's the boss," said Angus.

I rolled my eyes. Not usually one to worry about competitors, Angus seemed hung up on this guy. I dismissed his comment.

"See you boys." With Cal, I left meal hall and walked towards our cars. We drove towards Greening Drive.

* * *

Back home, Neuffer was studying, sitting on the red couch. I filled him in on our game of chance. "This race is going to be a joke. No Will Russell, no you, and no Scott. Jérémie is not on his game yet, and neither is Jake Wing. This will be nice and chill."

Neuffer picked his eyes up from his binder. "I wouldn't be so sure, Cyr. You four can obviously sweep the podium, but you're not exactly fresh. What was last week for you, 130km? And your workout of yesterday was over 12k of tempo. I don't know. The legs may be tired come Saturday."

"Ahh, just give me a couple of your almonds you always eat and I'll be fine. The body will hold up, really."

"Just saying," said Neuffer. "There is a reason I took this race off. I'm feeling dead. I can't imagine you guys will be feeling as sharp as you did two weeks ago."

"We'll see. One thing is for sure. Plan or no plan, I am not letting anybody without an X singlet cross that line ahead of me," I said, before thrusting my weary, mid-season body down the stairs of 18 Greening to my bedroom. I fell asleep within seconds.

Dalhousie Invitational

October 8th

"Hey Beef, feeling fresh?"

"Well, I may have a sore ankle and a weak knee that has been giving out on me from time to time, and the fatigue I'm carrying in my legs from Thursday's tempo is very present this morning, but I feel good enough to take it to a few plugs today, that's for sure," rambled Angus in one of his trademarked long, windy, sarcastic sentences. "How are you feeling, Cyr?"

"Ready to finish third. No higher, no lower." I was not willing to let anyone know about my current state. Waking up this morning, I had realized that Neuffer might have been on to something. I was just about to finish off my second week of 130+ kilometres, and the mileage was taking its toll. My legs had not yet responded from the beating I had put them through over the last week. I knew I was not at my best. But, I did not want to be – that was to be saved for the important races. Perhaps for that reason, no part of me felt the slightest bit of pre-race anxiety. The race was so meaningless to me that I had trouble working myself up enough to care. The only thought that struck fear into my psyche was the potential for this tempo run to hurt. The pace should be easy to handle, but then again, I was beat.

"O'Regan, what about you?" asked Angus.

"Well, I just have to get used to racing. We'll see," he said, lacking his usually confident tone.

We rolled into Point Pleasant Park and exited the bus as a unit. I put headphones in my ears and tried to get myself hyped up for the race. Along with all the others, I began the long march towards the cross-country course.

171

Point Pleasant Park was easily the most beautiful destination in the AUS. The races began by the water of the Halifax Harbour, and followed along wide and well-packed gravel trails in the nearby provincial park. Situated in an urban area, the races held there often attracted large crowds.

"Cyr, I need to pee, is there a washroom nearby?" asked Addison.

"Look around dude, we're in a park filled with trees. The bathroom is all around us." "No, but Cyr. I have to go number-two," he whispered. "I don't like doing that in the woods, it's gross. I don't have my ten-ply toilet paper with me. I don't like the wilderness."

I sighed. Addison would not have survived a day in Point Pleasant Park, let alone the wilderness. "Ok fine, come with me. There is an old outhouse close by."

"Oh, is that it here? Argh! It stinks in here! Eww...gross!"

I turned to Paul MacLellan who had come with us for the walk and shook my head.

He mimicked my gesture. "You know what they say, Cyr. If you can't take the smell, get out of the park," Paul dead-panned.

Most of the upperclassmen had agreed about one thing in Addison's regard: he needed to harden up. Cross-country was an unforgiving sport, and so far, Addison was feeling its wrath. After a decent performance in Maine, the hills of Moncton had killed him, and other than during the final rep of our hill repeats, he did not seem to have regained his mojo. Since that race, he had decreased his easy-run length, and his workout paces were increasingly troublesome. His young body, deprived of sleep and Mom's cooking, was growing tired. The workload was now breaking him down physically and mentally multiple times per week, and everything pointed to the possibility that he needed a break. He was, as the upper-years would say when they referred to rookies getting buried by Bernie's tough mid-season training, feeling the "Bern."

I dropped off Addison at the outhouse and, with Paul, ran back towards our team, which had set up camp under the shade of a massive tree to the left and about a hundred metres up from the start line. The tree was the very one by which I had met Bernie in the fall of 2012 when I was a high school senior. Like our group was doing now, the 2012 version of the X-Men and X-Women were gathered around the tree to stretch, listen to music and swap old spike pins for new ones, in preparation for their race. I had been attracted by the uniformity of such a large group of men and women. All wore white and blue, and all looked fast. The men's team had dominated that year, led by then-AUS champion, Connor McGuire. After my brief chat with Bernie after their race, a visit to the campus was arranged for me. Soon after, I was hooked. Since then, St. FX always used that big tree neighbouring a picnic table as their setup spot. Now a part of that sea of blue that had mesmerized me from the beginning, I still felt hints of nostalgia sitting in the same tree's shade.

I snapped out of my daydreams when I noticed that the sea of blue was moving. People were changing into their warm up gear.

"Boys let's go, we're fifty minutes out. Hurry up!" said Favero, pacing back and forth.

People were stripping down into t-shirts and singlets – the thermostat read eighteen degrees; hot for October. We followed the spectacles-wearing sociology major out onto the trails. When we finally got going, we noticed the coarse sound of feet hitting the ground amidst our more quiet steps.

"Paul, are you wearing your spikes during warm up?" asked Angus, perplexed.

"Well, yes. As you all know, I have had this calf cramp over the last few weeks. I want to see if I can run in spikes before racing in them," said Paul in his usual highly inflected speech.

"Ha ha! That is the stupidest idea I have ever heard." "You're just risking more injury!" said Cal and Angus. A few others jumped in on it.

"Well guys, if you have a problem with this, I do not care. If you could all shut up, that would be great," said Paul, between loud foot strikes.

Angus and Cal, along with others, snickered behind him. Warming up in spikes was a faux pas in competitive running, kind of like racing with a water bottle belt. Unbothered, Paul shuffled to the front of the pack, carelessly dulling his racing pins.

"Neuffer, could you make sure my stuff stays on the line while I do five minutes of tempo before the race?" asked Cal, who had decided that running an eight-kilometre tempo run would not suffice for today's workload. He had not worked out on Thursday, so his legs could take the pounding. He would roll into the race straight out of a five-minute tempo run. If our lack of caring for this race was already apparent, Cal had just taken it to a whole new level. Now, it was obvious that we were simply treating today as a workout.

"Got it Cal." Though they were not racing, Neuffer and Scott were present to watch us race, catering to our every pre-race need.

Bernie called us. "Ok guys can we just gather round for a second? Quickly!" Now fully stripped down to our racing gear, we gathered by our starting box. It was warmer than it had been in Moncton – where the thermostat had read thirteen degrees.

Guys, the girls ran great but they got separated completely. I don't like that. I think it is much easier when you run with your teammates. Today is a good opportunity for that." We were unsure if Bernie knew of our plan, but it was consistent with his instructions. "Stay together as much as you can out there and communicate and so on. Practice those skills in these races so that you know how to race as a group by CIS. Go out there and run smart. This course has one big hill. Work it hard, and when you get up the hill, what do you do Paul?"

"Give fifty."

"That's right. Fifty hard metres and just like that you break your opponents. Beat them and move on. For those of you who are on the fence, I want you to show me today why I should be taking you to Fredericton for the Interlock meet next week. Let's show them what X is all about!"

I ran a stride, and then walked back to the start line. Cal came back from his short tempo, barely touched the start line with his spikes, and sped away for a stride.

"Dude, what's Cal doing?" someone near me asked. I turned to see Josh Shanks to my left.

Embarrassed, I replied, "Cal wanted to run a bit of tempo before. This is our hell week of training, so he's really trying to make himself work."

Josh shook his head, smiling. "Well, whatever floats his boat, I guess." His long, wavy hair swayed from side to side. The third-year runner for University of New Brunswick had been close to committing to St. FX. We had recruited him as best we could, as he had been the most sought-after recruit to come out of Atlantic Canada since Mike Tate. His participation at the World Youth Track and Field championships had solidified his rank among the best in the world, following his grade-eleven year. Alas, two years of severe and unlucky injuries had forced him to take a monumental step back in his training. The entire conference rooted for the calm and friendly third-year runner and hoped he would remain healthy and once again be able to reach his potential. Shanks giggled. "That Cal is something else. Best of luck, Cyr."

"You too, let's mix it up out there."

Cal trotted his way back to the start line, looking focused.

"All right buddy, just chill and relax" I told him. "We got this easy. Angus, Favero, let's just roll."

"Runners on your marks! POW!" The gun was off and we dashed to the front. Controlling the pace with Cal, we had the entire AUS on our backs. After 500 metres of jostling, Angus and Favero pulled even with us. I was comfortable; I ran alongside my training partners like I had done so many times. We did not expect many people to drop in the first few kilometres, as the pace we had set was pedestrian. Nobody dared to pass us. Jean-Marc Doiron, the Université de Moncton head coach had entered the race as an unattached athlete. In his late twenties and still fit, he held a 1:49 personal best in the 800 metres. I had not anticipated his presence in the race, but he was a stronger track runner than a cross-country one. When racing the man we called JMD, however, you never knew what you would be in for. He saw our blue and white cluster leading and controlling the race.

"It's time for this conference to have more than one good team," he said between breaths. Though we knew other teams had good runners, none could match our depth. Jean-Marc had done wonders with his team in Moncton, but they still were not at our level. A few years of recruiting and development were still needed.

At 3km, Angus took the lead. Cal and I ran alongside him, with Favero close behind, but not running as smoothly as he had been in practice. We still were not clear of the pack. In our tracks were Jean-Marc, Jérémie Pellerin from Moncton, heavily recruited high-schooler Andrew Peverill, Jake Wing and Angus MacIntosh of Dalhousie, Shanks of UNB, and finally Matt Power from Memorial University of Newfoundland. Casual observers still wondered where Power would stack up against our runners. The rumour around Point Pleasant Park on that day was that he would put us all in our place. I was growing impatient with all this Power talk.

"Nic, stay with them!" screamed Bernie, as we ran past our coach. One steep, unforgiving hill broke up the 2.5km course in two. By four kilometres, we were cresting its top for the second time, and Jean-Marc and Jérémie were nowhere to be seen. Neither was Favero. I was shocked. He had looked so smooth and fit in practice on Thursday, and now this. He must have been having an off day. But, he was not the only one still worn down by the Thursday workout. I thought to myself that my legs were awfully heavy for midway through a race, especially for this supposedly easy pace! I looked over at Cal, and he did not look very comfortable, either. I calmed myself down by thinking of all the mileage I had done in the week and told myself that my being more tired than usual was anticipated.

We approached the big hill halfway through the third loop. I trudged to the top alongside Cal. I could now hear him breathe, along with the others directly behind me. At the top, I glanced over my shoulder to see how Angus was looking. To my utmost surprise, he was off our pack. I re-entered my state of panic.

"Angus gone" I muttered at Cal.

"Shit," he said.

What was happening? The only footsteps closely following ours were those of Jake Wing, Josh Shanks, Matt Power, and Andrew Peverill. How were there only two X-men left in the lead pack? This was not good enough. To add to Cal and my mutual panic, we were struggling. In panic, we decided to pick up the pace. We ran side-by-side, slightly losing command on our own fatigue threshold. Our prance was in no way controlled and looked increasingly ugly. Luckily, the injection of pace was too much for three of our followers. Entering our final 2.5k-loop, I could only hear one runner's patter behind me. I assumed the footsteps belonged to Jake or Josh. We ran down by the water, where spectators cheered. "Good job X!"

"Way to go, Cal!"

"Don't give up Matt!"

I flashed a look behind me and was mortified to lock eyes with Matt Power – the runner we knew nothing about. Instantly, I looked at Cal. Slight eye contact was all we needed to communicate. We had perhaps run together more often than any other two members of the team. I knew exactly what was running through his mind. It was the same thing that was running through mine. We needed to surge immediately to clear ourselves from Power and make this race ours. No way were we going to let a runner from MUN take the win. Their superfluous self-hyping on Trackie made them the last team to whom I wanted to lose the individual race.

Cal and I went to work. In the next loop, we distanced ourselves by 100 metres. Still running side by side, we were equally tired. So much for a tempo effort. I peeked behind me.

"Is he there?" Cal asked.

"Fifteen seconds back. We're good," I replied, trying to preserve as much oxygen as possible while conveying my message. Cal was red in the face. My quads were on fire. If Scott or Neuffer had been in this race, they would have easily handed it to the both of us. This win would certainly not be Cal's prettiest. "End is here. You take it," I continued, honouring the ceremonial draw of the names. We cruised into the last downhill and took a hard left to the finish. Sweating, red, and mentally defeated, Cal and I crossed the line in first and second. Power came in thirteen seconds later.

Cal hung his head low and scanned the results, embarrassed. "Cyr, what the heck? Look what we ran."

"Wow. I think we've run faster in workouts," I said, looking at the results sheet. Our times were barely under twenty-seven minutes for 8k. We had known our bodies would be tired, but neither of us had imagined such a disappointing result. Our confidence was shot. We waited at the line for Favero to cross in ninth in a time of 27:34. He was equally distraught. The fourth member of our supposed tandem, Angus, was limping by our sitting spot with a bulky wrapping around his knee. He had dropped out.

"Cyr, I was barely faster than two years ago when we raced here. That's ridiculous! This is not good." Cal was the most vocal about the communal disappointment.

Scott offered some moral support. "Guys, it's all right. Try to stay positive about this. You all knew today would feel hard. Heck, you guys ran a 12k tempo run not even forty-eight hours ago. Forget about this one. Back at it next wee..."

"YEEEAHHH!!" Scott had been interrupted. "Woah, guys did you see where I finished? And my time? I am back, baby!! Wahooo!" Clearly, Addison was not concerned with mood matching. Rightfully so, as the rookie had run a much stronger race than any of his workouts had indicated he could. His time of 27:48 was good enough for twelfth place, and fourth on the team.

"Happy for you man!" I said, trying to hide my individual disappointment.

"Oh thank God! I was getting worried. I'm back!"

At least one of us was happy with the result. To the sound of Addison's cheers, we grabbed our stuff and walked towards the bus. I met up with Neuffer, who still held multiple pieces of warmup gear.

"Guess you were right. Tougher than we thought."

"Yeah, guess I was," he said. "I was not trying to be pessimistic, but these training weeks are so tough, I just saw it coming. You can't read into it too much, though. You and Cal have been running and working out well. This is just a bad day to put behind you." "Yeah, you're right. Oh well, on to the next one. Are you getting a run in before you leave?" I asked.

"Nah, taking today off. The shin was acting a little weird on Thursday. It's probably nothing."

"All right," I said. "I'll see you at home, Neuf."

Aches and Pains

October 12th

The next few days following the Dalhousie meet were taken very lightly. Sleep was cherished and runs were slow. Even though the tapering had not quite yet started for the AUS and CIS championships, bodies needed a few easy days to fully absorb the strenuous training to which they had been subject over the past week. I was finishing off a week of 140 kilometres; an all-time high. Workouts over the week had still gone well, because our easy-run pace had been taken down a notch. Bernie would tell us to, "Make your easy days easy, so you can make your hard days hard." It was especially true in this gruelling time of year. We were walking on a tightrope of two edges; the ones of injury and burnout. The former seemed to be plaguing 18 Greening more than the latter. Ice bags were found all over the house. Therapy bands and foam rollers had become hot commodities.

"Cyr, do you have that little ball for under the feet?" asked Angus, walking into the living room.

"Yeah, it's in the basement. Do your feet hurt?"

"Hmm, not really. But my ankle's starting to be sore again. I was told it could have something to do with my arches being stiff," said the sophomore runner, worried.

"Oh, yeah go roll that as much as you can. How's the knee?" I asked. He had taken a few days off since dropping out of the Dalhousie meet, citing sharp knee pain.

"Ahh, it's manageable. I can grind it out for another four weeks. What about you? You're looking like you're in one piece, somehow."

"Yeah, I'm as surprised as you are," I said. "My arches are hurting me, though. Both feet. I've been taping up."

"What kind of tape do you use?" asked Scott, coming out of his room.

"Just whatever tape Laura gives me."

"Man, use kinetic tape. It's the best. My knee is acting weird again in some workouts, but this tape keeps it quiet."

"You're a big kinetic-tape guy, you use that stuff all the time," I said.

"Well, you know what they say, Cyr. There are only two things that kinetic tape can't fix: a broken heart, and illiotibial band syndrome. Unfortunately, I constantly deal with one of the two."

"Can your kinetic tape fix a sore shin?" asked Neuffer, overhearing our conversation. "Uh oh. We've heard that one before," I said. "Is it bad?"

"It's fine. Just kinda weird," he said, while retrieving an ice bag from the deep freeze. "Well, boys, you know what Bernie says: you can run when you're hurt, you can't run when you're injured," shouted Cal, from his room. The tall philosophy student was slowly working away at a paper, dividing his attention between his reading and the dialogue coming from the 18 Greening house living room.

"Cal, come ice with us!" yelled Angus, laughing at the sight of four broken bodies sprawled on our couches. Neuffer and Scott sat on our red three-seater, while Angus and I occupied a green checkered sofa to its side.

"No need, boys! This body is an injury-free machine. Running close to the fire, but still not burnt!" he said, before knocking the top of his head for good luck, as he often did. Cal was not as prone to injury as were the rest of us. He was, however, wary of falling back into a state of burnout. For that reason, he had not pushed the envelope in terms of mileage this week, like some of us had done. "Speaking of burnout, has anyone seen Favero lately? He is HURTING."

"He told me his Achilles tendon was kind of flaring up. Those crazy mileage weeks definitely didn't help," I said.

"Well, it's not just that," said Cal, still yelling from his room. "He is super tired on his runs. Same as every year. He whips himself into amazing shape by early October, and then his body can't take the huge training load anymore."

"So, how much had he been running?" asked Scott.

"Oh! He must have been pushing 150 kilometres some weeks. He should have been doing that in the summer, instead of balancing it with three work-outs per week. He's burning!"

"Well, in the event that Favero doesn't make it to the end, Paul becomes our sixth, and who's our seventh guy? Addison?" I wondered.

"Addison has a different injury every day," said Angus. "Calf, quad, butt, pinkie toe…I wouldn't put my faith into him."

"At least Ferg is healthy."

"Ferg is never healthy," pointed out Neuffer. "Ferg just pops insane amounts of Advil. You know he'll run if we need him, though."

"Yeah, I'm aware. The thing is, if we want to achieve our goal at CIS, we need the five of us on the line," Scott said. "If we want a medal, we need five guys capable of cracking the top thirty."

"That won't happen if we're already broken."

Scott reassured me. "Cyr, we have five weeks. That sounds like a long time, but really it's not. If we've made it this far, we'll muscle our way through. It would take a pretty nasty injury to prevent me from forcing myself through this last part of the season."

Cal's thoughts echoed Scott's. "None of us would be willing to stop at anything. This is our last year together. We just have to take care of the little things. We'll make it there." "Oh, there is no injury I can think of that would keep me away from the big races. Not again. Even if I'm popping pills too!" said Neuffer. "And come on, Cyr. We're in good shape now. I'm not hurt, you and Scott have been dealing with the same little things all year and they haven't stopped you. Angus is on the mend…"

Neuffer was grimacing from the cold ice on his shins. "Neuf," I said, "if you say you're not hurt, I believe you. But keep it that way."

"Neuffer buddy, you worry me a bit, I'll be honest with ya," laughed Cal, nervously.

Alex Neuffer had fractured the periosteal layer of his tibia more times than he cared to count. He had missed many seasons due to stress fractures. All his injuries started with shin "tightness" as he would describe it, only to aggravate and elicit sharp and deep pain. "Like I said boys, no injury will keep me away. And this is nothing, really. The shin is just a little tight – it'll go away."

The rest of us exchanged nervous looks. I hoped he was right.

Night at Boston Pizza

October 12th

"Guys, wanna do BP tonight? It's wing night!" said O'Regan, waking up from a nap. He had skipped our icing session; his body was indestructible.

"Some of us are still doing sober season, O'Regan," said Angus.

"We can go and not drink, come on! It'll be fun! We could go for supper and stay for an hour or two, just the guys. We haven't done something fun in a while."

"I'm down!" said Scott, springing off the couch. "We need to de-stress a bit. I do, anyway." We were almost through the dog days of the season, and minds were growing as weary as bodies.

"I'll come too," I said. "I'll post in our Facebook group to see if anyone else wants to join."

Turns out, many of our teammates were also in need of a getaway. We were racing for the fourth time of the season on Saturday, and the training had kept piling on.

In two cars, we left for Boston Pizza. I drove my Honda Civic with Neuffer as my co-pilot. O'Regan, Scott and Paul sat in the back. Cal was in his Volkswagen Golf with Angus on the passenger side. They picked up Jeffs, Matt, and Favero from the Acadia Street house. As they were about to leave the historical team abode, Cal's phone began ringing. It was Edward and Fuller.

"Hey Cal, do you think you could come pick us up?" They were at their apartment off Church Street, in a student-dominated residential area people called "The Village." They lived together with a friend of Edward's, Andrew Bekkers. Normally, they would have walked – Boston Pizza was barely 500 metres away from their house – but a violent rainfall had confined them to the house.

"Uhh, sure I guess," said Cal. I just don't have much room in the back of my car."

"It's ok, we'll squeeze!" said Edward.

"All right. I'll be there in a sec."

Cal showed up at The Village with a full car. "Sorry guys, I told you it was tight back there."

"All good! I've fit eight people in my truck before, ten if you count the trunk!" proudly claimed Ed. "This little thing can definitely fit six if we're creative. One of us will just have to get in the trunk."

"Fuller, you're too big to fit in the back with three guys already there," said Cal. "Do you mind hopping in the trunk for the ride while Ed squeezes with the guys in the backseat?"

"Uh, yeah it's fine." The giant squished himself into a ball to fit in the back crick of Cal's car. He pushed aside a few stray pairs of shoes, an Intro to Philosophy textbook, and a box of granola bars and ducked his head. Soon, the group of seven had made it to the Boston Pizza parking lot.

Meanwhile, at the restaurant, our group had saved seats for Cal and his passengers. "Cal's on his way, I'll text him to let him know we're on the bar side," said Neuffer.

"I'm surprised we made it before him and his reckless driving," stated Scott. Maybe the Acadia boys held them back."

"Oh, here they are now." I said, as I spotted Cal, Angus and the others walk towards us.

"Hey boys, nice table!" We had landed the big table with booths at the far right corner of Boston Pizza's bar. As soon as we all grabbed our seats, the waitress was already taking orders.

"Hey everyone, can we get you guys started with some drinks?"

"A glass of water for me," said Neuffer.

"Me too, please," said Cal.

"Yeah, same here," mimicked Favero.

"Ok, do you guys just all want water?" The group nodded in unison.

"Wait! I'll have a Rickards' Red!" said O'Regan.

"Coming right up."

"O'Regan, starting the night off early?" teased Scott.

"Hey I'm going to Wing Night at the Inn after this. It won't hurt to have a few drinks. We're getting at the end of these nights, you know. We're fourth-years, Scotty. Can't miss out."

"It's also our last cross season. We don't want to miss out on that either," our captain reminded him.

"Yeah, yeah, yeah...well..."

"Ok man," interrupted Favero, addressing everyone. "Scott brought it up, and this has been on my mind for a while. Think about this: it's our last cross-country season. Once this year is done, Scott, Cyr, Cal, Jeffs, Ferg, Neuffer, Matt, O'Regan, myself, Heidi, Mary, Liz, and Ellen are all gone. That's a huge blow. It's going to be the end of an era, man. Things are going to be so different; the team is pretty much starting back up from scratch. And then, there was all this talk about St. FX trying to recruit Gillis or Lee McCarron or someone to come coach. Yo, I think Bernie is going to retire soon."

"Can't see it," said Neuffer. "I might be back at X next year if I decide to do my bachelor's in education, and Bernie knows that. He's said nothing to me about retiring. He likely would have let me know."

"Plus," I added, "I got the vibe from Lee McCarron that if X hires a new coach at all, it will be Gillis. He is the only candidate as far as Bernie and St. FX Athletics are concerned, so if Gillis is not ready to start coaching now, Bernie stays."

"But, Lee McCarron could apply," said Angus.

"I don't think X will hire Lee."

"Why wouldn't they hire Lee?" asked Angus. "Did something happ..."

"The point is," I cut in, "Gillis is the only candidate, and as long as he is still training and competing, I don't think he's going to want to move away from Guelph and put a bunch of time into something else."

"Yeah, he said so himself," said Scott. "It would be difficult for him to uproot his family, too, let alone leaving his coach and training partners."

"He said he might want the job eventually, just not now," said Cal.

"Then there's Bernie, too. Are we even sure he wants to retire?" asked Edward.

"Yes! Of course, he's ready," Favero was defending his point. "Bernie is seventy. He's going on trips with Brenda, he likes spending time with his grandchildren... he doesn't want to deal with twenty-year-olds for the rest of his life!"

"I don't know...he does seem to love it still," said Scott.

"I guess time will tell," concluded Cal.

"Ok, Cyr, so why would X not hire Lee?" asked Angus, again. "He's a great coach."

"Water for all of you here! And, a Rickard's Red for you, sir" said the waitress as she distributed our drinks.

"O'Regan, pints are like seven dollars here," said Neuffer. "Are you sure you have that kind of money?"

"I don't, but DJ always finds a way, you know that," he said, taking a sip of his beer. One could never have guessed that he had been unemployed longer than we could remember. Indeed, he always found a way to pay for anything he wanted.

"Ok, Cyr. Tell me," said Angus, impatient. "What is it with Lee Mc..."

"Hang on, Angus, I'm getting a text." I looked down at my phone, and gasped. My eyes nearly popped out of my skull.

"What is it?" asked Angus.

"Oh my God, guys. We messed up."

"Messed up how?"

"That was Fuller. He's still in the trunk."

"WHAT???" shrieked Cal, as he and Scott got up and ran out towards his car.

Favero started laughing. "Woah, man! We've been in here for at least fifteen minutes, that's wild!"

"I can't believe we left him in there," said Ed.

O'Regan had the giggles. "Yeah how the heck did you forget him?"

"He never said anything as we got out of the car, I don't know. I figured Cal or Angus was going to get him," said Jeffs.

Cal rushed back inside, followed by Fuller, blank faced.

"Fuller, we're so sorry, man!" offered Ed. "What was it like in there?"

Fuller wiped a few beads of sweat off his freckled forehead. "Hot."

The Ostrich

October 14th

"So, can anyone tell me how to differentiate development from adaptation in young athletes? We briefly looked at this during our last class." Dr. Angie Kolen, was trying to jog the memories of her students of her Human Growth and Development class, whose minds were nearly squashed to mush by the weight of mid-semester stress. Midterm season was upon us, and though these examinations rarely matched the extensiveness of finals, students were expected to study for them while still attending class and writing assignments. Not to mention that midterm season coincided with the late part of the cross-country season – the part that mattered. "Anyone? Eric!"

Eric Locke, the captain of the hockey team and honour roll student offered his answer. "Well, development is behavioural. It's like, when a kid learns how to behave in certain situations, or in society, I guess. Adaptation is more physiological. It's how the body accommodates to its environment."

"Good!" said Angie, relieved that someone had been listening. "Adaptation has to do with the body; it is physiological! Training often elicits types of adaptation. Could someone give me an example of a training adaptation? Alex!"

Startled, I tried to come up with a quick answer. "So, uhh, athletes who live at high altitude need to adapt to the air quality, which is less rich in oxygen, and become more efficient at transporting oxygen. So, to deliver enough oxygen to their muscles as they train, the body has no choice but to produce more red blood cells. Then, when they come down to sea level, the enhanced amount of red blood cells makes them more efficient at transporting oxygen, and they run faster," I said, with running on the brain.

"Very good, that's a great example, Alex! Where did you learn about this?"

"I read *The Sports Gene* for Dr. Kane's exercise metabolism class and they talked about altitude traini…"

"But, Alex isn't completely right," said Scott, sitting beside me. "He failed to mention that the adaptation isn't permanent. The duration of the benefits of high-altitude training is dependent on the time spent at altitude. Eventually, the effects wear off. I guess he wasn't paying as much attention in ex-metabolism as I was." A few classmates giggled.

"Oh, very good, Scott. Do we have a little bit of academic rivalry among runners, here?" Angie asked playfully. Scott and I both were writing our theses under her supervision, so she knew that any banter between the two of us was playful.

"No rivalry, just a bit of correction where it is duly needed," said Scott, with a finger in the air.

I countered, "Well, you see Angie, there is a saying in research that goes like this: in order to advance science, you must stand on the shoulders of giants. In this case, I had laid down the base theory behind altitude training and Scott was advancing that theory. So, I was the giant and he was standing on my shoulders."

"Yeah, and I was right. I'd rather that," said Scott.

"Ahh, whatever."

Angie chuckled. "Hmmm…I know you guys are taking off for a race in Fredericton. Good luck tolerating each other for a five-hour bus ride."

"Ugh, I hate him. I'm going to sit with the girls," I said as class ended.

Our mock banter elicited some laughs, and some good luck wishes from a few of our classmates. With Alex Neuffer and Ryan O'Regan on our heels, we walked out of room 207 of the Oland Centre.

The University of New Brunswick was hosting the AUS-RSEQ Interlock meet, a unique race that featured teams from ours and Quebec's conference. It would give us the opportunity to measure ourselves against new teams and paint a better picture of how we stacked up against the rest of the country. The number-one ranked team in the CIS, Le Rouge et Or of Université Laval, would be present.

"Ok, when do we have to be in the front of the Oland Centre?" I asked Scott as we walked out of class.

"Be there at eleven. Bus leaves at 11:15. I think we're supposed to get to Fredericton by five."

"All right, I'm going home for now. I'll meet you guys later." It was 9:15. I had just enough time to go home and pack the rest of my things. I walked back to 18 Greening at a brisk pace, realizing that I only had my singlet and shorts stuffed in my travel bag. Bernie hated tardiness, and I had been late before. They likely would not leave without me, but I did not want to test him. He had left a late O'Regan at home in our second year. Remembering this, I picked up the pace of my walk once more.

As I walked down James Street, I thought of the last class I had sat through. I recalled how Scott had amused the class with his remarks. I was surprised he had spoken up. Usually quiet, his piping up was nothing but a successful attempt at injecting a bit of humour into our hour of class. Come to think of it, that was typical Scott. He never liked to get too serious about things. Casual observers who only knew Scott as the current star of our cross-country team would have been shocked at how laid back he was. An easy class schedule permitted him to laze around the house on most mornings in colourful sweat pants. He would take his sweet time eating his Honey Nut Cheerios and fit in a few games of NHL 2017 between spoonsful. By early afternoon, he would eventually stroll to the library, where he would search the web for new music to add to his party playlist (he had owned the turntables for every cross-country team party I had attended since my rookie year), while casually picking away at his thesis. Nobody would have guessed that he, among a heap of more high-strung type A runners, had been the St. FX athlete of the year in 2015, and had held a winning record against every single one of his teammates save for Connor McGuire since his arrival in 2012. And if watching him move around campus at a tempo starkly contrasting his running pace was not enough to mask his astounding ability on the cross-country course, a conversation with Scott would then suffice. He was humble and unassuming, enough to delude one about his prowess. In fact, a few teammates had named him Ostrich, because "Ostriches are deceptively fast." He did not consider himself a runner above all else, as some of us sometimes did. He would not talk about his so-far-spotless cross-country season unless somebody asked him about it. Some presumed that he avoided the topic out of humility, but I suspected that it simply would not even cross his mind. Up until five o'clock practice every day, he was not "Scott the Runner" – he was just some guy.

Perhaps that was the key to his prolonged success as an X-Man. Since finishing third at the AUS championships in his rookie year, and being named co-captain in his sophomore year, he had assumed an important role on the travel team in its every function. I suspected he had captained more teammates than anyone in St. FX history; he had been there for Bernie and the boys through thick and thin. He had finished fourth at the 2013 AUS championship while stricken by mononucleosis – the only one of two career AUS cross-country or track championships he'd participated in, in which he had not won a medal. He went on to dominantly win the AUS conference cross-country race the next year. He rode that momentum into track season and snagged gold in the 1500 metres and silver in the 3000 metres. Later, in 2015, he finished sixteenth at the national championship – the best finish spot any member of our current group has to their credit. On a team oozing talent from every corner, Scott led the pack in experience and pedigree. He had been expected to show us the way when Cal, Neuffer, Favero, and I were rookies. He was expected to outdo himself on the racecourse year after year. He was expected to be immaculate under the pressure of being a good captain to a sometimes-dysfunctional ship. Year after year, the expectations we placed on him were raised and, year after year, he met them. Perhaps, I thought, a more high-strung individual might not have been right for such a distressing task.

I walked up the Greening hill and into the house where Angus was playing NHL in the living room. "Cyr are you packed yet?"

"Not really, I have to start. Are you?"

"Nope. I thrive under pressure."

"Good, because we're leaving in ten," I reminded him. I ran downstairs and packed the belongings I would need for the overnight trip. As I looked at my singlet, I imagined how the blue and white would stack up against the black and red of national favourite Université Laval tomorrow – the headliners of the event. I also wondered how these singlets would stack up against each other. With only one race to go before AUS, tomorrow would be a great foreshadowing of our showdown for the individual conference title. I wondered which blue and white singlet, if any, would eventually be able to threaten Scott's still-perfect season, and further speculated about whether the thought of losing to one of us tomorrow had crossed his mind. I presumed it had not.

AUS-RSEQ Interlock meet

October 15th

"Arm sleeves, or no arm sleeves?" Scott asked from his room, still tangled in his sheets.

"Sleeves. Then throw them to Bernie when you get warm."

"Or, I could just start without them I guess. I get super warm in races."

"Well, you finish them redder than a boiling lobster, so that doesn't surprise me." We often joked that Scott was so red after a hard effort due to the excess haemoglobin travelling in the bouncy Ontarian's bloodstream. We figured he had to hold some genetic advantage over the rest of us to so often emerge on top. Even when he came back from injury, three weeks of training was all he needed to run with the leaders. No matter what he did, Scott Donald improved. He responded to any kind of training. We jokingly speculated that he would get faster simply by having someone tickle his testicles.

I looked out the window of the Quality Inn to try and gauge the temperature. The weather looked dry, but crisp. I put on my racing kit, and draped myself in a long-sleeved shirt, DRI-fit pants and a St. FX raincoat. We ate a quick breakfast downstairs and hopped on the bus to drive to the course as a team. The boys were apprehensive. We had done nothing but win all year, and now, we were expected to face the best team in the country in Université Laval. Our race plan had shifted from leading the pack to chasing the leaders, given our slim chances of winning the race as a team. On the way to the course, we began studying their line-up.

"Ok, let's think about it this way. They're very deep, but they only have a few standouts. We could challenge for the win, here." Angus was desperately trying to lift our spirits. "So Yves Sikubwabo will likely win, but after that it's up in the air. They're sitting Thibeau, Hoa Mai, Raymond, and Morin. They're pretty much just half a team! I guess Igor Bougnot and Emmanuel Boivert will be tough to beat, but we can hang with Tedeschi and Racine."

"Don't forget Lavoie-Gilbert. He has a 30:09," said Cal.

"I heard he's been hurt," said Neuffer, sitting a few seats behind us. "Same for Emmanuel."

"All right then," said Angus, dusting off his spikes. "We will let Yves go when he wants to, but we have to stick with that chase pack. Some of them may just have freak bad days. Realistically, we should lose, but it could happen that we'd pull an upset. Imagine how Trackie would blow up if we were to win this meet."

"We'd likely just move up from eighth to seventh in the rankings," sighed Cal. "They never give AUS teams any credit."

"If we beat Laval today, though," added Scott, "the CIS will at least be aware of us as a real threat. We'll finally get some kind of respect."

Slowly, we started liking our chances.

As the bus came to a stop, Bernie addressed the crowd of anxious runners. "Guys, Laval's coach has been telling people that all he needs is half a squad to win this meet. Let's show him what we have to say about that." As usual, he stood at the front, giving each runner a fist bump as they exited the bus. Spirits were elevated. We strutted on the UNB course with newfound confidence, ready to slay seven powerful French dragons.

Once off the bus, we noticed that Odell Park seemed more crowded than usual. Along with Laval had come seven other schools from the Quebec conference. McGill and Sherbrooke would likely contend with Dal for third spot. On a bad day, McGill could perhaps usurp us for second. Teams in green, blue, and red strode along together, starting an early warm up. But, intertwined with the French teams were those we already knew so well. Dalhousie was down the hill past the park's hospitality building, as per usual. Saint Mary's and UNB were parked close to the start line. From a distance, I could see the green and white uniforms of UPEI hop off their bus and head over towards the park, and on the other side of the building was Université de Moncton.

"St. FX, there they are in the blue and the white jacket! Ready to chase Marathon Man??" Jérémie Pellerin's raspy voice boomed out of nowhere. He was often heard before he was seen. Today was no exception. His Acadian accent and slang were unmistakable. "Mr. Cyr are you ready for the big showdown of the century? Laval, there there, they look fit and fast and I don't know if St. FX has the deepness you know?"

"Ha ha, we'll see, Jérémie. Why don't you focus on your race instead of sizing us up against Laval? Where are you going to finish in all this?"

"Well I know what I am going to do. I am super fit right now. Super shape. Hey, who are you?"

"Hey Jérémie, my name is Paul." The sophomore runner had come to see what the ruckus was about. "I thought it was a good time to introduce myself to Cyr's French friend." "Well Paul, you're going to see the spark flying on the course today! Yves will be way ahead, but then it's going to be Cyr, Cal, Scott, and me battling for AUS win!"

"Oh really? What about Neuffer?" I asked.

"And Angus?" added Paul.

"Oh, no no no no no. They are not on same level. I am faster than them. I need to win a medal at the AUS, and I am going to beat one of the other three. Look out! Mo Pellerin is back! See you at start line boys!" As quickly as he had entered my aura, he was gone.

"Why does he always think he can beat us?" asked Paul, puzzled.

"I'm not sure. But if you ever lack confidence in yourself, ask Jérémie for his secret." "Do you think I can stick with him today?"

"If you're not afraid of randomly placed surges and an unsustainably fast start," I told the sophomore, "it's worth a try."

"Scott!" Bernie called from behind us. "Go get the guys and get a pre-race huddle going. We go in ten minutes! I'm seeing the girls finish." I was standing next to the hospitality building, about two hundred metres away from our start line. Cal and Neuffer were striding along. Scott was doing leg swings. Addison was switching into his spikes. It was race time.

"Guys, we have ten minutes!" Scott said, trading in his warm-up shoes for his spikes. "Let's roll!" We slowly made our way to the start line. Half of us had exposed our singlets, while the other half still wore short sleeve St. FX cross-country shirts, waiting to strip down immediately before the sound of the gun.

"Ok guys bring it in!" yelled Scott. I could already tell that his game-time pep talk would be more intense than at past meets. We formed a wide circle, resting our arms on each other's shoulders. "All right, we're almost there," said our captain, calmly. "This is the last race we have before championship season. Last 8k. You guys are aware that today will be different. We will not have total control of this race. Instead, we're going to be chasing guys down. This is not our race to lose; it's theirs – Laval's. So, let's pretend like we're at CIS. Let's practice racing with guys we don't know right until the end, and not give an inch. Just because they're wearing red and black doesn't mean they're better than us. Their coach is telling people that he sat half the team because he doesn't think we'll be any threat to them, so let's make them know better. Today is a day to prove ourselves, so let's go out there, have fun, and race hard. Ready? HAIL AND HELL!"

"WHITE AND BLUE!"

"HAIL AND HELL!"

"WHITE AND BLUE!"

"HAIL AND HELL!"

"WHITE AND BLUE! 1, 2, 3, X" we chanted in unison.

"LET'S GO!" screamed Scott. For a guy so laid back, he had the ability to turn it on when needed. We lined up right next to Laval. They immediately began their chant. "OHHHHHHH! OHHHHHHH! GO LAVAL, GO LAVAL GO! GO LAVAL, GO LAVAL GO! GO LAVAL, GO LAVAL GO!" The coach jumped in, then the girls' team. I was uncomfortable – we were usually the loudest team on the start line, but we were outnumbered. Laval was roaring despite having left four big players at home.

"Runners, on your marks."

We stood two runners abreast. Cal and Scott took the front two spots.

"POW!"

I rushed towards the front, with Cal next to me. Neuffer and Scott followed. A herd of one hundred runners jostled for positioning while running the small gravel downgrade kicking off the Odell Park 2.5k loop. The front was crowded. It seemed as though fifty runners in this race were aiming for a top-ten finish. A few big, bulky runners from Sherbrooke and Concordia were annoyingly hogging the lead, only to get sidestepped like pylons within the next hundred metres by a herd of coiled-legged aerobic wildebeests. I ran on Scott's shoulder, not conceding an inch of ground. We used the momentum of the downhill to power up a windy gravel path leading us to a trail in the woods. Thanks to the difficulty of the hill, the front pack thankfully receded in numbers. We were finally settling into our appropriate places. The lead pack was suddenly saturated with St. FX and Laval singlets. Francois Jarry of McGill and Lee Wesselius of UPEI were the lone exceptions. To keep myself out of trouble and avoid any collision, I ran at the front as we descended the woodsy, narrow trail while dodging trees. Cal ran next to me. Emmanuel Boisvert and Jonathan Tedeschi of Laval matched our strides from two metres back. We rounded the first loop and passed in front of the crowd. 2km complete.

The cheers were loud for our pack of ten. We changed positions with Neuffer, then Scott, then Emmanuel. I spotted Scott on my shoulder. We shared the lead going up the start hill a second time. On the other side of me was Neuffer, pumping his arms, looking around. His perplexed look confirmed that he was thinking what I had been thinking. *Where is Yves?* Yves Sikubwabo, the Rwandan refugee, was Laval's star runner. He had run for the University of Guelph in prior years but had now transferred to the powerhouse Rouge et Or, making the rich even richer. He was a favourite to win the CIS national championship, but today, he was nowhere to be seen. This conservative race tactic was textbook for Yves.

We got to the crowded part of the course once again. Angus and Cal had fallen a bit behind, but Neuffer, Scott, and I were still in the lead pack, running comfortably next to Lee and Laval's army of slender men. Upon ending loop-two, we passed in front of the crowd. French screams were interspersed with English ones.

"Vas-y, Jonathan!"

"Nice and steady, Scott!"

"Parfait, Manu!"

Then, one cheer caught my attention. Being French-Canadian had its perks. "Ok Yves, il est temps!" is what I heard as I climbed the hill at the start of lap-three. Translating to "All right, Yves, it's time." I knew this could not be good news. As if he was fired from a cannon, Sikubwabo shot past our leading group, and strode comfortably to the front. Seeing him run made my stride look choppy and forced. Immediately, the pace increased. Igor Bougnot, an athlete from France picked up by Laval in August, bounded behind Yves. Cal caught up to me and was now keeping the lead pack in check. Neuffer and Scott stuck behind Bougnot, as did Lee. I ran at the back of the lead pack. Yves led our group as we charged down the rooted and rocky path for the third time. The pace was intensifying. Jarry and Angus had fallen off our group. I focused on Yves' back, not letting him gap me by more than approximately thirty metres.

I relaxed my body going down the slope and let my legs fly. I thought of trying to move past Neuffer and Lee to not let the gap between Yves and me elongate. For that to happen I'd have to relax my body, and let my legs coast down this hill, to pick it up at its bottom and surge. But, Odell Park's flora had other plans. For a split second, I looked up to see who was now running with Yves and let my guard down. BOOM! Before I knew it, I was on the ground with Laval's Dany Racine and Angus leapfrogging over me. My face was covered in dirt – my palms ripped and bloody. I had caught my foot on a tree stump and carried my momentum from the downhill stride straight to the terra firma. Shaken, I took my time to get back up, but the pack was long gone. I was stranded. We had under three kilometres left to run – I would not catch them. Luckily, however, I was in one piece. I kept running.

Up front, Yves strung out the pack even more. Cal and Neuffer dropped off the pace. Lee Wesselius, Emmanuel Boisvert, Igor, and Scott were still chasing the slender Rwandan. As they passed in front of the crowd, all eyes of the St. FX cheer squad consisting of the girls' team and parents were on Scott.

"Come on Scotty! Yes! Stay with them!" For the first time this year, Scott was showing his full deck. He had won in Maine and Moncton, both times looking great. At Point Pleasant Park, he had not raced. Now, he had judged that it was late enough in the season to loosen the reins and truly test himself against four worthy competitors. Up the final hill, Yves was long gone. Perhaps the best runner in the country, he was untouchable. The battle for second, however, was fierce. Scott ran next to Igor and Emmanuel, Laval's second and third men. As they exited the woods, Scott was leading their pack, and Emmanuel was falling behind.

"Make him hurt Scott! Now! Now! NOW!" Bernie was fully invested in the race.

"Give fifty!!" Up the long grass hill, Scott injected some pace and dropped Emmanuel. Igor stayed on his shoulder. The wiry Frenchman ran neck and neck with the red-faced, scrappy Ontarian. Both darted towards the finish.

Laval's head coach was running alongside Igor screaming. "Finis-le! Enwaye! C'est à toi!"

A sea of blue was cheering for Scott on the other side. Grinding their teeth, neither was able to break the other. They crossed in almost-perfect synchrony. Later, chip timing showed that Igor had beaten Scott by 0.29 seconds, an incredibly marginal victory in cross-country racing. Cal came in fourteen seconds later, in seventh place – another strong showing. Like in Maine, he was our second man. Seven seconds behind Cal was Neuffer, in ninth. I had managed to pass Angus again on the last loop, and finish eleventh. The sophomore was fourteenth. Favero and Paul had run together for a good part of the race and had come in twenty-sixth and twenty-eighth, respectively. Addison had fallen way behind in fifty-second, and Warren, who had been feeling sluggish under the weight of hard workouts, was fifty-fourth.

"Scott! Great work! You looked awesome out there!" said Laura, helping us clear the finish-line chute.

"Thanks, I felt good. But I thought we'd give Laval a better challenge." Scott was right. A score of nineteen for them and forty for us was not what we were looking for, especially since they had left an important part of their team at home. "We have some work to do."

"Cyr, are you ok?" Brenda Chisholm asked, noticing a few cuts on my leg.

"Yeah I'm fine. Just pissed. I should have gotten up faster after falling – I kind of gave up. If this were CIS, I would have been screwed."

"Well, get dusted off or something. You look like an oak tree." She brushed the dirt off of my back. "Ugh, it would be easier for all of us if you stay up on your feet next time." "Guys, let's cool down, no sense waiting around," said Scott, all business. "Neuffer, are you coming?"

"Ahh, I'm good. I think I'm just going to stretch. My shin is really sore." His tone sent a chill down my spine. We had heard this bad news many times before today. Neuffer was so prone to stress fractures that it was a miracle he had made it to the middle of October on healthy legs. But now, the injury bug was catching up to him at the worst time. He limped off the course and met up with his parents with an ice bag on his shin.

Nervously, Cal and I began cooling down on the course. "Oh God. There it is. Well, we're screwed for CIS," said Cal. I did not want to agree with him, but he was being realistic. Without a healthy Neuffer, we did not stand a chance to rival with the best teams in the country. He was good for twenty to thirty points. His replacement, Favero or Paul, would more likely score sixty to seventy. That forty-point gap was all the difference.

"I can't believe this is happening to him again. He's been so cautious this year," I said. "What if it's another stress fracture?"

"Here is what scares me," said Cal. "He could take two weeks off right now and get healthy for CIS, but that would cause him to miss AUS. Bernie should step in and take Neuffer out of AUS, but Neuffer won't let that happen because he wants to win. But, he is going to get severely injured if he doesn't take a break right now, and if he's hurt, we don't stand a chance as a team at CIS."

"I know. You're right, but we both know that's not going to happen. Bernie knows how much Neuffer wants to run at AUS – how much he wants that individual gold like we do."

"Yeah, but AUS is two weeks away, Cyr. Look how we're running, and how Scott has been running. If Neuffer thinks he, or anyone else for that matter, stands a strong chance to win the gold over Scott right now, they're delusional. Neuffer needs time off."

"Yeah, you're right, I guess. The way he's limping, it seems like he'd need more than two weeks," I added. "And then, if it's more than two weeks, he loses considerable fitness." "Maybe, but if someone can put something together off weeks of cross-training," Cal reminded me, "it's he." That, we had learned from experience.

Possible Eventuality

October 17th

"Guys, I have a secret!" I stopped doing my pre-run activation exercises and looked up to the change room door entrance. Cal had barged in, giddy. Barely two days recovered from battling Laval's men, he seemed to have replenished his energy stores. "This secret is a good secret. It will go for twenty dollars!"

"Wait, so you're selling a secret?" asked Matt.

"Yup! And I'm willing to negotiate down to fifteen dollars, but no less because this one is juicy!"

Angus stood next to him, giggling. "He's right. I bought it and it was worth every penny."

"You bought Cal's secret for twenty dollars?" reiterated Matt, confused as to why this secret was making Cal a small fortune.

"Well, ten dollars. Roommate Discount. Hey Cyr, the discount could also apply to you if you want it!"

"Nah, I'm going to get it out of him some other way," I said, curious. "Can you give me a hint?"

"Nope. Well, a small one. It involves a member of our team."

"Fuller? No! Paul?" asked Ed.

"Ah! I'm saying no more! Hmm...I may have to increase the price of this secret if the demand is so high. Get it now while it still sits at twenty dollars!"

"Ok we'll figure this out on the run. Let's go. Who's missing?" asked Scott.

"Neuffer, but he doesn't run on Mondays. O'Regan, but he has not been coming for a while. Wait, where is Ferg?" I said as I scanned the room.

WHOOSH. The door burst open and a flustered Warren Ferguson stormed in the room in a shirt and tie. "Sorry I'm late, guys. I'll be ready in thirty seconds," he said, changing in a stupor.

"Ferg you look like you're dressed up to go to the ball!" joked Nathan Jeffs. "What's the occasion?"

Before he got to answer, a second body stormed through the change room door. It was Bernie. "Ok guys, it's 5:18 and I still don't see one of you out there! Pitter Patter, come on! And Warren, why are you dressed like you're going to your grandmother's funeral?"

"Uh, well I-I, uhm. No reason, really. Ahh, today came with a possible eventuality or a-uhm well nothing really, it's nothing. I-it-it doesn't matter. Nothing consequential. Nothing important." Warren always rambled when pressed with questions that made him nervous.

"A what?" asked Bernie, puzzled.

"Just a-uhm… a possible eventuality – it… it doesn't matter. It is in the past."

"Well, either way, you guys are going to be leaving in the dark again. One of you should be wearing those reflective vests because we're getting into October and cars get cranky when they see a group of runners taking up the whole street."

"Especially when one of them is 6'4" and running on the middle yellow line," quipped Angus, staring at Fuller.

The giant did not acknowledge the remark, likely oblivious to the fact that it was directed at him.

"Ok guys I have the vest, let's go!" said Warren, feeling bad for having held the group back. We were off and quickly separated into two groups. I ran in the front group with Cal, Addison, Angus, and others.

"Ok, so anyone else in the secret pot?" asked Cal.

"I'm not paying you twenty dollars for a secret. You can forget about it!" I said, laughing. "But I want to know what it is."

"Ok! One more hint, then. It is the following: the happenings of the last five minutes should serve as a lead."

"What's happened in the last five minutes?" asked Addison. "Oh! Bernie telling us to hurry up! He's cranky for some reason. Something happened to Bernie! He lost a cribbage game or something?"

"Nope."

"We were late to run. Late... does it have something to do with O'Regan??"

"Wrong again, Addison."

"Ferg!" said Paul, running to Cal's right. "He was dressed up for something! And there is a reason he was late for practice!" Angus and Cal started to laugh.

"What, was he at another one of those academic luncheons he always gets invited to?" asked Favero.

"Nope," giggled Cal.

"Did he have to sit in on a hearing with the student ethics board?"

"Nope!"

"Was he presenting a thesis? Listening to a thesis?" A nicely dressed Warren Ferguson could have meant a million things.

"Ok Angus, want to tell them? No way I'm making twenty dollars off these guys," said Cal.

Angus looked around to make sure that Warren was running with the second pack. "Well, it appears as though Ellen and Cal ran into Ferg at the Tall and Small today, and he was with... A GIRL!"

"Ohhhhh," the rest of us chanted in unison.

"She was cute, too," added Cal.

"Did it seem like it was going well?" I asked.

"Well, I don't know, but he got all red in the face and kept putting his hands in his pockets and then taking them out as soon as he saw Ellen and me. He quickly muttered something to the girl and then pretended to ignore us."

"Ha ha! Probably because he knew that this would happen," I said. Our team had grown so close that there was no such thing as confidentiality, and kept secrets were things of the past. If you were to tell one brother or sister, the rest of the family was bound to find out. In this case, I decided to not ask Warren about it because he, especially, tried his best to remain quiet about his dating life.

"Ferg, what an animal. I knew he could pull," added Edward in a proud tone. "So then is there a second date? Is that part of the secret, Cal?"

"I don't know, maybe. It's a possible eventuality."

"The Days"

October 19th

"Fellas!" Patrick Marlow kicked off his shoes and plopped himself on the red three-seater in the middle of our living room.

"Yo Pat!" I yelled, from the kitchen. "Coming for the run?"

"You bet! I was bored, so I figured I'd drop by before to kill some time."

"Hey buddy!" Scott called while coming out of his room. "I feel like I haven't seen you in years."

"Well, it's been at least a week. I was travelling with Dad, so you're almost right," the blonde, twenty-three-year-old answered. Born and raised in Antigonish, Patrick Marlow was well liked by all of us. He had been a member of the team in my first and second year, before taking a break from running competitively. Injuries in his Achilles tendon had slowed him down. Last year, he had graduated from St. FX with a degree in human kinetics, and was currently working at Boston Pizza, weighing his options for the years to come. "Figured I'd hop in with the boys for one of their last runs before the AUS champs. Are you guys feeling good?"

"Well, Neuffer is downstairs, and he likely won't come. His shin has been giving him a hard time," I said.

"Again? My God that boy has bad luck. Will he be good to race?"

"Race? He wants to win," said Scott. "I think he'll be just fine. He's popping pain killers apparently."

"Well, as long as he doesn't try to kill himself. The AUS team race won't even be close. He wouldn't even have to run and you'd still win." Patrick had been following our season closely. "But Cal and Angus are coming? O'Regan?"

"You bet," groggily said O'Regan, waking up from his daily nap – or was it morning for him? "Wow, is it almost five? I must have slept for, like, three hours. What's up Pat?"

"Get your running shorts on, we're taking off!" I urged him. "Cal and Angus will meet us there."

Jogging slowly down the Greening Hill, we tried to get our legs warmed up. My arches were sore, but thanks to Laura's tape jobs, I was managing.

"Scott, is your knee still bugging you?" asked Patrick.

"Not really, I think putting on some kinetic tape is just ritualistic at this point."

"Well, not even three weeks out of CIS, and everyone seems ok, save for Neuffer. Those are some pretty good numbers, guys! I've seen worse." Patrick knew how badly injuries could ruin a team's chance at the national championship – especially a team as shallow as ours. We were deep compared to other AUS schools, but to have only six runners run under nine minutes for 3000 metres would make us candy for bigger schools as soon as we lost one or two of our key runners.

Against the October sun and a slight breeze, the four of us jogged by the fast-food restaurants on James Street, crossed the intersection of Convocation and West, and rounded the Oland Centre to meet the rest of the team at the starting point. It was a beautiful autumn day. Leaves had fallen and made the grass areas multi-coloured and squishy.

"Gentlemen!" greeted Bernie. "You're just in time. I think everyone is here. Do you recognize them all, Father?" He was addressing Father Stanley MacDonald, St. FX athletics' most passionate fan.

"Well, I do recognize most of you," he said, as he gazed at our pack of X-Men and X-Women. "Usually, when I see you though, you are moving much faster, so now I'm confused!" Father Stan would often watch us do drills and strides on the outdoor track while on his morning walks. He revelled at how well we were doing in conference races thus far; he loved seeing St. FX win. He had tasted success of his own, back in his undergraduate days in the 1950s, serving the X-Men as a dual-sport athlete in hockey and rugby. I figured he had been a bit taller and more upright at that time in his life. His love for our school was contagious; he rarely missed an athletic contest on campus.

Now mostly retired from priesthood, he had even more time to attend games and races. This weekend would be no different.

Bernie addressed us again: "Father Stan is quite excited to get the opportunity to see you race at the AUS championship this weekend, given that we are hosting the event."

"Yes! We have not hosted the AUS cross-country championship in years! Boy, I love watching people run. It requires discipline, patience, and... guts. Yes! A combination of all three." Father Stan had of way of preaching everything he said, so that his listeners became mesmerized by his wisdom. "So, I came here today to wish you luck. Saturday is coming up, and I may not see you before your race. Please know that when you line up on the start line, you are not alone. You have coaches; teammates, and most numerous of all, community members watching and supporting you. Believe in their power and know that you are well surrounded with people who care about you – people who want to see you succeed. So run like you can, I am anxious and excited to watch you go."

As a group, we thanked him.

"Father, we appreciate your guidance here," said Bernie. "And the runners are excited to show you what they can do. Now it's 5:15, so they have to go. Where to, Angus?"

"West River today!"

In long-sleeved shirts and shorts, we shook Father Stan's hand before rolling out for an easy Thursday night shuffle. He sent us off appropriately, using his distinct cheering voice: "GO X GO!"

The run was peaceful. For once, we remained in a single pack for the duration of the run. We were thirteen runners, moving in synchrony between the leaves. The thermometer read five degrees Celsius – comfortable running weather. Nobody pushed the pace, given that we were racing in two days.

"Ahh, I miss this!" exclaimed Patrick. "Guys, I'm seriously thinking about coming back next year. I'm about to apply to the St. FX Bachelors of Education program. I want to get back to running with the boys."

"Really?" said Warren, jumping into the conversation. He knew Neuffer had more strongly been considering taking the same route as of late. "Do it. I'm sure it would be nice for Neuffer having another senior around."

"Yeah, I think I want to. I've really been missing these times with the guys. I've been feeling great, too.

"Yeah, it feels nice to slow down to my pace, doesn't it guys?" teased Scott.

"Now that Neuffer's not here, the pack doesn't separate. Nobody is pushing the pace. We've found the culprit!" exclaimed Cal.

We kept strolling along to the sound of our footsteps crushing leaves. The run seemed to fly by. By the last stretch of the loop, we were running along James Street and its long, steady down grade. Nobody felt tired, and nobody felt strain.

Nic Favero ran with a smile, giddy. He was bouncing off the ground, as he surged to the front. "Ah man. You know what guys? These days are the days, man."

"Huh?" I asked, confused.

"Yo, you know. You know what I mean."

"Uhm... no Nic, I don't think I follow."

"Cyr, man! These are the days. It's still nice out, but not too nice. It's getting cold, but the boys are all together and still grinding. I feel really fit and skinny. It's like we're hardened now. Man, cross-country just feels so good, you know? It's the days! These days! The days!"

"Uhm... I guess I know what you mean," I answered, still muddled.

Teammates exchanged looks of semi-confusion, trying to make sense of Favero's observations. He did not care. He just smiled to himself and whispered under his breath once more, "The days...these days," and led the way all the way to campus.

Living Room Stare-down

October 28th

The few days before the conference championship flew by. Mid terms were written, assignments were passed in, and a few seniors presented their thesis proposals. On the running side of things, intensity was ramping up. Our volume had hit its peak a few weeks beforehand, but we were now focused on nailing every workout and, especially, staying healthy – perhaps the most challenging aspect of a cross-country season. The workout on the Saturday between both races had not gone as smoothly as we would have liked. Neuffer had to sit out to rest his shin, and Cal was away for an academic conference in Halifax, so he ran the workout on his own. Our lead group consisted of Scott, Angus, and me. We all felt beat up and tired. Angus had developed a cold. Behind us, Favero and Paul were hitting slower times than they had earlier in the season, and Addison was nowhere to be seen. Ferg grinded hard, but he struggled. We hoped that our bad day was out of the way, as we toned down the difficulty of our workouts until the AUS championship.

We were at now Friday – one day out of our conference showdown. Uncharacteristically, it was quiet in the Greening household. Pre-race nights were usually loud and fun. We would open our doors to all team members for pasta nights and X-Box tournaments of NHL 2017. This night, however, knew no activity. The following day was one we had been anxiously awaiting. For many of us, it would be our last time running in front of the home crowd. We knew we would win the race; winning was not the challenge. Since the Interlock race, talks of the perfect score – referring to a sweep of the top five individual places – had infiltrated our conference. Cal, Scott, Neuffer, and I were expected to occupy the top four spots, and if one of us faltered, Angus was projected to be right on our tracks as the fifth runner. Favero, though not in his best form at Interlock, was not expected to finish too far behind Angus. On a good day, he could challenge him for fifth spot. Then, our seventh runner, Paul, had been the tenth AUS runner at the Interlock meet, and had started gaining on Favero. Needless to say, the lead pack on Saturday would predominantly be dressed in white and blue. Of course, Will Russell, Jake Wing, and Angus MacIntosh of Dalhousie would show their best cards to split up our top five, and for them to accomplish that feat was in no way out of the question. Then there was Jérémie Pellerin from Moncton. His walk had yet to match his talk, but he was a perpetual wild card, and we knew it. The version of Jérémie that had once run 31:09 over 10k was becoming an increasingly rare sighting, but it still came out to play every once in a while. Aside from them, Matt Power of Memorial University of Newfoundland posed a threat. Although he had been overhyped on the Trackie forums by, as one could easily infer, his friends, he had given us a run for our money in Halifax a few weeks prior. His confidence was sky high.

Our pre-race preparation was done. Cal and I had gone to the girls' house to wish them luck. I had also gone with the ulterior motive of borrowing Heidi's spare spike pins. She had spare nine-millimetre pins that were longer than the five-millimetre ones I had in my spikes. I would copy the rest of the guys who had already transformed their spikes into lethal weapons. Heavy rain was expected to fall and make a slip and slide out of our course. Now holding them in my hands, I was inspecting each individual pin. The slightest detail could dictate the order of the top five; a minute mishap could cost one of us a medal, or worse, a title. One single second could perhaps solidify one's fate as the ultimate victor, and another's as the forgettable runner-up.

By this time, we had all acknowledged that five members of our house could cross the finish line before anyone else in the conference, and it was an exciting thought. The idea of the perfect score was sexy and novel, but my thoughts had begun to wander elsewhere. I was realizing that in slightly over twelve hours, I could be the AUS cross-country champion. Even though Scott and Cal so far had gotten the best of me in races, I did not consider anyone out of my league. I had a shot at winning the individual title. As Fuller, hiding behind one of his infamous avatars, had put it on the Trackie forums: "The

AUS championship would be a pure dog scrap." I glanced around, and they were all there, resting their legs on our couches.

Next to me was Angus. He was the longest shot to win the title, mostly because we all were at least two years his senior. On top of his paucity of race experience, his nagging knee and ankle injuries had robbed him of important base mileage weeks in September. But, Angus was resilient, and had looked increasingly fit in workouts. We all knew that if one of us were to falter, he would quickly be grabbing a higher spot. Next to him was Neuffer. The fittest runner of late August had been playing compromise with his broken body as of late. His goal of winning the AUS championship was becoming decreasingly realistic as the days passed. That being said, nobody was counting him out to finish on top, including himself. A proven grinder, he seemed just as confident as usual, despite the injury. We all knew that his plan would not waver; he would push the pace from the front.

"Think your shin can hold up, Neuf?" Angus asked.

"Oh yeah, it's fine. Popped a Neproxin, all is good. "

"You're well rested, anyway. That's a good thing."

"I'm more than well rested, Beef. I think this body is ready to roll. But it's not like I'm the only rested one. Heard Cal sandbagged the Wednesday workout."

"Me? No way. I wasn't any worse than Cyr. We did it together! Who told you that, Neuf?"

"It was me," said Angus, smirking. "You guys all took it down this week. It's like if you're trying to peak for AUS or something."

I hid the fact that I had lowered my mileage this week. I didn't want people to think I was trying to taper now. That was not the case, but I also wanted to come into the race rested. A taper was tempting, because tomorrow came with an opportunity for individual glory. But to try to peak now was to be dishonest to the team and betray our end goal of peaking at CIS. So, I'd elected to bring it down a bit to be sharp for Saturday without trying to make it my best race of the year. I suspected that Cal and Scott had done the same.

Cal confirmed my theory. "Ok, yeah, I took this week a bit easier, but it makes sense! We're two weeks out of CIS and we're racing a 10k tomorrow. I'm not trying to peak for AUS. You'd be crazy to assume that."

"Oh yeah, no way! We've done all about the same amount of training this week. Nobody is peaking," affirmed Scott.

"I hope not. It's not our end goal, remember." Angus had reason to worry. I knew very well that it was everyone's goal to be individual champion – especially because we were hosting. Who wasn't chasing the feeling of crossing the finish line first in front of a multitude of their peers watching? We wanted success for the team, but a bit of self-indulgence had never hurt anyone. I hoped none of my teammates had let themselves get caught up in the hype about the conference championship around campus. I hoped I had not.

"You know," said Neuffer, rubbing his shin, "we're going to have to place ourselves in the front from the very start tomorrow. The course does narrow out pretty quickly. I don't feel like weaving around people." The others in the room anticipated his impatient racing style.

"Here is my plan," said Cal. "I'm just going to all-out sprint! I'll get to the squiggles first and take the best tangent." Cal was quietly having a strong season. For a guy who had dealt with severe burnout a mere five months prior, he was responding exceptionally well to the training load. I expected to see him around my vicinity in the late stages of tomorrow's war. He had won one race, Dalhousie, but I was not sure if he would have been able to truly take top spot had we been racing. We were always so close that it could have gone either way. He had never really stood out from the pack, but he also had never fallen behind it. But as we knew, it would take more than a steady performance tomorrow to clinch the title. If he ran as he had at the Interlock meet, Scott would surely beat him again.

"I think if we just run as a pack, people from other teams will fade," said Scott. Surely, as a fifth-year runner, he was speaking from experience. "I'll start strong, but I think it will be pretty controlled." As usual, he was radiating calmness. Scott was attempting to win his second AUS cross-country individual championship, having won in 2014. If Angus had the smallest chance at the title among us five, Scott was the favourite. He was undefeated in the AUS in 2016. All he would have to do tomorrow is beat the same competitors he had beaten all year. It was his race to lose, but somehow, none of it seemed to faze him. Whether his stiff upper lip was a product of extreme confidence or unparalleled nonchalance, none of us knew for sure.

In the midst of all this talk and speculation, I remained silent. I did not feel the need to say much. Tomorrow, my team would win. We would punch our ticket for the real race, the CIS championship. I would probably finish in the top five and battle for placing with my roommates. For thirty-two minutes, we would become bitter rivals. These were all given facts; easily predictable truths - truths that needed no elaboration. I had no reason to dwell on certainties. Instead, I was focusing on what was not certain, what was improbable. Tomorrow, I would do my all to emerge as champion. With a bittersweet sentiment, I would rob my closest friends of an elusive title. I would place a gap on Cal and Neuffer in the later stages of the race and charge towards the front to challenge my last opponent. Tomorrow, I would defeat Scott Donald.

La Bamba

October 29th

A ray of light pierced through my eyelids at 9:06 a.m. I had thankfully been able to ignore my pre-race anxiety for almost ten hours and doze off. I could not remember the last time I had slept so well. To the sound of "Novacane" by Frank Ocean, I got dressed in the way I usually would on race day. Shorts first, then singlet. Short sleeve, long sleeve, tights, jacket, and pants. I put my lucky orange Burke residence tuque on my head and made my way up the stairs to meet up with my competition in the living room. I came face to face with O'Regan, who was undergoing a Cal-led inquisition. Apparently, O'Regan had stayed out late the night before, and had disrupted the sleep of a few roommates in drunkenly stumbling back to his room at three in the morning.

Cal was too peeved at his roommate to think about today's race. "O'Regan, we asked you to sleep somewhere else last night if you went out!"

"Cal, it's my house too, I have the right to sleep in here. Plus, I had a friend with me."

"Doesn't matter!" shouted Cal. "We agreed that you could sleep in here on one condition: that you do not wake any one of us up. If you did not respect this, there was a consequence. This consequence was that we would get to shave off one of your eyebrows. You woke me up at three in the morning, therefore, I get to take the shaver to your face!" His frustration had morphed into excitement at the prospect of shaving his roommate's eyebrow.

"Ugh! I was super quiet," said O'Regan, lying on the couch. You probably didn't wake up because of me. I made sure to not even make a little sound; I knew you guys were all racing. No way you shave my eyebrow!"

"Guys, let's settle this after the race," said Scott. He and I liked our silence while mentally preparing, as did Neuffer. In the midst of the morning commotion, the most brittle member of our group was quietly sitting on the couch with an ice bag wrapped around his tibia while eating a bowl of oatmeal.

Angus soon emerged from his room with a head full of messy hair that gave him the allure of a sheepdog. He had been growing his hair for this very reason: to look shaggy by the time the championship races came around. He looked out the living room window.

"Guys, it is going to be a mess out there. I heard rain hitting my window all night. We better be ready to grind." I knew very well that the weather would not affect his performance – or any of ours. We had all become immune to external distractions. I was not a perfect runner in terms of mental toughness, but in October and November, my mind became impregnable. It would not matter if burning lava were falling from the sky; our individual hopes of winning the race were not subject to change.

After pre-race meals and little talk, five sets of focused eyes left the Greening household and made their way to the Oland Centre in Cal's Volkswagen Golf. Campus was already buzzing. The AUS championship was held in conjunction with an open cross-country race for high school students and open, non-varsity runners. Amidst the cars and people, we luckily found a parking spot near the Oland Centre entranceway. To minimize our time in the rain, we ran towards the door.

"I think we should stay in the change room for as long as we can," said Scott. "We get out to watch the girls while we warm up and that's it. It's cold and gross out there."

The guys agreed, except for Neuffer, who would go on to brave the rain a bit longer to witness his younger sister Maddy race in the junior girls' high school division. The rest of us found refuge in our warm change room. There, we met Favero, Paul, Addison, and Warren. The nine of us composed the official team – Warren and Addison being the alternates. Today, the senior and rookie would be racing in the open race, which would take place at 11:30, seventy-five minutes before our start time. It was currently 11:00, and they had finished their warm up. They were only in the change room to grab their spikes and wish us luck. Then, they would be leaving for the start line. We all threw a variation of "hey boys, good luck, run hard!" at them before they ran off. They did not approach this day with as much intensity as did we. For Warren and Addison, there were no stakes, except for the one of proving their fitness to themselves. After this race, their season was over, barring injury to one of the seven starters come CIS.

Before leaving, Warren reciprocated our wish of fortune. "Good luck everyone. If you need anything from us, we'll be around before the race!"

"Yeah boys, go kick some dirty little Dalhousie Tiger butt!" added Addison, in a way only a seventeen-year old rookie could utter it. They ran off, shorts already splashed with mud from their warm ups.

As soon as they left the room, Bernie walked in. "Hey guys, let's head over to the classroom here for a little chat before you get going with your warm ups and drills and so on." As a pack, we made our way to room 104 of the Oland Centre, where we usually held team meetings. Kevin and Bernie both wore the blue and white St. FX raincoat we had gotten last year. Bernie was holding a clipboard, and Kevin carried a kit filled with spike pins. We followed them in and sat in seven desks.

"All right guys, just grab a seat here, I won't be long."

Immediately, I could tell that Bernie was not taking the stakes of the meet as seriously as he had done so in the past few years. This was a good sign – we were on the same page. Bernie had made many of his past teams hit their peaks at the conference championship simply because he was not sure if they would win and move on to the national championship. This year, it was not the case. We were on the same page as was our coach today – we all knew we needed no peak.

"Ok guys, so I'm not going to beat around the bush here, you all know what you have to do today," said Bernie, sitting down at the professor's desk and folding his hands together. Unlike what was seen in most university class-rooms, we crowded the two front rows and listened attentively. "Guys, we've worked for this for weeks. Even though the big race or big dance or whatever you want to call it is still only in fourteen days, today carries importance because this is your first 10k. Today is a huge stepping stone towards what is to come, and I expect you guys to get out there and race hard. I know I'm preaching to the converted here and so on, so there isn't much that needs to be said about your racing strategy. Remember, even though you are competing against one another, you can still help your teammates during the race. I don't want to see one guy leading the whole thing. If on the first lap, Cal is leading, then Neuffer should take the lead on the second lap for a while, and then Cyr or Scott and so on. Share the workload. At some point, it's going to get hard and you'll be breathing heavy and telling yourself you're tired and sore and so on. Fight that with your mind. I've said this a million times but it is true. Run the first 7-8k with your head, and the last two with your heart.

"The conditions are not great. I hope you guys have taken care of the whole spikes situation. If not, Kevin has the spike kit. You have many people out there ready to see what you guys can do. Friends, colleagues, family, and so on. I'm not worried, and neither should you guys be. You all put the work in, and you're all physically fit. Mentally, I don't think any other team holds a candle to you guys. Working out in tough conditions, on grass, up hills, it's our bread and butter. So get out there and do what you always do. That's all I have to say. Kevin?"

"I think you covered most of it, Bernie. Get out there, run hard and things should go well. I have bibs here for you guys. I'll call out your numbers and you can come get them."

The seven of us pinned our racing bibs on our chest and marched out of the classroom back towards our change room hideout. I noticed Paul walking beside me. He had been quiet all day. At any time, I was dying to know what thoughts were festering in his peculiar mind.

"Paul, how are you feeling?" I asked.

"Well, Cyr, I feel quite good. But, the thing is, I don't think I will be keeping up to, like, you guys. But, I think that if I have a good day, I could give the top twelve a go. I just hope the course is not too slippery and wet, because I tend to fall quite a bit. My dad says he's seen me fall on the cross-country courses more times than he can count. He always tells me, 'Paul, it's a good thing you're not a dancer, because you're not so nimble.' Thankfully, he's never really seen me dance. Now that's a spectacle."

I just smiled and shook my head. I kind of had a better understanding of what was going on up in Paul's head, but I was not much further than where I had started. I was not interested in seeing Paul dance, but at least I now knew he had a clear goal. The sophomore was quite talented, and he had made big leaps since his rookie season. Squeezing inside the top twelve was not outside of the question. Paul was fearless in races, sometimes to a fault. I just hoped that he would run his own race, and not bite off more than he could chew.

We all entered the change room and Favero decided to take control of the stereo system. He blared an expected blend of J Cole and Kendrick Lamar while rapidly tapping his feet on the ground. "Man, I haven't been nervous like this in a while. Like, I don't know about you guys, but I'm losing it here," he said, rocking back and forth on a bench. His words echoed what some of us were feeling. We had placed pressure on ourselves. An AUS promo video made by Matt Eliot had circulated around social media, and its message was clear: that we were not only looking to win, but we were out to obtain the perfect score by occupying the first through fifth overall spots. The video had been liked and shared multiple times, and word had even gotten around the community. Rumours of seeing five X-Men cross the finish line before any other runner in the conference had propagated. It was exciting. Running fans were expecting a show. So many students had come to watch; curious to see if our countless miles run around campus in weird clothing would actually amount to something.

"Cyr, can I borrow your headphones?" asked Cal. Even he was not in the mood to talk much. We plugged music in and sunk into our own individual mental spaces for a solid half hour.

Things stayed quiet until Warren stormed in the room. "Guys, make sure your pins are screwed in tight, it's very slippery out there."

"How was the race, Ferg?"

"Ah, not terrible. Not great. I'm just psyched to watch yours to be honest." Warren wiped some dirt off his jacket. "But yeah, it's bad out there. Many people fell. You may actually gain an advantage by simply wearing longer pins than the people around you. His hectic delivery and presence brought everyone out of their slumber. He grabbed his cool-down sweats and left the room as quickly as he had entered it, leaving us to Favero and his stereo once again.

"Guys, I feel like this one is a staple," he said as he played "No Church in the Wild" by Jay Z and Kanye West. Everyone pulled their headphones out and listened to the now communal music stream. Head bobbing and feet tapping,

I was getting into the zone. Angus was sitting by me with his arms dangling to his side, glaring at the ground. The intensity had risen to a point that could only be sustained for another ten minutes. Then, we would emerge from the building to begin our warm up. I began doing a few activation exercises to loosen my legs and hips. Scott did the same. Soon, Jay Z's voice faded to signal the end of the song. Still amped, we waited eagerly for Favero to select a song of the same intensity. Feet still tapping, I waited for the new track to take over. Nothing was playing.

"Fabs, are you goin…"

"PARA BAILAR LA BAMBA. PARA BAILAR LA BAMBA SE NECESSITA UNA POCA DE GRACIA!" That did not sound like Kendrick.

"Ho ho ho! Oops, it was on shuffle!" said Favero. "But you know, I think this is what we need. It's going to calm us down a little bit." Ritchie Valens' classic tune never failed to lighten the mood. We respected Favero's mastery as DJ enough to let it happen. With tense smiles on our faces, and jitters in our stomachs, we all picked up our spike bags. To the sound of "La Bamba," seven men in blue and white walked out of the change room, and onto the battlefield.

Internal Battle

October 29th

Walking over to the course, I noticed the breadth of the crowd. I spotted classmates at all corners of the soccer field. Despite the damp weather, many members of the community were also present, wanting to see what kind of team Bernie had managed to put together this time around. Parents were interspersed between athletes having already run the open division race. Then, there were the familiar faces. Alexa Zarins was by the finish line. She had run for the X-Women until 2013 and was now working in the Alumni department at St. FX University. She never missed a home event. Krista McKenna, the sport information coordinator, stood by her, as did Leah Bond, the marketing and events coordinator. Pacing near the start line was Leo MacPherson, our athletic director. Leo's 6'7" frame and booming personality was deeply intertwined with St. FX Athletics' ethos – proud, loud and confident. He loved winning, so he had become a passionate fan of our cross-country team and of Bernie's.

"Gentlemen!" he said in a deep voice. "Feeling good?"

"Feeling fast," replied Scott.

"This is your day. Show all these people what you've trained for. I'm not worried in the slightest." After handshakes and good luck wishes all around, the boisterous behemoth rushed over back to the start line to catch the beginning of the women's race. As soon as we placed our stuff on the ground under our small St. FX tent by the start line, we began our warm-up trot of twenty minutes. The race would begin in fifty minutes. My legs felt bouncy, so I jogged to the front of the pack with Neuffer. We eventually broke away from the rest, running at a slightly faster pace.

"How's the shin?" I asked him, expecting the worst.

"It's just all right."

I had known Neuffer long enough to know that "just all right" meant awful.

"I popped a dangerous amount of pain killers so I'll be able to finish, if my heart doesn't stop. I obviously won't feel it during the race, like you don't feel those things when you're racing. I'm just nervous for the feeling afterwards. Like I probably won't be able to walk too well, and then I'll take a few days off." He was thinking out loud, as he often did when he was nervous.

"Well, take it day by day, I guess. You know you're fit, so as long as the pain is tolerable today, you'll run well," I said.

"How are you feeling?" he asked back, changing the subject.

"I feel ready. Little sluggish right now, but it's probably just the nerves. Oh! The girls are passing!"

We rushed to a part of the course where we could see our female teammates battle. Liz MacDonald was in a pack of three, battling for second, and she looked strong. She was poised to become the first X-Woman to win an AUS medal in cross-country since Melissa Hardy in 2013. She was gaining on Jenna MacDonald from Dalhousie. Close behind was Mary MacDonald, in sixth at the time. Hana Marmura, Zoe Johnston, and Heidi MacDonald followed in twelfth, thirteenth, and fourteenth spots.

"We'll miss the end if we go do our drills at the track," said Neuffer.

"Yeah, but we'll hear results coming from their sound system." We pranced down towards the track and joined the other guys, doing drills.

"Ok, guys, this day is going to go well. I feel it!" said Cal, hopping in place. His anxiety had, as usual, finally been transformed into agitation. Favero and Scott were doing drills, both looking bouncy and slender. Paul did leg swings, as Neuffer skipped back and forth. As a group, we ran a few fast strides across the turf, and began gathering our things before jogging back towards the soccer field where the race started.

"Feeling good?" Scott asked me.

"I'm ready to go. My legs feel great now. You?"

"Perfect, mine too. Let's run a smart race. Nobody will stick with us four or five if we run it right," added Scott. In contrast to Cal's pre-race rambunctiousness, Scott's presence was calming. He was in full control of his emotions and had an uncanny ability to think in all positive terms and themes. I had learned a lot from him in that regard.

At once, the sound system began screaming. "And it looks like Liz MacDonald will grab third place!!! Give it up for your first X-Woman!!"

The girls' race was ending. We couldn't hear how the others had finished, but it was our cue to leave the track, walk past MacIsaac Hall, and make our way towards the start line at the end of the auxiliary soccer field. We threw on our spikes and shook out our legs with the help of a few strides. I weaved around groups of spectators, female finishers, and competitors to stride out past the start line and towards the gate that led runners outside the soccer field and between Riley and O'Regan Hall – the two newest residences on campus. Running on the wet grass already torn apart by spike pins, I looked around me. The competitors were there. Will Russell, Jake Wing, Jonathan Peverill, Jérémie Pellerin, Josh Shanks, Matt Power, and company were striding about, also shaking out their legs one last time before the take off. I looked farther and saw the girls cooling down, stress-free. I saw Colleen Wilson, the winner of the girls' race, walking with silver medallist Sarah Myatt, both from Dalhousie. On the sidelines were the coaches. There was Rich Lehman of Dalhousie, Jean-Marc Doiron of Moncton, Kevin Heisler of Saint Mary's, and Bill MacMackin and Jason Reindl of UNB, among many others. Those coaches, whose names were revered and well respected in the Atlantic Canadian running community, had all been on dozens of start lines before. Their giddiness may have been a product of their excitement for their respective athletes coupled with the relief of not having to line up alongside them. Too well, they knew how it felt to wait for a race of high stakes to begin – to do their best to control their anxiety. Now, they had the pleasure of watching others do it. Also watching the race were some well-known personalities of the local running scene. Lee McCarron, Ashley Ryer, Alex Coffin, and others were anxiously waiting for the crack of the gun. If, in the real world, distance running was trivial, the setting and crowd at this present moment made it seem direly relevant. Today, a new page in the book of AUS cross-country history would be written. Today, the Atlantic Canadian running scene stood still.

"All right, boys, let's gather round," said Scott, calm but stern. Our seven gathered in a circle. Warren and Addison joined us. Following them were our practice team runners. After them was the entire girls' team. We made a circle of forty people, standing ten metres in front of the start line, where everyone could see us. Scott, as the captain and lone fifth-year runner on the boys' team, again knew his role as speaker. Like only he could, he traded in his calm and peaceful aura for his hellish grin and confident eyes.

"Ok boys, we raced four times for practice. Now, we start showing our stuff. This is the best simulation of CIS we will have before the real thing. We talked ourselves up enough, now it's time to deliver. Everyone is here to cheer us on, let's treat them all to a show. I have nothing else to say. Matt's video said it all. Today, we enter a new realm. It's championship season, baby. Let's race with heart. Hands in. HAIL AND HELL!"

"WHITE AND BLUE!"

"HAIL AND HELL!"

"WHITE AND BLUE!"

"HAIL AND HELL!"

"WHITE AND BLUE!"

"One, two, three, X!"

Like that, we took our spot on the start line.

"Boys, let's do it! Perfect score!" screamed Cal, before darting off the start line for a stride. University of New Brunswick was standing next to us. They chuckled at our blatant confidence. Some would have called it cockiness.

"Cal seems pretty confident. Ha ha... good luck today, man." I turned around to find Jonathan Peverill of Saint Mary's University to my right, extending out his hand. I shook it and wished him a good race.

"Yeah, well, let's hope he's not bluffing," I said. Like many other individuals in our conference, and in our sport in general, Jonathan was a merciless competitor, but above all, an athlete with integrity. We would battle for our half-hour, and undoubtedly congratulate each other by the race's end. His good luck wish calmed me down, as I stared into the ten-foot wide gate at the end of the soccer field, one hundred metres away. Soon, seventy runners would attempt to clear it at the same time. I dug my spikes into the ground, ready to duel with my roommates.

AUS Championship

October 29th

"RUNNERS, ON YOUR MARKS."

POW!!"

Furiously, our group of seven bolted off the line. None, however, as hastily as Cal. The lanky, 6'2 runner had somehow managed to put a forty-metre gap on the entire field in the first twenty-five seconds of the race. He was so jacked up on caffeine pills and adrenaline that he could not contain himself anymore. He was swinging his lanky legs and wiry arms so fast that he looked like an inflatable tube man in a car dealership commercial. I looked at Favero beside me and couldn't help but laugh. It was perhaps the fastest I had ever seen Cal run, and it was at the very start of a 10k race. He, however, had a method to his madness. He knew very well that soon, right after rounding our beloved grass three-minuter loop, that we would enter the squiggles. The squiggles made up 800 metres of gravel on each course loop. They were affectionately called such because of their wavy and maze-like configuration. To get to the squiggles first was to avoid jostling around its many turns and corners with a pack of runners. Knowing this just as well as Cal, I caught up to him, and the two of us led the pack through the first loop of two kilometres. The course was made up of two two-kilometre loops, and two three-kilometre loops – the longer loops having an extra kilometre of gravel trails to cover. As we emerged from the trails to complete the first loop, we passed an impressive crowd of cheering fans. I used their screams as feedback to know who had decided to hang onto the lead pack.

"Yes Cal!"

"C'est bien, Alex!"

"Scott, Angus, Neuffer right there!"

"Right on Will, Jake."

"Good job Josh!"

"Parfait, Jérémie!"

"Wooo good work Fabio!"

"Yeah Matthew!"

"Steady, Jonathan."

"Paul get up there!"

The sea of screams led me to conclude that we had not dropped any major players. Only two kilometres in, I was not surprised.

Entering the second lap, Angus placed himself in front of me. He now shared the lead and ran next to Cal, who enjoyed running from the front. I settled behind the two tall runners and ran alongside Scott. Like I had planned to do, I let my brain shut down between kilometres two and four. It was late enough in the race for the initial adrenaline jolt to dissipate, but it was too early to feel pain. It was best, then, to go through the motions and do minimal work up front. Naturally, no moves were made. Our X clan exited the woods and ran through a crowd at three kilometres. The people cheered at the sight of a blue and white pack leading the rest of the conference. Many others were still attached, but we looked dominant and in control. We would soon finish lap two, and begin the third, and first three-kilometre-long loop.

By the end of our second lap, I noticed some heavy breathing on my right shoulder. To my surprise, it was coming from Neuffer. I turned to face him. He sported a terrible grimace. *He's hurting already?* I thought. The extra effort he was expending to not think about his tibial stress fracture, along with the low mileage he had been forced to run was catching up to him. I instantly felt for him, but I had to keep focusing on my race.

"Boys, you're about halfway. Looking good!" The cheer came from Lee McCarron. He was standing by himself in the woods, by the entranceway to the squiggles. The former assistant coach of the Tigers had reason to cheer us on. He had recently parted ways with the rest of the coaching staff at Dalhousie, but still coached a few of their runners. He also had a vested interest in our runners, being an Antigonish native. Given that he held some sort of connection with nearly every runner in the pack, his cheer was for nobody in particular. This pack, however, was narrowing. Jake Wing, Angus MacIntosh, Jérémie Pellerin, Favero, Paul, and Matt Power had lost contact with us. We were six.

To my amazement, the lead pack of twelve had dwindled down very quickly. We had dropped six runners in the span of two minutes. And now, Neuffer's breathing was increasingly heavy. Angus, who had conceded the lead to Scott, had dropped to the back of the lead pack. We made it past the squiggles and charged for the trails around the soccer field. An increase in pace from the front made Neuffer and Angus hurt a bit more. Sensing a breaking of the pack, Will Russell – the lone foreign runner in our tandem of X-Men – inched towards the front to break up our sea of blue. His plan worked. By the start of our third lap, Neuffer and Angus let a gap form between them and the pack. Will tucked in behind me, and the four of us ran away from the rest of the conference.

We rounded the grass loop for the third time. I glanced at Cal and Scott. They looked comfortable. I then glanced at the fourth member of our pack. Will Russell was running smoothly, confident and focused. The muscular runner from Dalhousie had come to play. We had spent the summer competing over 1500 metres and had become the two fastest metric milers in the conference. Now in full cross-country mode, rumour had it that he was logging huge weeks of mileage. Fresh and tapered, he was poised for a strong performance. His blonde hair and broad frame gave him the allure of a European cyclist or cross-country skier, rather than that of a distance runner. He had never beaten any of us over 10k in the last few years, but he was a grinder, and appeared stronger than ever before in a cross-country race. We rounded the grass loop and ripped through the squiggles for the third time, running towards the spectators.

Passing by crowds, we heard that the chants were now only directed towards two teams: St. FX and Dalhousie. We still had control, but it was not complete, and some people were beginning to smell an upset in the individual race. We exited the crowded area and disappeared between the trees. Empowered by chants from his disciples, Will had inched his way into the front, leading with Cal. Scott and I ran comfortably behind them. Nobody was showing any sign of weakness. Then, with four kilometres left to run, Will did something none of us expected. With the help of twenty powerful strides, he surged in front of us all, and gapped us by nearly fifty metres without any warning. Thinking that Will would be content to merely run behind us and finish in fourth place had been foolish. Will hated to lose. But, was this move a bluff? Was he showing all of his cards? Would he come back to us? Or was he simply fitter?

After an initial wave of panic, the three of us looked at each other and realized what had to be done. Will could not win on our home course. The prospect of individual glory was briefly forgotten. We had to run as a team to catch him. By reading each other's modified sign language, consisting of hand waves and facial expressions, we communicated. *Stay together, run steady for now. If he is not coming back to us, we will pick it up on the last lap.* We chased him in the trails with three and a half kilometres to go – he led us by six to seven seconds.

The baffled crowd of St. FX supporters stood in silence, only to listen to the group of Dalhousie fans going crazy. For the first time in the race, my body became tense. I did not feel like we were in control. I did not feel like *I* was in control. Will looked strong. If our plan were to work, it would require patience. A hilly part of the course was coming. *This is on me*, I thought. I was a strong hill runner, so I judged that this moment would be the best one to strike fear into Will's psyche. I took the lead and injected a minimal amount of speed into our already-fast pace. Scott and Cal easily slipped right behind me. To my surprise, my plan was working amazingly. At the same rate as we were increasing our pace, Will was slowing. Within two hundred metres, he was suddenly a single arm's length away. Once again, the lead pack was of four. This time, however, Will looked weaker. We exited the woods for the last time to signal the end of our third lap. We rushed past the sea of people by the loop's end, which had now forgotten about every other unravelling storyline of the race. The perfect score was out the window. Only one question was on everyone's minds: who would take the gold medal and be conference champion?

As we cleared ourselves from the crowd of spectators, a steep hill was awaiting us. It was not a long one, but the fifteen steps it required to surmount it were enough to suck the energy out of tired legs. I remembered the significant ground we had made on Will on the last hill, so I again took a slight lead and increased the pace. Cal matched my stride with Scott on his back. Will slipped in behind me. Once past the hill, the pace continued to increase. I remembered one of Bernie's most famous training tips. "When you get up a hill, run the next fifty metres hard. It will break your opponent."

I tried to ignore my brain's command to slow down; it was too early for head games. *Give fifty*, I told myself. I tried to focus solely on the sound of our footsteps and ignore my increasingly shallow breathing. In the midst of my quasi-hypnosis, I had not noticed that the eight legs forming the pack were becoming six. I glanced over my right shoulder and saw Scott on my tail. Will, however, had let a gap form between him and the three of us. There it was. The break. We sped up. Such a gap late in the race would be difficult to make up.

"He's gone," I said. There were not as many of us in the front as expected, but it was time to negotiate this title between three X-Men. With Scott and Cal, I entered the squiggles one last time and attacked the last half of the loop.

"Fifteen hundred metres left. Focus boys!" Once again, Lee McCarron's cheers had no specific recipient. They were for each one of us. They briefly made me lose focus and mentally step outside of my current state. Here I was, in a real battle for an AUS title. The only two who stood in my way were Cal, my long-time competitor and close friend, and Scott, a mentor of mine whom I had very rarely beaten. With a kilometre to go in 2014, Scott had pulverized Matt McNeill of Dalhousie en route to a first AUS cross-country title. Both had been grinding and were looking equally tired until Scott found an extra gear and ran away from his closest competitor. I had watched it all, injured, wondering if one day I too would look as strong at the end of a gruelling cross-country race. As the lactate was building inside my legs, I started to think that I would look more like McNeil.

I held on tight. Like he had done two years prior, Scott chose his spot to increase the pace. Now in front of Cal and me, he stretched out his short, springy legs and surged ahead. Cal covered the move and did not let him leave his vicinity. The two sprung up in front of me, both looking strong. The competitive juices began flowing, and I held on. One kilometre left signalled the final push. Mental fortitude was needed more than ever.

The next five hundred metres were a game of cat and mouse. Scott would spring ahead. Cal would respond. Cal would spring ahead, Scott would respond. I remained a single metre behind them, tired, but strong. Though laboriously, I matched every one of their moves, growing too weary to make moves of my own.

We exited the woods as a unit of three. Three hundred metres were left, and the entire crowd formed a line starting at our current spot and ending at the finish line. Cal and Scott began pushing harder, and the two pulled away from me. My juices were running low, but the cheers of hundreds elevated me. I could not let them win! I put my head down and lifted my knees at a higher cadence. My arms flailed. My only hope now would be for both of them to hit a wall.

Maintaining a ten-metre lead, Cal and Scott were neck and neck. Cal began pushing harder, and gained one, two, three steps on Scott. Our captain was grinding but slowing. Seeing my counterpart revealing an extra gear got me pushing harder, and I was soon matching Scott's stride. With pumping arms and a distorted face, I caught up to him, and passed him. I was now chasing the lanky runner ahead. I had gotten my second wind. There were a hundred metres to go, and I was now sprinting. My teeth were out, and my face was tense. At first, I couldn't tell if I was making gaining on Cal. He was digging his spikes to the ground, swinging his arms and driving his knees to the sky, his head bobbing violently on every step. His body was destroyed, and pure will was all that was left to carry him across the line. I put my head down and summoned the negligible amount of strength there was left in my beat-up, mud-stricken legs and gave one more push towards the front, eying Cal's back. Instead of closing the gap, however, I simply held it, and could do nothing other than enjoy the spectacle ahead from the discomfort of my front-row seat – the spectacle in which I wished I had been starring. Mouth agape and fists clenched, Cal's look of pain and sufferance slowly transformed into one of elation as he crossed the line in first place. Too tired to throw his arms up in the air, he just screamed. Like Scott Donald in 2014, and Connor McGuire in 2011 and 2012, he had become the AUS cross-country champion.

I crossed the line a single second behind him, and Scott, three. I gave Cal a bittersweet, but euphoric bear hug. We had spent four years inching each other out in workouts and races. For most of that time, we had been mere seconds apart in fitness. Neither of us had been blue-chip recruits upon arrival at St. FX, but we had shared the same level of ambition and passion for the sport. And here, four years later, he was champion, and I was finishing a slight second behind, hungrier to beat him in our next duel.

"You, you did it! We did it!" I yelled at him, elated.

Between screams and suppressed tears, Cal was rambling, uncharacteristically. "I can't believe this happened! Oh my God. What a race… wow… I can't even speak right now." He was as shocked as he was thrilled. "Where is Scott?"

All it took to dampen our mood was a quick, 180-degree turn. In one glance, I spotted Scott sitting with his head bowed down between his kneecaps, and Neuffer limping towards the finish line. The former was trying to come to terms with his third-place finish – his worst since 2013. He was not one to dwell on things but getting edged out by teammates for the first time of the long fall season had to hurt. He had been expected to win, and anything less than top spot was deemed a failure of sorts. He was clenching his legs, teary eyed and distraught. I was surprised at how devastated he was. He rarely got worked up about a bad race. But if Scott's qualms seemed mostly mental, Neuffer's agony was direly physical. The fissure that had formed along the periosteal layer of his tibia had surely deepened. He had endured the pain for a thirty-three-minute mudslide, his body pleading him to stop after every step. Somehow, like only he could, Neuffer had secured fifth place on a broken bone, finishing twenty-dour seconds behind Will. He was one of the pillars to our structure as a contending team, and we could not afford to have him injured for the national championship. Somehow, I hoped that the slight, red haired runner, currently being carried off the course by both his parents, would muster up the strength to put it together by CIS.

Next to cross the line was Angus – his face twisted with discomfort. The sophomore runner cruised in his usual loping stride. The pain he was feeling was purely lactic. He had put in his best effort to catch a fading Neuffer, only to finish sixth, one spot higher than in last year's championship. He had raced fine on the day, but he knew that a more consistent season without sickness and injury was needed for him to reach his potential. "Who won?" he yelled, barely five seconds after crossing the line.

"Cal, then Cyr, then Scott," said Leo Jusiak, from the sidelines. "It was fast until finish. All three kick at the end!"

Favero was the sixth X-Man to cross the line. He had finished in tenth place. "Oh man, that went way better than I expected," he told the crew of spectators surrounding him, his hair in a muddy mess. He had gone through a rough patch, toying with the limits of his body in October. Thankfully, he seemed to have overcome it, putting up a strong performance.

"Favero, do you have another one in you for CIS?" asked Angus.

"Oh yeah, man. I feel fit. I was so nervous before today, but now I know I can race."

Soon after, Paul crossed the line in twelfth. The arrival of the Antigonish native elicited several cheers from the home crowd. As usual, Paul just walked off the course without making a scene. People often wondered if racing tired him out at all, or alternatively, how hard he was even pushing.

"Paul! Great race! How was it?" asked Hana Marmura.

"Well, Hana, it was difficult."

* * *

We rushed to Greening to shower and change for the AUS banquet.

In one of the conference rooms of the Charles V. Keating Centre on St. FX campus, Leo MacPherson greeted us. "Guys, great showing! Man, was I proud to don the X Jacket today. Awesome job!" said our imposing athletic director. He somehow dished out handshakes even firmer than before the race. My hand was still sore from the first one. "Coach Bernie! Great work again. You know when I say that St. FX punches above their weight class? This is EXACTLY what I mean. Proud of you all."

The nine of us sat at a table and listened to Alexa Zarins call out names of award winners. Five of us were conference all-stars. Three of us were individual medallists, and Cal was named AUS Runner of the Year. The nine of us were called up to accept the championship banner for the sixth consecutive year in front of Father Stan, Leo, AUS president Phil Currie, and other respected figures of our conference and university. Through clapping and cheering, we sat pretty around our banner and took pictures.

Once the cameras stopped flashing, I returned to our table to gather my belongings. Brenda Chisholm, dolled up for the occasion, sat near me. "Do you have anything more in the legs, Cyr?" she asked.

"Well, I hope so."

"Good. People get caught up in all of this. Make sure there is some left for the big show." She was referring to the CIS championship in two weeks. By way of travelling to championships with Bernie for years, she had seen many teams get blinded by the limelight of the conference race, only to let their guards down before nationals. "Just remember, Cyr. The real season starts now."

She had a point. The banquet had a way of wrongfully inflating our egos. Winning our conference was exciting, but there was still more to do, and larger beasts to slay. In two weeks, none of this would count. We would be squaring off against Declan White, Jack Sheffar, Corey Bellemore, Connor Darlington, and all of their teams. We would get to race against Yves Sikubwabo again, this time accompanied by Laval's full roster. We would see University of Victoria, Calgary, Queens, and other teams for the first time. We would have to be a better team than what we had shown today. But, despite Neuffer's injury, Scott's vulnerability, and Angus' worn out body, we were curiously content with our current standing. The awards, recognitions, congratulations and catharses of the day threatened to blind us from the truth – we still had accomplished nothing.

Two full loops

November 3rd

"Hey, what time is it?"

"Two-seventeen."

"Oh. Okay. Hey Cyr, are you going to campus anytime soon?" asked O'Regan, still in his boxer shorts.

"Yeah, like now. Do you want a ride?"

"Well, I have a class. So yeah, sure."

"What time is your class?"

"Two-fifteen."

Angus started giggling on the couch. "What Beef? It's an easy class! I have like an eighty in it probably. It's so chill."

Nothing seemed to bother O'Regan. In fact, if he were any more relaxed, he would probably be dead.

"Put your pants on, DJ, I'm going!"

"Yeah, one sec. I'm coming."

I hopped in my Honda Civic. Its top and windshield were covered with red and yellow leaves.

O'Regan entered through the passenger door, with a banana in his hand – probably his breakfast. "So what's the workout today, Cyr?"

"Ten times three minutes on the three-minuter loop. Same as a few weeks ago, but two more this time."

"Oh, ok nice."

"Are you going to join us?"

"I don't think so. I've started feeling like myself again, but I'm still not ready for workouts. Probably starting next week." Since the time trial, O'Regan had been dealing with racing issues. Whether they were due to his minimalist diet, his sporadic training techniques, or something entirely different was still up for debate. Unfortunately, he had not been able to put together a solid 8k, so he had taken a step back from training. Bad news for him – great news for Piper's Pub. Finally, he was coming back to form, hoping to find consistency again before the indoor track season.

"Thanks for the ride, Cyr. I'll probably be out to watch the workout tonight. So wait, if the warm up starts at 5:15, you'll be done at 5:35. So you'll probably start running the first rep at like, 5:45. Or maybe 5:50, depending on how long Bernie giv…"

"O'Regan, it's 2:22, get to class," I said, laughing.

"Oh! Ha ha, right. Uhh… yeah ok I'll see you later!"

I drove off as he began slowly shuffling towards the Keating Centre, staring down at his phone. I sometimes wondered how he was going to be able to get through an undergraduate degree with such a low-stress threshold. We lived opposite realities. I was driving to campus for 2:30, because I needed to finish an assignment and print it off at the library. From there, I would go meet my thesis supervisor on the top floor of the Oland Centre at 3:30. I would then rush down to the therapy room for an appointment scheduled for 4:00. By 4:30, I would be in the change room, doing my activation exercises in preparation for the workout. October had no breaks.

When I finally walked into the change room, Scott, Cal and Angus, who already were changing into their running gear, greeted me. By 5:05, all the guys had made it, and we were standing outside the change-room doors, waiting for Bernie's orders.

"Wow, nice to see everyone is ready on time. That's a change. I like it," said our coach.

"Must be because we're not waiting on O'Regan!" said Addison.

"All right guys, it's Thursday," said Bernie, leaning on the Oland Centre radiator. The warm air it deployed was more appreciated by the day. "We've had plenty of time to get that AUS 10k out of our legs. We are currently nine days out from the championship. We want a good one today. We will have a little chat before the workout. Off you go!"

Without a word, our group left the Oland Centre as a unit. Tights and running jackets were broken out. The temperature barely surpassed zero. It was, however, calm and sunny. The entire team was present for the workout, with the exception of Neuffer, who was nursing his shin. We ran two laps of the cross-country course, skipping the squiggles to make it an even twenty minutes, and then congregated behind MacIsaac Hall, by the start line of our beloved three-minuter loop.

"All right now guys, I don't want people bickering about start time, did we reach an agreement?" asked Bernie.

"Ten minutes!" Favero and I answered back in harmony. We had settled our disagreement as a team since the last three-minuter workout. Ten minutes, and that included bathroom time and time putting on spikes. Next to Angus, I did my leg swings, skips, and accelerations. Ten minutes soon passed.

"All right guys, just like last time. I want the first five to be taken a bit more conservatively – 3:10 pace. Then, pick it up for the last five. It's more about the effort than the pace, but just try to make it a bit farther in the loop on every rep after five. Cyr, Scott, Cal, Angus, Favero. You should be running together. Paul, Leo, Addison, you should all be close to that pack for at least the first five."

"Hey Paul!" said Scott.

"Yeah?"

"None of this branch-flinging shit today, eh?"

"Nope. You have my word."

"Three, two, one, go!"

Steadily, we took off.

"Switch leads for these?" Scott asked.

"Yeah. I got first rep," said Cal, as he surged towards the front. I took the second rep, Angus the third, and Scott, the fourth. The branches remained untouched.

"Good! Rolling well boys, hitting 3:07 average for the first four," said Cal, checking his GPS watch. We were already finishing parallel to the highway traffic sign, and the pace was very comfortable.

"Guys, if you don't want to lead, I take number five." Leo had come to play. He was visibly hurting more than the rest of us but was willing to give us a hand by letting us take a break from leading the intervals.

"All yours, buddy."

"Three, two, one, go!" The fifth one was steady, with Leo holding down a consistent pace. He ran a step ahead of Cal and me, then Scott and Angus, then Favero and Paul. Once again, we rounded the branched tree with no hiccup.

"Yes, boys! Work together! Let's go!" I spotted Patrick Marlow, O'Regan, and Neuffer, now present to cheer us on for the toughest part of the workout – the second half.

"Ok! That's rep five. Throw on your spikes. Now is the time if you want to do so!" called Bernie.

"All right, you guys good to crank it up a bit?" asked Scott.

"Yup. I'll take this one," said Cal. Number six and seven saw us average 3:02 per kilometre. Favero and Paul were beginning to drop back a bit, but still ran strong. Leo had fallen behind since leading the fifth rep, too. But all three had now formed a chase pack with Addison.

"Come on boys, number eight! The grind starts now!" yelled Kevin as we passed. This time, Angus led the interval, and increased our pace again. The sophomore runner was looking much stronger than at the AUS championship. He was running with confidence, daring us to keep up. He ran far past the street sign and hit three minutes. I jogged back with Cal, Angus, and Scott to the start line.

Neuffer was timing. "That's it guys! You have sixty seconds left before nine!"

"Looking great boys! These ones are those that count!" cheered Patrick by our starting point.

"I'll take nine!" I said, as I lined up on the start line. Scott, Angus, and Cal lined up next to me. Directly behind were Favero, Leo, Paul, and Addison. Behind them were Warren, Edward, Fuller, and Matt. Finally, Fuller was finally lining up with his training group.

"Go!"

The grass was getting torn apart. We avoided the muddy areas for better traction. In front, I led the guys around the tree and up the hill. I ran with focus and calmness, synchronizing my steps and breathing with Cal, who ran beside me. We rounded down the hill to finish the first lap.

"One thirty-three, 1:34. Work! Work! Let's go!" screamed Bernie and our spectators. Usually, Scott would break away from us by the ninth interval.

This time, however, we still ran by his side. We charged up the hill and finished as a unit.

"Time," said Scott, between breaths.

"Almost there, boys," I encouraged.

"Boys, I'm taking the last one," said our captain, dialled in. I figured he had been holding himself back during the last interval. Though we were approaching his level of fitness, Scott had the ability to really turn it on in these early weeks of November.

Slowly, we walked back to the start line. The girls' team had finished their workout and were waiting to cheer us on for the last interval. Twelve of them stood by Patrick, Neuffer, O'Regan, Bernie, and Kevin. Again, we lined up in our groups, and the last start was flawless. Tucked in behind Scott and next to Cal and Angus, all I could hear was focused breathing and light steps. We rounded the first tree, up the hill. On top, I pulled up and ran next to Scott. We went stride for stride, fast but controlled. Like migrating birds, we switched formations with ease to go down the narrow downgrade to signal the end of the first loop.

"One thirty-one, 1:32!" read Bernie from his stopwatch. "That's it boys!! Last one of the year!" Our observers had formed a crowd. Patrick had taken out his Go Pro to get footage of our last rep. The sun was setting and the air had reached a peak level of calmness, paralleling the monotony and focus within our pack. We rounded the tree one last time and powered up the hill.

"Two ten, 2:11."

Scott picked it up again. Cal and I matched pace. To the chants of our watching teammates, we reached the three-minute mark all together, once again.

"Woo!" I screamed.

"Boys are fit!" added Cal.

Scott stayed quiet but gave high fives all around. We grabbed our knees to catch our breath, and then turned around to congratulate the rest of our teammates. Angus was not far behind, and Favero and Leo were following him closely. Paul and Addison ran the last rep together. Warren and Edward ran a few metres ahead of Matt and Fuller. All had finished the high-volume workout. I just wished Neuffer had been here to run it with us, but he could not afford to punish his shinbone again until CIS.

"Well done guys!" said Bernie and Kevin. "The legs are ready now. This was the last truly tough workout before the show. Now, all about recovery!" added Bernie. He was excited with how strong his runners had looked. "All right, get your cool down done and we'll see you tomorr..."

"Uhh, can I just cut in for a sec, Bernie?" Edward MacDonald said, excitedly.

"Yes, of course. What is it, Ed?"

"Well, I just wanted to tell you guys that it's official. St. FX athletics is paying for two vans so that we can all come watch you guys at CIS! So far, there are about eight of us who've committed to the trip, and we still have room!"

The group cheered. "That's great, man! Always nice to have your support," said Scott. Our group of alternate runners had made the trip to Newfoundland for the 2014 championship, and it had been a blast to have them present. They had brought posters, flags, and even costumes. I figured that this time would be no different. Our team was every bit as passionate as it had been two years ago.

"St. FX has the reputation to be the loudest, so I figured we shouldn't disappoint!" said Ed.

"Great! So it's settled," concluded Bernie. "We will have more X-Men and X-Women around than Quebec City can handle. Just how we like it! All right, go cool down before you get cold!" He and Kevin watched us trot off past MacIsaac Hall and through the cross-country course. It was now dark, but the night was calm.

"Well, Bernie, this one went a lot better than the last three-minuter workout."

"Oh did it ever! Finally the guys are in tune with one another; none of this bickering and branch flinging and so on. Fuller even started towards the back today."

"Just in time. It always comes together by the end."

"Yeah," our head coach agreed. "I think we have a real team on our hands here, Kevin."

Icelandic Glacial, Neproxin, and the Burke Tuque

November 8th

The end of the week flew by. Every day spent in class was a carbon copy of the previous. Focus ran low, except for during practice hours. We were closing in on Judgment Day. With another week to go before the race, and only three full days until departure, the packing of essentials slowly began. Cal and Angus kept some Icelandic Glacial water inside the refrigerator. It was the only water they would drink in the days leading up to the race. When asked why, Angus answered as if the science behind their weird ritual was evident.

"We drink it for the high pH. The more basic the water, the better." The bottles went for seven dollars per litre. After ingesting other brands of expensive alkali water for the Maine and Dalhousie races and feeling unsatisfied with their performance, the two lanky runners had settled on Icelandic Glacial after successful races at the Interlock meet. Since then, they swore by it. I had suggested that they simply could have just been getting fitter as the season went on. They disagreed and cited the change in refreshment selection – Occam's razor at its finest.

Neuffer had a different set of essentials. He packed his prescription of potent painkillers, bags, and wrap to ice his shins, and the bone growth-stimulating device he'd bought from a shady website for which the jury was still out on whether it actually worked. His shin was now very sore. Time off had not done much to help. He did not need a physiotherapist to tell him that he had a stress fracture. He knew from experience. Staying true to his word, he still would be racing come hell or high water. Given his obvious limp, that water was dangerously high.

I packed my caffeine pills and my Burke residence tuque – the former for performance, the latter for luck.

Scott was at my door. "Hey Cyr, you have caffeine pills with you, right?"

"I do, want me to save you one or two?"

"Yes please. I want that extra boost." He was standing on one foot and supporting himself on my doorframe. He did not usually take caffeine before a race, but regardless, I would give Scott as many pills he needed. As he waited, he was excessively rubbing the sole of his foot.

"Feeling all right?" I asked.

"My foot's been feeling a bit weird. It's fine – it's been a long season."

I agreed with him. The last few days had made me realize how long we had been at it. We were stiff, sore, and skinny – not built to last. But, a bit of adrenaline and caffeine would get us to a hundred percent once more – a final hard effort was all we needed.

"Here, they're tiny pink pills. Take two."

"Thanks, Cyr."

Outside of Greening, Favero and Paul were getting prepared in their own way. Paul loaded his suitcase with clothing for any foreseeable circumstance. Jackets, pants, hats, long socks, short socks, boxers, briefs, bathing suit, sweater, gloves, mittens, balaclava, bandanas, and a morph suit for good luck. Nic's packing was simple in comparison. Racing gear, a ball cap and plenty of sociology literature. He had been walking around campus carrying a little brown book as of late, enthralled by its content. We knew better than to ask what exactly he was reading about.

***

On Tuesday, everything was packed by the time we met for practice at 5:15 pm. It was cold; the temperature now routinely dipped under zero. Winter had come early. Bernie looked around him to see perfect attendance from his men's team. Even those who were finished with their season came for one final run to send off the seven runners and two alternates, before hopping in their vans and driving up two days later. Bernie gave his directions for tomorrow – departure day – including take-off time and pit-stop locations. To our dismay, we were taking a bus to Quebec City instead of flying. A flight into the city was expensive for our budget. That was why we would be leaving on Wednesday, rather than Thursday. The trip would be ten hours.

"You guys ready? It's 5:15 and you should be going home afterwards and double-checking everything you've packed, so I won't keep you," hastily said Bernie. "I think Edward has something to say, before you all leave."

"So uh, boys? I know we've talked of having a fan bus following the team. Final numbers are in, and it looks like twelve of us are driving up!" said Ed, excitedly. The team clapped in unison. Our cheer squad was going to almost double the Newfoundland numbers. We had put in countless miles with Edward, Matt, Fuller, O'Regan, David, Leo, Jeffs, and Cullen. It felt right to have them, among others, there with us.

"Ah! That is fantastic!" cried Warren. "It will be like CIS in Newfoundland a few years ago! We had such a great time."

"Yeah, but this time Ferg, you'll have to worry about racing in the alternate's race instead of just kissing the cod on George Street," I joked.

"Ahh, nobody is watching that race. I can kiss as many cods as I want!"

"Ok off you go!" interrupted Bernie. "Tomorrow we ride on the bus. We roll into Quebec on Thursday. Go run!"

Thursday

November 10th

"Hey are we in Quebec yet? Uhm, I mean, est-ce que je sois le Quebec? Je... le... Français pas bon. Oh, Leo viens vite!" I shook my head and laughed at Addison's nonsense.

"Looks like I'll be ordering your food for the next few days."

"Wait, don't the people here speak any English at all?" asked Addison. "Will I actually have to speak just French? That's as good as I can get, I'm not making this up! What about at the Superstore, do I have to say anything to the cashier?"

"Addi, all you need at the grocery store is some rocket fuel!" said Cal, while taking a sip of a large water bottle.

"Also known as Icelandic Glacial!" added Angus.

"Oh no, this is going to be terrible," said Addison. "I can't talk to anyone! I'm supposed to bring back some 4 Locos for my roommates."

"Why can't they just buy those things themselves?" I asked.

"Because it's an energy drink and it's so high in alcohol content and caffeine that it's banned in all the other provinces!" said Addison, turning back towards the front of the bus. Next to him, Angus shook his head.

"Ok guys! We are here," said Bernie. "Get your stuff out of the bus. The hotel is overlooking the cross-country course. It's that big building on the right. Let's get settled into our rooms and meet in a few hours for supper. For those of you who want to run today, I suggest you go now. It's supposed to rain later, and it will be dark. Deal?"

"Oh I can't wait to see what kind of rooms we have. Maybe we can connect them like we did in Newfoundland!" said Neuffer, excited about the prospect of inviting over a large contingent of runners following the race. St. FX had earned a reputation over the years; we had become notorious for hosting the post-race festivities in our rooms. The tradition had been born well before our time, but we felt as though it was up to us to withhold it, much to Bernie's dismay.

As if he had heard us, he turned around and addressed the boys and girls in the lobby. "Ok guys. As you can see, this is a pretty pish posh place and so on. The lady at the front desk just warned me about post-race parties and drinking and things like this here. There will be zero tolerance in this place. This is not coming from me, but from the hotel staff. I will simply enforce it. Sure, you can have a few drinks once the race is over. You're all adults, and that's fine. But I don't want any noise complaints, or broken appliances." With these last words, he glanced in Scott's direction. The usually flawless captain had contributed to the dismantling of a hotel room in Newfoundland in 2014 that had left the cleaning staff in tears. "I want none of this 'St. FX is hosting this and that this year.' I don't want to have to come down from my room with my guests and tell you guys to keep it down." This time, he glanced at me. In Guelph for the 2015 edition, he'd had to shut down our party by himself while dragging his guest, Eric Gillis, along with him from the comfort of his room on the top floor. The rare sighting of an angry seventy-year-old accompanied by a confused Olympian slowly sipping on a cider had been enough to oust the other teams from our room. "Got it?"

"Got it," we said in unison.

"Great. Scott and Angus, room 614. Neuffer and Nic, room 618. Paul, Addison, and Warren, room 623. Cyr and Cal, room 612." Bernie handed us the cards. "Go settle in, do your shakeout run, and then we'll get ready to go eat. We are two days out of the biggest race of our year. Let's make good decisions this weekend. Good nutrition, long sleeps, and so on. Now, feel free to go unpack in your rooms."

With that, Bernie and Kevin were gone, leaving us alone with our keys and our judgment. Like a group of excited children, we crammed into the massive elevator of Hotel Le Concorde and rode it to floor six, to go explore our rooms.

"Ahhh, what do we do now?" said Favero in a hushed tone, as we hopped onto the elevator. "I really don't want to disrespect Bernie. He's made this clear. We can't just go behind his back."

"Yeah, I know. But it's going to be so hard," said Cal. "People from other schools already expect us to host. Like, how are we going to keep them away? It's probably still going to happen."

He was right. The party was an integral part of the championship. Three hundred skinny and mentally exhausted runners came from across the country for one final test after months of preparation. Such pressure would inevitably elicit feelings of elation or despair, depending on the end result of each individual's race. But in either case, the runners would then seek the elixir having eluded them for the entire cross-country season: alcohol.

"Guys, it's Thursday. We race on Saturday. I don't think that this is the conversation we should be having," said Angus, tired of all the party talk.

This ended our elevator chat and we separated to find our rooms. Cal and I picked our beds and ventured out to the hallway to see Addison, Paul, and Warren's three-person room, as it was supposed to be a suite.

"Woah, you guys have it made!" Cal said, as he peeked inside the massive suite.

"This is great! Two king-sized beds and a pull-out couch. I wonder who gets the couch..." said Warren, staring at Addison.

"Hey I'm not sleeping on the couch!"

"I wouldn't bet on it, rookie," said Paul, asserting his dominance as a sophomore. "Hope you can make yourself comfortable."

"Awhh... ok fine."

"Wow, look at the size of this room!" said Scott, as he was walking in with Angus. Neuffer and Favero followed them. The suite had a gigantic window behind closed, green curtains. I opened the curtains and realized that the room had a perfect view of the course.

"There she is, boys," I said, motioning towards the window. "For those of you weren't here two years ago for Interlock, prepare to meet a nasty old course."

Cal looked at the course, mouth agape. "Oh, those rolling little foothills, they killed me last time."

"Look, you can see the first downhill from here. It's huge," said Scott.

"Oh, that's a downhill. Thank God. It looks about as steep as Brown's Mountain. I swear the first time Riley took…"

"Ferg! We know!"

"Look at how quiet it is down there. In two days, the place will be buzzin'!" said Angus, excited. "I hope I finish higher than last time." He had endured a rough race as a rookie, battling a cold and allergies in Guelph last year.

"If we all run a bit better than last time, and add Neuf in there, we can win a medal," said Scott, as he tallied projected points in his head.

"Scott if you run any better, you'll be All-Canadian top fourteen," I said.

"I know. That's the goal. As it should be for you guys too," he told Cal and me. I had finished thirty-eighth last year, and my training partner was thirty-second. Top fourteen sounded like more of a dream than a goal, but who knew what a good day could bring? The race included 150 to 200 of the best varsity runners in Canada, all peaking for this weekend. Most of these runners, we had not yet seen this year. So, we could speculate all we wanted, but nobody really knew where they would stack up until Saturday. We raced in less than forty-eight hours.

Friday

November 11th

"This place is ridiculous!" gasped Angus, as we were walking down to the hotel lobby.

"Everywhere you go, you see big-deal runners and coaches! Hilary Stellingwerff was by the breakfast tables this morning, then I saw her talking to Steve Boyd and Dave Scott-Thomas."

"It's not a real CIS championship until you see Taylor Milne from Guelph," specified Scott. "The guy's probably been around since 1999."

"I saw Corey Bellemore walking to the course yesterday. He's so tall!" said Addison.

"Careful, though. We can't pay too much attention to those people. We have a race to run tomorrow," said Scott.

"Fabs, did you see Taylor Milne?" I asked.

"Taylor who? What?" My question had abruptly interrupted the sociology student's reading from the same small, compact textbook that he had been carrying everywhere, even at the mall yesterday. He was wearing a flat ball cap to cover up a messy head of hair, and glasses with thick frames. He looked more ready for a Ted Talk than for a race. "Uhm, no I didn't see him." He plunged back head first into his reading.

"Boys, anyone going for a shakeout soon?" said an unfamiliar voice. It was Jonathan Peverill, Saint Mary's University's lone representative at the championship. He sported a slicked back Mohawk.

"JP! Yeah, we're going at around twelve," said Cal.

"Great, I may join you guys. We're going out to breakfast now though. Are you guys all going then?"

"Yeah, provided that we can pull Nic away from his book," I half-joked.

"Oh, what are you reading?" asked JP.

Nic, not hearing the question, finally picked his head up, aloof, when he sensed eight guys staring at him. "Uhm, uhum, yeah. Oh, hey JP." He returned to his reading once again.

"Jeeze, I hope this book gets him focused. What even is in there?" asked Peverill.

"Your guess is as good as mine."

"All right, time's ticking," said Scott. "Let's go get breakfast. Where's Cal?"

"He's talking to Rich," said Angus.

Cal had scored very high on the standardized test for law school admission (LSAT) and would likely be accepted to Dalhousie University and run for the Tigers next year. Since hearing the news, Rich Lehman, Dalhousie's head coach, was giddy. Though losing the AUS champion would be a tough pill to swallow for Bernie, one could not study law at St. FX. Cal had no choice but to switch schools. By the look on his face, he seemed to be hitting it off with Rich. He sensed that we were waiting for him and rushed back to our group. We walked down Quebec City's busy streets to find a breakfast place, and quickly returned to the hotel. A few hours were spent digesting, and soon, we were in our running clothes, ready for the afternoon shakeout on the unforgiving course.

"Holy, this thing is hilly," said Addison, struggling and flailing his arms. "I am so happy I'm just an alternate! My legs are already sore!"

I usually made fun of his softness, but this time, he was right. No part of this course was flat, other than its very start. A hazardous downgrade shot us down and to the right, crashing into a series of little gravel foothills. A few little ups and downs continuously broke our momentum, until we reached the bottom of a steep, fifteen-step climb, followed by a bumpy descent. From there, we would serpentine our way back to the starting area, where the surface was rough and uneven. We would have to run this loop four times in sub-zero temperatures. Tomorrow would not be a day for the weak.

"Hey guys, feeling good?" Bernie had come out to greet us on the course as we were finishing up our run and doing a few strides. He wore a St. FX raincoat on top of a thick sweater and pants.

"I feel bouncy!" said Angus, right before throwing himself into a long stride.

"Perfect. Keep doing your thing and get used to this course. Tomorrow, it's going to be a lot mental. Many teams haven't run on something like this. Make this course an advantage. Most of you ran here last year for the Interlock meet. You know what it's about." Bernie waited for Angus to come back from his stride. "I have to go, guys. Coaches' meetings start soon. Tonight, I'd recommend Maison du Spaghetti for supper. Good food and portion-size. Brenda, Kevin, and I checked it out yesterday. Eat well and rest the legs – we'll meet tomorrow morning and go over a few things. Keep preparing yourselves. It's time."

Like that, he was gone. Nothing else needed to be said or done. The hay was in the barn.

After a few strides, we took off our spikes, and walked back to the hotel as a unit of seven. It was mid-afternoon. The temperature had reached a daily high of zero, but a frigid gust still struck our face periodically. According to the forecast, tomorrow would feel a lot like today. I shivered at the thought of racing in a singlet and shorts in this cold. I jogged back into the hotel lobby a bit behind the rest of the guys, my shivering body glad to find refuge.

"Alex Cyr?" inquired a man with thick-lensed glasses and white hair to my left.

"Yes?"

"Hi, I'm Gary Malloy. I think we spoke via email a little bit. I am the head coach of the Windsor Lancers." As a fourth-year student, I had begun searching for a destination to work on my master's degree. St. FX did not offer graduate programs. Since October, I had been emailing a few coaches and professors to try and narrow down the application process. "I just wanted to introduce myself so that you could associate a face with my name."

"Yeah, really nice of you. It's good to meet you!"

"Alex, I don't want to distract you from your weekend of racing, but I just wanted to let you know that we'd love to have you down for a visit at some point. We have a very tight-knit group of guys, and great facilities," said Gary.

"But like I said, we could talk about a recruitment trip sometime after the weekend, if you're open to it."

"Uhm... sure. Absolutely! I will be in touch," I answered, intrigued.

"Great. Well, I won't keep you. It was nice to meet you, and good luck tomorrow!"

"Yeah, thanks. Same to you and to the Windsor guys!" My brief interaction had separated me from the pack of guys. I broke into a jog to catch up and slid into an elevator with Scott.

"Where were you?" he asked.

"I just met the University of Windsor coach. He wants me to come down for a recruitment trip in the near future."

"Oh wow. That's cool, man," he answered, lacking his usual enthusiasm.

"Everything ok?" I asked.

"Well, yeah – of course. Like, this is an awesome opportunity for you, if a master's degree is what you want to work towards. But everything is moving so fast. You're talking to schools, Cal is likely off to run for Dal next year, and I'm done at X too. Tomorrow is our last race as a team. This chance will not come back."

He was right. I thought about never racing on a team with this group again, and the thought briefly saddened me.

"And that's not even the craziest part, Cyr" he continued, somewhat grim. "Our entire time here, our legacy, will be defined by our best CIS finish."

Tomorrow's race was momentous. A good one, and we would go down in St. FX history. One slip up, however, and this team would be quickly forgotten.

"I guess you're right," I said. "That's why tomorrow has to be the best race of our lives."

"Uhh, yeah. Well, either way, tomorrow marks the end of an era." We walked into my room. I screwed my pins into my spikes, apprehensive to move forward, though still not fully understanding how right he was.

In another part of the hotel, Bernie and Kevin were talking. "Well, Kevin, these coaches' meetings haven't shortened in length over the years, have they?"

"No, they certainly haven't, Bernie. At least all this talk about equalizing distance is put to rest now."

"The girls' race is 8k next year, and that's that. They finally got their point across." The two coaches hopped on the first elevator and Bernie pressed the number 6. "I'm getting jittery for the guys. They set a pretty lofty goal for themselves. I just hope they get it done."

"Well, Bernie, they've been coming together as a team. Cal and Cyr are in the best shape of their lives. Scott had a hiccup, but we all know what he can do at these championships."

"Yeah, it's not them I worry about. It's Neuffer. We need him healthy. If not, we don't stand a chance."

Kevin knew his elder was right, but he was optimistic. "I know. But Neuffer won't let the guys down if he can help it. He's said so multiple times. He's ready to hurt."

Bernie exhaled, hopeful. "I guess."

"Bernie, these guys have been preparing for this. You saw how our last three-minuter workout went. You saw how the guys are approaching this race. They're finally a team. Neuffer is willing to risk seriously injuring his body for the good of the team. Scott's foot is sore, but he hasn't said a word about it to keep people positive. Cal and Cyr plan to race together instead of facing off. You've been preaching to them about the importance of coming together as a team all year. They're finally doing it. Do you think Neuffer would have put his body on the line for the good of the team weeks ago? All he wanted to do was to be top guy. It's going to work out for them."

Bernie sighed again. "I hope you're right, Kevin. I know how much they want it. I want it for them, too."

They walked into their hotel room. It was ten o'clock. Tired, Kevin got ready for bed, as Bernie paced around the room before sitting down by the desk, studying start lists. "Dear God," he prayed, "let tomorrow be our day."

Saturday Morning

November 12th

Cal was meticulously planning out his day leading up to the race. "Ok. So, breakfast at nine here in the hotel. Then, small lunch at eleven to make sure I have enough in the tank. At twelve I'm walking towards the course, making sure I have everything. I take my caffeine pills at 12:45 or so, and then start warming up at one. Race is at two."

More quietly, I was doing the same thing. I would also take a caffeine pill, but at 12:55. I would eat a big breakfast at nine, but no lunch at eleven. I would instead eat a tray of raspberries at 12:30. After countless trials and errors, we each had our respective pre-race preparations down to a perfect science. There was no room for error at the CIS championship.

I was lying on my bed and looking at the lanky, wiry man twisting about like a nervous child in the bed next to mine – the 2016 AUS champion. He had risen from the ashes of burnout, and up until now, had put together his most dominant season. But, none of it mattered anymore. The other races were mere practice trials. Today was the show. This race was what people cared about. A high finish at the CIS championship was what one would treasure in their arsenal of racing credentials. It was a nugget, a token of a varsity runner's relevance within his or her sport. It tacked on meaning to the abstract nature of cross-country running. Winning random open meets meant little; finish times meant less. It was all about placing at nationals. I wandered out of my room to let Cal slip into an almost meditative state. I met Angus and Scott in the hallway. It was 8:30.

"Hey man. Good sleep?" asked Scott in a yawn. He was mind-numbingly calm.

"Yeah. I dozed off. Had a dream about today. It involved me leading with 3k to go."

"Then what happened?"

"I woke up. We'll have to wait and see. I'll take the lead today to try and find out," I joked.

"Cyr, if you plan on taking the lead, you need a 2:45 first kilometre, if last year can serve as any indication," said Angus.

"We're getting breakfast right now," said Scott. "Then, team meeting at 12:30 down at the lobby. From there, we'll walk to the course."

"I'll go tell Cal." I got my roommate, and the four of us walked down to the breakfast room. There, we met up with Neuffer, Favero, and Paul. We ate little and said less. I then walked back up to my room, immersed in thought about today's battle. Cal and I watched TV, while slowly getting our racing gear ready. He packed navy-blue arm sleeves. Mine were black. Our shorts were matching. At 12:27, we walked down to the team meeting room. Bibs were pinned on the singlet, spike pins all new. Cal sipped on his Icelandic Glacial water and I was eating raspberries. In the hallway, we picked up Neuffer and Favero.

"Ok man I'm freaking out more than I was before AUS. This is big." Favero was not teaching me anything new. I was relieved that he had temporarily ditched the sociology book.

Neuffer was concerned about other things. "Ok, so the meeting Scott called is just for the top seven right? Because Ed and the guys are here now, and as much as I'm excited to see them, I don't want to talk about the after party before the race."

"I think the boys will be on the course," I said. "I can't wait to see O'Regan and the guys, but I agree. No talking about that shit right now."

"We're going straight downstairs, I just want to focus," said Favero. The four of us hopped off the elevator and walked down a staircase on a far side of the lobby. A stuffy little room with hard benches and red carpet awaited us. It felt right to walk in with Cal, Neuffer, and Favero. We had run our first strides as X-Men together, and we were about to run our last ones side by side. A lot had changed since our first steps on the St. FX campus in 2013. We had matured as runners – as people – and not only because our facial hair game had dramatically improved. We were older, and with many races run together came the appreciation of how special our trial of miles had been. All the hard work was now done – it was simply time to capitalize. Along with my fellow seniors, I grabbed a seat.

Our only fifth-year runner quietly sat alone at the corner of the room. Though he made no noise, and took up negligible space, his presence was haunting. This was it for him. Unlike the rest of us, he had no years of eligibility left. This race was certainly his last on the varsity circuit, and he knew it. We hurried to sit around him. Angus walked in quietly. Following him – quickly running down the stairs – was Paul, covered in winter clothing from head to toe.

"Arctic expedition or what?" I asked him, breaking the silence.

"Stripping down is always easier than stripping up, Cyr," he replied. I was too focused to try and make sense of his reply. As we waited for Paul to sit down, we spotted the University of Victoria runners passing our room and walking upstairs. It was now completely quiet. Scott, as our most decorated and experienced member, took control of the situation.

"How's everyone feeling?" The question was genuine, but rhetorical. There was but one possible answer. "I'm feeling like this is our day. We have not only waited all year for this, but this group has envisioned this moment since freshman year. The senior-year CIS championship." Something was different in our captain's demeanour. He would usually address the team with a smile and a few jokes before races. Today, he was stone cold. "There is no hiding the fact that this is the most important moment of our running careers. It's not about chilling out and just hoping for the best and having fun today. That was Maine. That was Moncton. Today is about getting in there and grinding; giving it the best effort you can muster up. It's going to hurt. It's going to suck at parts. But, there is no way of avoiding it. We made it here. The seven of us earned this spot. We deserve to hurt for this.

"Our group is special and unique. I'm not just saying that, I would not want to attack this beast with literally anybody else. We're brothers, and we're ready to go to war. But, let's keep focused and calm. We have an hour and a half. We'll walk over to the course, get in the zone, and come together for one last huddle right before we go. Everyone with me?"

"Yup," we responded, in a calm, church-like tone. Without another word, we walked up the stairs, and made our way towards the lobby doors.

"Guys, let's wait," I said. For the first time today, we were about to come face-to-face with Mother Nature's wrath. The temperature was an even zero degrees, and Quebec's northern wind made it feel like minus eight. Cold rain, just shy of snow, was drizzling down from the sky. We had no reason to get out there before warm up time. "It's 12:48. Let's walk out at 12:55, find our tent, put our stuff down and then warm up right away. Otherwise, we'll freeze." The guys agreed, and we stayed in the hotel lobby, gazing at the battlefield through the windows in perfect silence. We cherished our last minutes in the warmth and comfort of Hotel Le Concorde, before Favero eventually got us all out of our trance.

"Ok boys, it's 12:55. Let's roll." Without a word, we got moving and marched in a file of seven, Neuffer in the front, onto our deaths.

"Be a hard-ass out there"

November 12th

* *Go placidly amidst the noise and haste, and remember what peace there may be in silence.*
— Desiderata — Max Ehrmann

It was cold and loud. Hundreds ran about, thousands watched. All screamed. The girl's race was underway. We skipped and stretched on the Plains of Abraham, amidst the noise. Our AUS co-representatives, Dalhousie, were given a box at the far left of the start line. The powerful Laval Rouge et Or were positioned in the middle box. They were both the hosts and the favourites. We lined up towards the right end of the start line, with University of Ottawa to our left, and University of Windsor to our right. I did a stride with Angus.

"Cyr, I feel good, man. This is my day."

I did not doubt it. Pressure situations seemed to bring out the best in the sophomore runner. He was a gamer. I also felt ready. My last race had been a good one, and workouts had been smooth. The only fear was to get lost in the sea of runners. I could not lose focus and let myself get passed by too many people off the start. Letting up for one minute out of thirty could mean losing ten, fifteen places. Each point counted. Striding next to me was Neuffer. His shin was taped up and he had taken his triple dosage of Neproxin. His face was still wincing with pain at each stride, but he didn't seem to care.

"Cyr, this is it. Let's do it buddy." Cal looked ready, striding past me at a torrential speed. The caffeine was kicking in. I turned around to walk back to the start line; Neuffer was already sprinting back. As I lifted my head, I saw him, surrounded by runners from Queens, Guelph, and Victoria. Angus was twenty metres to Neuffer's left, swarmed by a group of runners from Saskatchewan and Regina. The crowd of runners was thickening, with everyone now by the starting area. Our group of seven, usually loud, together and dominant seemed scattered and lost at sea. For each blue and white singlet, there were thirty to forty odd-coloured ones. I felt overwhelmed – alone.

"HAIL AND HELL, BOYS! TIME TO SHINE!" someone screamed behind me. As if they were heaven-sent, a herd of X-Men wearing the blue and white suddenly occupied important space on the grass ahead of us. Matt Eliot was uncharacteristically screaming from the top of his lungs. Soon, Edward joined in. The diminutive runner was carrying a huge St. FX flag. Following them were rookies Cullen, Leo, and David, seniors O'Regan and Jeffs, Fuller, Matt Murphy and Andrew Bain of the track and field team, and Gabe Quenneville and Stephen Deering, 2014 graduates of St. FX. The rag-tag gang of our biggest supporters had come to be loud and make noise – the only way they knew how to cheer.

Stephen walked towards me and placed his large hands on my shoulders. "Cyr, this is your last race as an X-Man. You only get this once. Be hungry and f*****g go."

I had never heard him speak with such emotion. The rest of the boys ran to the start line and stood behind us to collect the last pieces of clothing we would leave behind before the sound of the gun. They were boisterous and proud, and their enthusiasm was contagious. They had all driven from Antigonish to watch this race; to see us represent the school, them, and ourselves. We owed them a worthwhile performance. They were friends, teammates, and training partners – important parts to our puzzle.

"Whatever you boys need, we're here," said Ed. Bernie was also by the start line.

"Quickly guys, gather round!" Bernie was ready to give us his last words of advice. A few. "Guys, this is your moment. There really is nothing left to say. I know I'm preaching to the converted here. You executed at AUS, and you've only gotten better since then. When all the dust has settled, you will be happy with your result – whatever it may be – as long as you can say you've run as hard and as smart as you could on this day. You know what to do. Show them what we've worked for and get in your huddle. Scott, take it away."

"HUDDLE UP!" yelled Scott, appropriately out of character. He was fired up. Addison and Warren, having finished the alternates' race, also joined in. Our supporting crew followed them, and then some of the girls who had made their way back from the finishing chute enlarged the circle once more. We were now a unit of thirty – larger than every other huddle on the start line – even Laval's.

"Boys," he was screaming at the top of his lungs, "this is where we fire up. This is where we race with guts, heart and instinct. You want to work. You want to hurt. That's what today is about. I won't sleep tonight if I know I didn't leave it all out there for my boys, and I know you're thinking the same. Every place counts. When there is a guy ahead of you, remember that they must be hurting just as bad, and get up there. We need everyone. Hands in." The fifth-year runner had communicated his emotion and passion to all thirty mesmerized St. FX teammates and coaches, ready to witness our ultimate performance. As loudly as he could, he chanted. "HAIL AND HELL!"

Our choir answered, "WHITE AND BLUE!"

"HAIL AND HELL!"

"WHITE AND BLUE!"

"HAIL AND HELL!"

"WHITE AND BLUE!

One, two, three, X!"

I immediately darted for the centre of the grass bed for another stride.

"Two minutes, ladies and gentlemen!!" announced a man with a large bullhorn.

I loosened my legs and walked slowly back towards the start line. Then I took my place at the front of our pack, next to Cal. We could only line up two abreast. Scott stood behind me.

"Cyr, you have to get out fast, here. If not, you get burned, and I'm behind you. I'll also get burned. Be aggressive." I nodded to Scott. No way was I letting him down. I pivoted to hand my long-sleeved shirt to Ed, and a hand grabbed my arm. It was Brenda Chisholm.

"Alex, be a hard ass out there." Nobody could have said it any better.

CIS Championships

November 12th

"Ten seconds, runners!" They felt like minutes. I heard breathing behind me, beside me. The cacophony had dissipated, leaving place for 150 quiet, nervous runners and thousands of hypnotized fans. I looked down at my feet and saw twelve spikes surrounding them – the same twelve I had seen before AUS. Cal's white and blue Matumbos were on my right. Scott's shoes were behind mine. They were so beat that I could not make out their brand. My mind was bouncing from one thought to the next, jolted by caffeine, adrenaline, endorphins. It was time to shut it off.

"Ok. All attention on the starter!"

My heart raced. My body was numb.

"On your mark."

"POW!!"

At once, the crowd roared. Remembering what Scott had told me, I exploded out of the gate. I sidestepped runners, avoided potholes, and controlled my stride down the wide and treacherous downhill greeting the herd of runners before any separation could occur. When I arrived at the first turn, at 500 metres, I had passed all runners but ten. I knew I was closer to the front than I should have been, but it was better to be a bit fast than it was to fall behind and get stuck in a cluster of frustrated bodies trying to close a gap. This way, I was also sure that Scott could demark himself from the cluster of bodies off the start line. A teammate of mine must have shared my idea. One of the ten runners ahead of me was Cal. The anxious Nova Scotian was not only in the front pack, but he was leading the race! He and I had narrowly avoided a massive entanglement of runners the year prior in Guelph after getting off the line too slowly. We had learned our lesson – perhaps too well.

"Go Cal! Cyr! Scott!" I heard O'Regan's voice, then Ed's, then Matt's. The guys were all over the course, giving us reassurance. We approached one kilometre, still carried by a cloud of adrenaline. As we knew, the course was challenging. The foothills in the narrow dirt trail in the woods sucked more out of our legs while going at race pace. I pushed up each small hill, trying to preserve as much energy as I could in these early stages. Directly behind Cal now, I climbed up to the Plains' historic Martello tower – a fortress built for shelter in Quebec's period of fortification against the British army in the nineteenth century. There, I could see the girls.

"All right Cal, Cyr, Scott! Perfect! All downhill now!" I was reassured to hear my teammates' names called with mine, even if we were still only one kilometre in. I worried that Scott hadn't been able to have a fast start, given that he was not running ahead of me. But, then again, I was still holding down the fifteenth spot, and everything was a blur. Cal had relinquished the lead to a few of the favourites, including Yves Sikubwabo of Laval. He was now running alongside me.

"Yeah Angus!" shouted someone in my vicinity. Angus must have been in the top twenty runners – this was also good news. As expected, four of us were racing alongside the top tier of runners. Favero and Paul would likely run with a second pack, aiming to finish in the top fifty. I could not see or hear them, but I was confident that at least one of the two would provide a cushioning in the event that one of our top runners had a bad day. As I climbed past Martello hill, Bernie and Kevin screamed at Cal and me. "Yes boys! Perfect position. Top 20! Come on Scott, just like that!"

As I let my legs de-buckle down the hill, I realized there a name in our supposed quartet was missing from the screams: Neuffer. Immediately, I entertained the worst possible fate. It was uncharacteristic of him to start slowly. *If he could, he would be up here with us,* I thought. Was it his shin? Had he fallen? Maybe he was trying out a new tactic. I was worried but tried to focus on the task at hand. Twisting and turning up the final hill of the first loop, I had fallen back to twenty-fifth position. That was fine with me. Cal ran directly behind me. We had both settled into good paces after securing a safe path from the start line. I hoped that Scott and Angus were by Cal. Or perhaps, even, they had passed me and were running ahead of my pack. I could see nothing beyond the shoulders and backs of the runners directly ahead of me. The course narrowed in the last part of the loop, and it was difficult to see what was happening ahead. Without feedback from the screaming crowd, I could not locate my teammates, and amidst the madness of runners and cheerers near the starting area, there was now no way of knowing who was where. Roman Justinen of Calgary and Brayden Seneca of Guelph were a step ahead of me, Cole Peterson of Victoria and Eric Wynands of Queens, a step behind. This was all I knew. Someone yelled out the 2.5k split, but I was too focused to make any sense of it, let alone to do any mental math. Our group sprinted down the steep grass hill for the second time and passed the group of X-Men and X-Women attentively watching the race and counting places.

"Yeah Cal! Cyr! Twenty-third and twenty-fourth! Good placing!"

At least Cal was still up there, perfect. I could hear Cullen's boisterous screams, as well as Ed's deep, steady voice. Each cheer empowered me a bit more and I thought of picking up the pace, hoping that Cal would come with me. Three k into the race, I still felt no pain – the adrenaline rush was still carrying me over the hills.

Up Martello Hill for the second time, I picked off a few runners and found myself in twentieth place. In a field of 170, a top-twenty finish could go a long way in helping a team. Cal was only a few spots behind.

"Cal, get up with Cyr!" screamed Bernie.

I wondered where Scott was. He was likely in the thirties with Angus, and possibly Neuffer. Or, he was way at the front. If that were the case, we would be in great shape for a medal. As I approached the end of the second lap, I moved up, and started running next to Dany Racine of Laval and Ryan Grieco of Calgary. Both were picking up the pace. A bit of fatigue was settling in, but we were halfway. This feeling was expected. Besides, I knew I would be able to relax on the downhill and meet the crew of X-Men at its bottom. Gabe Quenneville had run up the hill and was waiting for me as I began lap three.

"Cyr, top twenty! Let's go buddy...right there, Cal!" We were moving up. As I rushed down the hill, I tried my best to hear Gabe's screams behind me. I could not hear him cheer for anyone else, still. We were past the halfway point, and I expected Neuffer and definitely Scott to get on my shoulder if he wasn't already ahead.

"Cyr, Cal! It's all you! Need a low stick!" Stephen's voice carried a hint of panic. I wondered why. Perhaps the guys were farther back than I thought. Was someone having a bad day? All I could do was to keep running. So many things could change in the second half of a race. I composed myself and turned right at the bottom of the starting hill for the third time. Though the panic was setting in, I still had to relax for a loop.

Without any warning, however, my panicking was validated a few hundred meters ahead. I rudely found out why hints of worry were lacing the voices of my cheerers. The St. FX cheer squad had gained a new member. As if in a nightmare, I heard my best friend cheer me on.

"Let's go Cyr, keep fighting." It was Neuffer. I looked at him in disbelief without breaking stride. He was now on the sidelines with chagrin in his eyes, and ice on his shins. Presumably, his stress fracture was too much to handle. The senior had been popping Neproxin pills for the duration of the trip, but despite the wishful thinking, he was in no condition to race. It dawned on Cal and me that our chances of medalling had dramatically decreased. We now needed everyone's best race. I picked up the pace. Battling with a few runners, I caught up to Emmanuel Boisvert of Laval and Nick Colyn of Trinity Western University. I crested the Martello tower hill and muscled my way through the serpentine course back to the starting point. With one lap to go, I was sixteenth.

"Two spots away from All-Canadian, Cyr! COME ONN!!" O'Regan shouted at me as I descended the long starting hill for the last time. I could be the first male All-Canadian from St. FX since David Gerych in 2008. My legs were now pumping on a new reserve of adrenaline. My oxygen tank, however, was running low. As I made my way to the foothills in the forest trail, fans of St. FX were screaming at me around every corner. Blue and white were ubiquitous. I listened for familiar voices in the crowd, needing all the will power I could muster. I tried to hide the fact that the pain I was feeling was intensifying. I hustled up and down the mounds of the trail in the woods, each crest seeming taller than the previous.

Justinen and Colyn were pulling ahead. Still no Scott. He had to be in the front. Perhaps top ten. We desperately needed it. Still no Angus, but he could be running at around thirtieth. Favero and Paul would have to come up big, but the chance for a medal was still alive. I hoped Cal was close behind me.

Thrusting my way up Martello Hill, Kevin Grant's voice pierced through the veil of white noise that had invaded my oxygen-deprived auditory system.

"One k left, Cyr!" I had never heard him scream so loud. I was now flailing – crashing. I ran on pure will. Ascending a small hill, my legs were buckling, my arms becoming heavy. Despite my will, I began to slow. I desperately tried to hold on, hearing footsteps behind me get louder. My legs refused to respond to my mind's urgent messages. The commands quickly stopped being "pick it up!" and "faster!" and transformed into "just finish, stay on your feet." I was in a pool of lactate. My quads cramped up, followed by my calves. My saliva foamed and thickened at the corners of my mouth. I was seeing red, then black. The only thing keeping me up was the possibility that I was counted on. Being an All-Canadian didn't matter anymore. What if we missed a medal spot by one place? What if I was the reason? I had to finish. I did my best to keep pace, exposing and martyring myself to an exponential increase in pain. I remembered the south hills. I remembered the three-minuters. I remembered Scott's guiding words: *you deserve to hurt*. I pushed on.

Soon, however, a few runners passed me. Seneca, Nebel, Ullman, Grieco. I lost my top-twenty spot, but I was in no position to count. Negative thoughts swirled around in my head. I was too weak. I was losing ground. I stopped thinking. With 500 metres to go, Cal ran past me. I did my best to keep up to him but fell back. He charged to the front, desperately trying to salvage a strong team finish. Head tilted and torso bent forward, I hobbled, and finally crossed the line a few seconds behind him.

I knew nothing. Placing, team-standing, nothing. I threw myself on the grass and held my temples. I fought the need to faint by taking deep breaths. I closed my eyes, turned to my backside. There we were – destroyed. But I could not stay down. I needed Cal. He was the only person who could tell me what had happened. I had to find him amidst countless shaking, broken bodies. I needed to know where we stood – needed to know if our efforts were worth it. A new runner was crossing the finish line every second and collapsing on the battlefield, but I had to find my training partner. I opened my eyes again and propped myself up with the negligible help of my failing arms. With his back against the rail separating the runners from the fans, he was sitting. His defeated, pain-stricken face was buried between his knees.

"How'd we do?"

"I don't think Scotty's in yet," he whispered, broken. "I was the first. I still don't see Angus." My heart sank. We were the two top runners. Scott was behind us. Neuffer had dropped out. We would not get the score we needed. I sat next to him. Distraught, we gazed out at the finish line, knowing that no matter where anyone else would finish, our hopes had died.

Soon, our captain and best friend threw himself over the line in sixty-third-place – a far cry from his sixteenth-place finish of last year. With tears welling up his eyes, he immediately clenched his foot in extreme pain and disappointment. He was also hurting. "I need ice. Quick," he said.

Laura quickly came to his rescue.

"It's the same as AUS. I can't get up on my toes." At that moment, it became evident that Scott had quietly been fighting intense foot pain ever since the conference race. He did not cry after the AUS race for finishing third, he was wincing and crouching to hide his discomfort. We had not caught up to his fitness by our final three-minute workout; he had instead regressed to our speed, unable to push harder. The caffeine he had asked me for was not solely for performance enhancement – it was to numb himself from the pain he was enduring. Today, to our collective chagrin, sixty-third had been all he could muster; he had tortured himself just to make it to the finish line.

Cal and I sat next to our captain and put our arms around him. "You did what you could," said Cal, on the verge of tears.

Next to cross was Angus, in sixty-eighth place, wearing a disgusted look on his face. A year of inconsistent training had finally caught up to him. Paul followed in seventy-fourth, and then came Nic in eighty-fourth, burnt to a crisp from his high-mileage weeks. There was no need to tally up the score. We had failed.

"Ah! Oh! How'd it go?" asked a defeated Favero, clenching his knees.

I picked my head up, body still drowning in lactate. "Not good," I said. "Neuffer DNF. Scott in the sixties."

"Shit," whispered Favero, as he stared at the ground. It took a few hours for officials to tally up the final score. Our top five had scored 240 points – good for eleventh place. Laval had taken the win, scoring an impressive 43 points. Yves Sikubwabo, who had earned top spot, led them to victory. Trinity Western University had grabbed silver, and the University of Western Ontario had finished in third place. Kevin Grant's facial expression mimicked ours, as our assistant coach walked towards me, looking defeated.

I was getting off the ground and attempting to walk towards the tent when he halted me. "Hey, you guys gave it all you had. Just not your day."

"Thanks Kevin. But it's not enough. We failed."

"I know. It seems that way, but don't judge your final season as an X-Man on one race. Let this one sink in, but then you have to forget about it. I know it sucks."

Behind him was Bernie, even more disappointed. "Cyr, you raced with guts. You went for it." Those words were all he could offer. He was choked up in empathy. Seeing one runner after another underperform brought him sadness. He knew we had worked hard. He knew how much we wanted to win a medal – he wanted it for us as much as we did.

"What did I finish?" I asked him.

"You were thirty-first. Cal was twenty-third." All I could do was shake my head. Collectively, it was not enough. After sympathetic pats on the back from our teammates who had watched, with the other six racers I retreated from the racecourse back to the hotel, feeling empty – ashamed.

The Value of Training

November 12th

After changing and showering, we walked down to the banquet in a conference room of Hotel Le Concorde. They served mountains of food. I was able to down a glass of water, but I could not eat. It was partly out of disgust, and partly because my stomach had rejected everything since being turned upside down in the last kilometre of the bloodbath. We then migrated back upstairs to the hotel rooms, and eventually made our way to the after-party bar. Despite our placing, or because of it rather, we felt it right to decompress. I ordered myself a drink with Favero and leaned against the bar, picturing how different the atmosphere would be had we perhaps finished in the top five – or even won a medal.

"Cyr, man, we have to forget about this."

"I know, Fabs, it just stings too much right now." Nobody remembered the eleventh place team. They cared even less for who finished thirty-first.

Though he was trying to move on, I could tell Favero was disappointed in himself. This was the first time since we had left Angitonish, save for the race, that he was not carrying his little brown sociology book. He stared ahead through his glasses with distraught eyes.

Amidst the crowded bar on the Université Laval campus, I saw Neuffer sitting on a barstool, nursing his battle wound. Scott was dancing with our girls' team but was not wearing his usual smile. His dance was leisurely – his mood and his foot injury slowed him. Angus was unhappily sipping on a mixed drink. He was by himself, still visibly bitter about the day's events. I noticed Cal in the corner of the bar, chatting with Blair Morgan, a CIS alumnus, about what had gone wrong. I caught myself wondering what he was telling him. The gleam he had worn in his eyes since the AUS championship was gone. Our team had disintegrated into – or returned to – a handful of individuals, looking for something to blame. We had come together as a unit against our own instincts, forgetting about any individual glory. Our intentions were the right ones, our preparation sound. Yet, we had not been rewarded. Bernie had not been rewarded. It was over. We would likely all continue running, but in the pursuit of other goals, other finish lines. Our days as members of the 2016 St. FX cross-country team, perhaps the deepest and most talented team in the school's history, had come to an end without tangible reward.

Away from the noise of the bar, Bernie was up in his room at the end of the hallway on the sixth floor of the Hotel Le Concorde, staring out his window. The Plains looked hauntingly calm. All garbage, sweat and blood had been cleaned off the course. Legend has it, Bernie used to join in on the CIS post-race festivities. Tonight, his heart was not into it.

He knew tomorrow would be the longest day of the year. He would have to spend hours in a bus with a number of athletes sharing his disappointment. He had not expected the end result to be as catastrophic, but it was out of his control. Both his captain and one of his ringers had become injured by the end of the year. Some of the others had run fine races, but it took more than fine to win. It took more than fine to be remembered.

Bernie had suffered losses, embarrassments, and harrowing defeats before – one cannot avoid such feelings in such a lengthy career – but none hurt quite as direly as this one. He struggled to remember coaching a team that had underperformed so woefully on the one day it counted. At the root of his displeasure was the vision of greatness he had believed in and shared with us. A small part of him had expected more out of us because he wanted to be recognized with a CIS medal, but the greatest part of Bernie Chisholm expected more because he knew we expected greater things out of ourselves. Bernie lived vicariously through his athletes. Our wins were his wins. Our losses, unfortunately, were also his.

He turned away from the window and reached for a document on the hotel nightstand. It was a printed copy of the day's results. He passively skimmed through the names, as Brenda amicably caressed his shoulder. Bernie saw Cal's name, then mine. He turned the page to find Scott's, Angus', Paul's and then Favero's. He reflected on the past four years spent with this group of athletes. The beginning of this era had been signalled by the loss of multiple-time AUS champion, Connor McGuire. Anticipating McGuire's departure by 2013, Bernie had worked hard at recruiting, and managed to land Scott and Lee Wesselius, two of Canada's top high-school recruits in 2012 and had begun building his team around them. With those two on the team, accompanied by McGuire, Riley Johnston, Bryden Tate, and others, his men's team had then been lethal.

The X-Men's success within the AUS conference in 2012 had attracted a trio of Maritimers – Cal, Neuffer, and me. None of us were highly touted recruits, but we had talent and the desire to work. We had progressed under Bernie's tutelage, along with Favero, to become some of the fastest undergraduate runners he had ever coached. From our group sprouted AUS individual champions, St. FX athletes of the year, and figures of dominance within our conference. Two years after our arrival, he had recruited both a young Calgarian and an Antigonish native; Angus and Paul were the future of the team. Whether Bernie would be around for the end of their careers as X-Men, he did not know, but he would forever be the one who had gotten their – and our – varsity careers started. Bernie would be responsible for the legacy – the culture – of St. Francis Xavier University's cross-country team for years to come. A culture, he hoped, that could eventually rekindle the magic of 2008 and 2009, the years in which the X-Men had stepped on the CIS podium.

"It could have been this year," he whispered to himself.

"Hey," Brenda addressed her still distraught husband. She was not used to seeing Bernie in this humour. "There will be other ones."

He was not so sure. Though he had not shared his thoughts of retirement with anybody, he was becoming increasingly certain that they were the right ones. "We'll see."

While his athletes were crestfallenly sipping on beer – or whisky sours in Angus' case – Bernie downed the remnants of the crumpled Aquafina water bottle he had been carrying around all day. "I guess we need to look at the positives," he told his wife, lost in thought. He needed time to find those positives, but they eventually would come to him. He knew that the building and maintenance of a team was a process, never defined by one particular moment, even though the day's events made it seem as such. To rest his mind, he pulled a worn-out piece of paper from his wallet, folded in four. He carried this small token of wisdom wherever he went. On it was a short passage from an unknown writer. It was written on the walls of several Canadian Olympic training facilities. Bernie had it printed before the games of 2012, in anticipation of Eric Gillis' first Olympic marathon. St. FX's winningest running coach reached for his reading glasses on the hotel desk and put them on. As he did most things, he read the passage quietly.

"The duration of an athletic contest is only a few minutes. While the training for it takes many years of hard work and continuous exercise of self-effort, the real value of sport is not the actual event played in the limelight of applause, but the hours of dogged determination and self-discipline carried out alone, imposed and supervised by an exacting conscience. The applause soon dies away, the prize is left behind, but the character you build is yours forever."

Epilogue

It's July 6, 2017 and I am making my way back to the St. FX campus for the first time since graduating, two months prior. It is Thursday, and I am driving from Halifax, where I am working and training for the summer. I am alone. O'Regan also lives in Halifax with me, but he will only be making his way to Antigonish on Friday with Cal, due to work commitments. I could not wait as long. This is Highland Games weekend – our best opportunity to reunite with our crew in the town where we grew close. The event offers a unique mixture of running and celebration, and it attracts runners and St. FX alumni from all over the Maritimes and beyond. The festivities begin tomorrow night, and a five-mile road race around Antigonish helps kick off the weekend. In my car, I see a road sign: Antigonish: 10 km.

This weekend, I will stay at 25 Acadia, which is now occupied by Scott, Nathan Jeffs and Edward MacDonald. 18 Greening has been signed away. Our lease is up, and new tenants – non-runners – have moved in. I will head over to Acadia Street later tonight and Patrick Marlow will be sitting on the couches with the current residents to live-stream the Canadian Senior Track and Field Championship, taking place in Ottawa. Angus Rawling is racing the 5000 metres. Warren, Favero, Stephen Deering, and others are in the nation's capital, and will be watching him race live. We, instead, will be tuning in from a distance.

The next day, Friday, I will make my way across campus to say hello to old friends and professors, before going to Subway with Patrick. There, we will run into Cal. He will come back to Acadia house with us, and Lee Wesselius will meet us there. Cullen MacInnis and his older brother, Neil, will make an appearance as well, and we will joke about everything and nothing at all until race time. We will then meet up with hundreds of other runners on the Columbus Field track, off of Main Street, to race the Highland Games five-miler through the streets of Antigonish. We will get to say hello to Bernie and Kevin and then drive over to enjoy a barbeque meal at Lee McCarron's mother's house – the house in which Lee grew up. The barbeque serves as a huge gathering for local runners. Nearly a hundred people will show up. Paul MacLellan, Ryan O'Regan, Heidi MacDonald, Ellen Burnett. and Hana Marmura will come with us. We will socialize with past, present, and even a few future St. FX runners. A crew from Dalhousie University will also be present. With the current X-Men, X-Women and Dalhousie team, we will then drive back to 25 Acadia for a night of partying. We will end up at Piper's Pub and stay up until three a.m. A few of us will wake up at 7:30 a.m. on the next morning to race the Highland Games elite mile. On tired legs, Lee Wesselius, Paul and I will put ourselves through our second trial of the weekend and race down Main Street in front of thousands of spectators. We will then host another gathering, once again at 25 Acadia. We'll invite many friends who are in town. From there, we will go eat at a close-by fast food place, and finally, head over to the beer tent, positioned on the field where we started the race of Friday afternoon. We will sleep like babies until the late hours of Sunday morning. As soon as I wake, I will grind out twenty more kilometres on the Brierly brook, but alone this time. Cal would have gone with me, but he will already have left for Bridgewater, his hometown, to work. Lee Wesselius opts for a run later in the day. After we've all run and said our goodbyes, I will drive back to Halifax with O'Regan, wishing we had more time to spend in Antigonish. Unfortunately, we both work on Monday. I am at a physiotherapy clinic, and he is working as a dentist's assistant.

"It's always tough, leaving this place," I will tell him, as we drive away.

"Yeah, I know," he'll agree. "But you know, Cyr. We'll be back. It's never the last time... it's never the end."

For once, I will take my friend's words as gospel, out of hope. The weekend as a whole will have fed my nostalgia, which becomes more pervasive every time I pass the fast food restaurants on James Street and see St. FX's Nicholson Tower from a distance.

Today, however, I drive slowly past the lights intersecting James and West Street onto campus. I pass Governor's Hall, where Warren resided for four years and two degrees. The sun was setting behind me, and the sky had aged pink. I park my car on Convocation Boulevard, and stiffly walk out. I am in the middle of a difficult week of training, getting in shape for the Canada Summer Games at the end of July. I am sore in my calves, and my back is behaving like a poorly oiled hinge, but I am finally injury-free. The months of May and June were trying. Slowly, I make my way to the Oland Centre doors. It is nine p.m. on Thursday.

Campus is quiet, and for once, I am able to stand in the Oland Centre without running into a friend or colleague. The building that was once buzzing with hype and passion for our sports teams is abandoned for the summer, and eerily calm. I enter through the main doors and come face to face with the St. FX Hall Of Fame, a long wall depicting the most successful X-Men and X-Women in history. It had always been an aspiration of mine to see my own photo hung on this wall next to those of Danny Gallivan, Wayne Synishin, Bernie Chisholm, Eric Gillis, and others. More specifically, I wanted to leave a mark.

I gaze at the photos, trophies and medals locked away in large cabinets, and it brings me back to my first sighting of this impressive vault of hardware. It has grown a bit since 2012, and I can now appreciate each piece more than I could as a senior in high school. I know stories now – I know the people behind those stories. When I was first introduced to this Hall of Fame, it was by Connor McGuire and Bernie. Almost five years ago now, I had been standing in the exact same spot, mystified by Connor's prowess as a runner and that of Bernie as a coach. With Ellen Burnett, Alex Neuffer, and Cal Dewolfe, I was on a recruitment visit. Right away, I hoped that one day it would be my turn to headline a team for a school with so much passion for, awareness of, and pride in their craft. I hoped it would be my turn to be top dog – to be Connor.

I was never Connor. We did not have a single Connor. We may have had six. But to have six Connors is oxymoronic. To be him, one had to consistently stand above the rest, as far as racing was concerned. Connor had been the uncontested face of the franchise in his years at St. FX. I had fought for that status with Cal, Neuffer, Scott, and Angus this year. Beforehand, there was also Lee Wesselius, Riley Johnston, Bryden Tate, and others. We had an army of men with Connor's talent – potential for an incredible team. But, we failed to realize it. It was perhaps because the stars did not align – or perhaps because of something else.

I shift my attention to two neglected, bland CIS (now U Sports) medals – one silver and one bronze – hanging in the top right corner of the smallest cabinet. The men's cross-country teams of 2008 and 2009 had won them. Lee McCarron, now the coach and face of one of the largest and fastest growing running groups in Canada, the Halifax Road Hammers, had been a co-captain with Brent Addison, from Halifax. They'd also had two star runners join them from the Czech Republic: David Gerych and Petr Doubravsky. Legend has it that most of the runners overcame H1N1, the swine flu virus, en route to their bronze medal finish.

As I scrutinize the print on the medals, I try to pinpoint and understand the difference between their team and ours. Why were they a podium team, and not us? Were we simply not as good? The numbers suggest not. While their team went down in St. FX history as the best one we've had, our era was highlighted by a seventh place CIS finish in 2015. While they will forever hold tangible proof of their prowess in the form of medals, our claim to fame will be the mismatch between our sheer dominance within our conference, and our mediocre showings at the national championship. But why? We had multiple runners under 8:30 for 3000 metres – something the 2008 team did not have. We ran the same workouts as fast as, or faster than, this team had done so. So, what was the problem? Perhaps we had too many Connors, and not enough Lees and Brents; too many people aspiring to be the AUS champion and not enough dreaming of climbing on the podium as a team. They had a common goal. We had individual ones. They had players. We had egos.

We had pedigrees needing embellishment, portfolios craving growth. I cannot fully generalize this statement, but I dare qualify it as the ethos of our era. Though Cal, Neuffer, Scott and I experienced glimpses of what it was like to be top dog, it never lasted. But we all liked the feeling so much that we spent most of our time chasing it once we lost it. Perhaps it was that time chasing each other that spent us physically and mentally. Bernie often said: "Not everyone can make the Olympics, but everyone can have an Olympic moment." We all sought our Olympic moment. The issue was that in our minds, the Olympic moments were perhaps too individual. The Olympic moments we longed for inevitably came at the expense of others.

Don't get me wrong. We became great friends. I would argue that our graduating class could rival any former cohort in the closeness of its constituents. We were so similar that we understood each other and respected one another. But, we were a group of leaders without any followers. All alphas, and no betas. We made for an impressive bunch of individuals, but, despite our efforts, a forgettable team with a pervasive power struggle. Perhaps that was why we failed to perform when it mattered.

I would be remiss, however, if I said that we did not become team players. Despite perhaps having a penchant for seeking our own good before that of the collective, we each, unknowingly, became working nodes within a grand network. We had no choice but to become a part of something greater than ourselves. During our time at St. FX, we were inducted into a large team – a team in which we will never star. A team for which we were taught to always go to bat for, always grind for. It is a team of current and past X-Men and X-Women, identifying with each other for years following their active period as runners. To wear the white and blue was to accept a membership to the team. To honour it was to preserve its legacy – a legacy of hard work, consistency, and hardiness. We learned – although perhaps only after our racing days – about the importance of being team players.

We learned that to be a member of this team is to understand what being a part of St. FX cross-country is about. It is about grinding around the Bethany nunnery in the winters, after powering over the South River hills during the increasingly cold days of late September. It is about not only avoiding scheduling classes during practice time, but also during our team meal hall time between seven and nine. It is about having Bernie tell you to suck it up and run every once in a while. It is about going to Kevin to confirm that your soreness was in fact too painful today to suck it up. It is about being unable to walk across the Oland Centre in less than ten minutes due to conversations with fellow classmates and athletes. It is about the supporters: Father Stan, Leo MacPherson, Angie Kolen, Krista McKenna, Mike Cavanaugh, Eric Gillis, Tommy Chisholm, Cathy Tulkens, Chris MacKinnon, Bernie Wallace, and endless others. It is about Kevin, Brenda, Bernie – the three main pillars of our culture. From these people, we learn of the worth of the program, and the value of being a member of its team. Someday, in some faculty, we will transmit what we've lived and learned to younger team members, so that it is preserved. Because of this transmission system and network, the zeitgeist of St. FX and its' athletics program has remained unchanged for years. It's about excellence, perseverance, and when needed, resilience. To accept our role as members of the team has shaped us into the people we are. It has helped us grow.

I slowly walk away from the Hall Of Fame and turn left to walk down the hallway of the Oland Centre. This is the direction Connor and Bernie had taken us on that snowy December recruitment trip of 2012. I'm still uncomfortable with the current silence in the building – I hear the soft patter of my shoes resonating against the empty corridor's walls. I walk towards our changing room and open the door. The padlock code on the lock is still the same. 8888#. A waft of old shoes, dried up sweat, and chalkboard dust strikes me in the face. It smells, like Riley and Nathan Jeffs described it, like mileage. Slowly, I begin looking at the names still posted on the lockers.

Paul MacLellan still has a few shirts in his locker. He is in Antigonish for the summer. He is taking running more seriously, after a solid result for a sophomore on the Plains of Abraham. He has run 8:49 in the 2017 indoor season and is increasing his mileage this summer. Once Scott goes back home to Ottawa by the end of the summer, Paul will move into 25 Acadia with Edward and Fuller, who both are entering their fourth year of study.

Addison Derhak has been back home in Waterloo, ON for over two months. He is enjoying his summer of eighteen years of age, increasing his mileage steadily. He has come to the troubling realization that the grade twelve runners he is actively recruiting to come to X are all older than he, thanks to his late birthday. An aggressive Facetime user, he has kept in touch with most of our senior class since convocation weekend, in May.

Warren Ferguson's locker is decorated with the reflective vest Kevin and Bernie urged at least one of us to wear during night runs. He had lived in 25 Acadia for a few months before moving back home to Ottawa. He is off to Queens University next year to pursue a one-year master's degree in economics on a generous scholarship. He plans to never study physics again for a day in his life. He still runs for fitness, but not like other people. His idea of a casual jog is a hellish tempo run on whichever treadmill he can find. Sometimes, he ramps up the incline, simply "because it's hard."

Nic Favero has had his locker cleaned out since November. Since cross-country, he was not seen at practice very often. Academic endeavours had been eating away at his free time, as he completed his honours thesis in sociology. Not fond of indoor track season, he decided to step away from running for a while. He currently resides in Hamilton, Ontario with his brother, preparing for his next challenge: a master's thesis in sociology and political economy at Carleton University, in Ottawa.

Angus Rawling is laughing at the memory of his lacklustre cross-country season. Since November, he has experienced a major breakthrough. He took the AUS by surprise by claiming top spot in the conference 3000 metres. His new PB of 8:25.80 now ranks top on the team. He secured his spot at the CIS track championship, where he finished eighth in the 3000 metres. After a mercurial spring of racing, he races tonight against the best 5000 metres runners in the country at Senior Nationals. He goes on to finish in sixth place in a time of 14:16, far and away faster than any runner vying for next year's AUS XC title has run. He is returning to campus for his junior year in the fall, now a threat to become a CIS All-Canadian. He lives at home in Calgary for the summer.

Alex Neuffer has cleaned out his locker, but not for good. He got accepted into the bachelor of education program at St. FX, so he will be running here for another two years. Bernie really hopes to have his most senior athlete healthy come September. Neuffer has dealt with shin issues since cross-country season. Recently, he has relinquished his spot on Team PEI for the 2017 Canada Summer Games, citing the same sort of issues. Though many teammates from the Maritimes are congregating to the Nish for the weekend, he stayed at home.

Cal Dewolfe is on his way from Bridgewater and will arrive tomorrow afternoon. He will finish third in the Highland Games five-miler. His fitness from cross-country carried over into the indoor track season, where he set new personal bests of 14:44 and 8:28. He finished second in the AUS 3000 metres but fractured his third metatarsal in the process. A quiet spring saw Cal recover and slowly return to running by early summer. He began to ramp up his mileage, training with Lee McCarron and the Halifax Road Hammers. In this time, he got to know his future teammates. He accepted the offer from Dalhousie Law School and will be a Tiger come the fall. He has one more year of eligibility and has vowed to do everything in his power to capture another individual and team title.

Scott Donald is waiting for me at 25 Acadia. His locker is empty, even though he has lived in Antigonish since the cross-country season. His foot injury took a long time to heal. Sadly, the former St. FX Athlete of the Year and two-time AUS champion was not able to compete in his last indoor track season. He did, however, earn the "Leader of Distinction award" from the St. FX Leadership Academy for varsity athletes – an award given based on coaches' and teammates' evaluation of one's leadership qualities. He is the first and only member of our cross-country team to earn this distinction. Out of eligibility, he hopes to run again, but he did not base his future schooling decisions on the sport. He is headed to Wilfrid Laurier University to pursue a master's degree in sport psychology. He will soon leave Antigonish to go back to Ottawa, Ontario; his hometown.

I get to my locker. I forgot a pair of socks in the top compartment. They are laced with this same aroma of mileage that has followed our team around for four years. I wisely do not touch them and leave them for the taking. The locker has been mine since 2013, but I had not exactly earned it in my first year. Bernie had given it to me because my high school times were respectable. I remind myself of my place on the team in that first year. I was irrelevant. Too young, too scared, too injured. But, like most others, I evolved here. As I aged, the team around me got younger, and I soon found myself amongst its senior members. At last, I had become a relevant piece of the puzzle – a leader. This year, I had enjoyed my best moments at St. FX University. I had earned my X-ring and my diploma. I had finally won an individual AUS title in the 1500 metres in the 2017 indoor season, and I went on to finish tenth at the CIS (now U Sports) championships. I had been accepted into the University of Windsor's masters in kinesiology program, and I planned to run for the Lancers this fall and learn to live the varsity cross-country experience away from Antigonish. Tomorrow, however, in front of friends and community members that I have gotten to know over my years at St. FX, I will win the Highland Games five-mile road race. As I round the track towards the finish line, with a lead on Lee Wesselius and Cal DeWolfe with familiar voices cheering me on, I will remember at once how special our time as the runners of St. FX University was. And at that moment, surrounded by friends, coaches, and vast academic and rural communities who didn't always understand, but respected what it is we did, I will consider myself lucky to relive a shadow of this feeling that may very well evade me for the rest of my life.

I exit the Oland Centre and walk towards 25 Acadia. I leave my car on campus. The walk is so familiar. The first person to lead me to Acadia Street had been Riley Johnston, in 2012. I since paid the favour forward to countless rookies, recruits, and new friends. I wondered if this very walk would be my last towards the team house. I was moving away, as were my friends. But, as O'Regan would say so wisely as we left Antigonish on Sunday: it's never the last time, it's never the end.

I use his words in describing my relationship with St. FX and its culture. It's never the end. Therefore, our story at St. FX should not be defined by our failure, but by our growth. We had potential for a medal, or at least, I like to think, a top five finish. We were dubbed the deepest team in the school's history, and we failed to capitalize. But, we grew in other ways. Eight of the ten graduates of our men's and women's team of 2017 graduated with honours. Remarkably, ten out of ten graduates of our cross-country team are advancing to professional programs or master's programs in the fall of 2017. Most are continuing to train in the hopes of bettering their PBs well into their twenties and maybe thirties.

Our days running under Bernie and wearing the singlet may be over, but our time as members of the St. FX cross-country team is unlimited. It is a membership my teammates and I , have taken on since donning the blue and white for the first time, and one we plan to keep. In part, it is this membership to the team that has driven me to continue running, to pursue my education, and to write this work. Equally, it is this membership that allows me to remain close to those I call my best friends.

Indeed, if there is one gift from my years as an undergraduate student that I cherish most, it is the bonds I built with my teammates and coaches. I hope to keep in touch with all of you for years to come. You have made me faster, but more importantly, you have made me better. I hope, that with the help of this work, you can appreciate the level of admiration I have for each and every one of you. Thank you for making my experience at St. FX one to remember, one to cherish, and one to take with me wherever I go.

Hail and Hell. White and Blue.

Printed in Canada